robert mitchum

solid
dad
crazy

damien love

B.T.BATSFORD · LONDON

"The beauty of that man. He's so still.
He's moving, and yet he's not moving."

Lee Marvin on Mitchum[1]

Acknowledgements

BFI Stills: 45, 59, 79, 134, 158
Associated Press: 25
Michael Ochs Archive: 192, 202
All other pictures and cover: The Joel Finler Archive

Chapter 3 is a revised and expanded version of an article originally written for *The Guardian*, August, 1998

Thanks to Tina Persaud and all at B.T. Batsford and also to Jeremy Theobald for his encouragement.
I am particularly indebted to Joel Finler for the use of his photographs.

This book is for Andrew and Norah, without whom nothing would have been started,
and for Alison, without whom nothing would get finished.

Volume © B T Batsford 2002

First published in 2002 by

B T Batsford
9 Blenheim Court
Brewery Road
London N7 9NY

A member of the Chrysalis Group plc

Printed in Spain

A catalogue record for this book is available from the British Library.

ISBN 0 7134 8707 0

Contents

Selected Bibliography

Bangs, Lester: *Psychotic Reactions and Carburettor Dung.* New York, Vintage Books, 1988

Bogdanovich, Peter: *Who the Devil Made It.* New York, Ballantine Books, 1997

Brown, Peter Harry and Pat H Broeske: *Howard Hughes: The Untold Story.* New York, Signet Books, 1977

Buscombe, Edward: *The BFI Companion to the Western.* London, Andre Deutsch/BFI Publishing, 1988

Callow, Simon: *Charles Laughton: A Difficult Actor.* London, Vintage Books, 1995

Downing, David: *Robert Mitchum.* London, WH Allen & Co, 1985

Eells, George: *Robert Mitchum.* London, Robson Books Ltd, 1984

Eisenschitz, Bernard: *Nicholas Ray.* London, Faber and Faber, 1993

Hayden, Sterling: *Wanderer.* New York, Alfred A Knopf, 1963

Hiney, Tom and Frank McShane (Ed): *The Raymond Chandler Papers: Selected Letters and Non-fiction 1909–1959.* London, Hamish Hamilton Ltd, 2000

Huston, John: *An Open Book.* London, Columbus Books, 1988

Farber, Manny: *Negative Space: Manny Farber on the Movies.* New York, Da Capo Press, 1998

McBride, Joseph: *Hawks on Hawks.* London, University of California Press Ltd, 1982

Miles, Sarah: *Serves Me Right.* London, Macmillan, 1994

Mitchum, John: *Them Ornery Mitchum Boys.* Pacifica CA, Creatures at Large Press, 1989

Roberts, Jerry: *Robert Mitchum: A Bio-Bibliography.* Westport CN, Greenwood Press, 1992

Silver, Alain and Elizabeth Ward (Ed): *Film Noir: An Encyclopedic Reference to the American Style.* New York, Overlook Press, 1992

Introducing

"You're like a pay toilet:
You don't give a shit for nothing,
do you?"[1]

It was late on a Tuesday night in the middle of summer 1997 I heard that Robert Mitchum had died. Although, actually, now I think of it I didn't hear he had died at all. The sound was off.

Flicking in that quick, late night zombie way through the five television channels with the sound off, my eyes read an image it took my brain a further two channel clicks to catch and identify: a young monochrome Mitchum, circa 1950, in a grey flannel suit, white shirt and black tie, a confused Mitchum, dishevelled fringe drowsing greasily about his eyes.

That's what memory dredges back now, at any rate, catching this unexpected splinter I associate with the only Mitchum film released that year, 1950, *Where Danger Lives*. Short of getting in touch with the BBC news archive to find out whether or not this fragment was in fact broadcast or is instead a trick phantom spliced into my own internal Mitchum obituary reel (an act that would destroy the whole fugitive power of the memory), memory is all I have to go on. Anyhow, I'd hate to learn it wasn't a clip from *Where Danger Lives*. This is a film linked essentially with the whole Mitchum experience, among the first I can remember actively seeking out on television in the dead hours of the night and anticipating purely because it was a Mitchum movie, and therefore a film to be enjoyed as a kind of secret knowledge.

The great thing about television is that it is so beautifully undiscriminating. They will put on any old shit. Which is not to say that *Where Danger Lives* is a piece of shit. Far from it. No. However, while at the local revivalist cinema you can see all sorts of beautiful stuff, for readily understandable reasons it tends largely to be only the Beautiful stuff that you can see, that which is recognised as belonging in the pantheon. Deemed Beautiful in whatever definition of beauty is called upon, a Beautiful bit of Blaxploitation, a Beautiful bit of low-budget horror, a Beautiful bit of Honk Kong kung fuey, dependent on the prevailing fashion. The certified stuff. The highest common denominator. On TV, in the dead hours, you can find the rest. And a lot of it is beautiful in other ways.

In the case of Robert Mitchum, well, Mitchum merits a whole other pantheon of his own, a hep extension with a password at the door. So many of his films fail so many of the certificates for so many reasons that, by necessity, the Mitchum fan draws up unauthorised new certificates, develops mechanisms of strange criteria, which only on occasion overlap with those understood and accepted by the rest of the world. That many of the films he made are ostensibly shaky and yet can be avidly watched by a core of people who, when it comes to other areas of cinema can be meticulously discerning, demanding and acutely critical – along with the fact that the greatest films he made, the certified, are utterly unimaginable without him – points him up as a performer who comes close to justifying an 'actor as *auteur*' theory.

There is pleasure to be had here, beyond the delight of seeing a great artist at work within the confines of often less than great art, although there is that too. At times it's recognising that all the reservations you have about whatever it is you're seeing, Mitchum has also, and more besides. But he has somehow moved beyond that knowledge without allowing it to colour the world view of the character he's animating, without declaring his own superiority over that character. To watch him in a bad film is to see a character vaguely wonder what the hell his life has suddenly turned into, and how come everybody's talking so weird?

This shift of his can take him, a film with him, to a number of interesting places. Mostly,

though, it's the pleasure of watching him inhabit the geography of each film, as though he was born in there, long before we showed up to watch. In even the least of his movies, there is a truth and coherence to Mitchum's acting whereby the smallest details reflect and recognisably fit the complete overall plan of a character. What is so extraordinary is the way that not only can he hold the truth of so many disparate lives (Irish village schoolmasters, marooned US Marines, Australian shepherds) but also somehow have them all balanced in some fundamental way, mirroring each other.

While it's a gross oversimplification to say a John Wayne or a Humphrey Bogart or a James Stewart played the same role in every film, it was the case often enough to allow people who haven't watched enough Bogart/Wayne/Stewart movies to believe this to be true, and to make the moments when they stretched or stepped beyond the accepted bounds of those roles doubly shocking. With Mitchum, the boundaries were nebulous, hazy. He was different every time, yet without disappearing chameleon-like; all his guys started from the same roots, but things had happened along the way, before the cameras had started rolling, to warp their growth. So in this life he became a sexual psychopath, in this a mild, impotent teacher, and in this a weird, goateed lecherous lecturer. It's like observing some endless cycle of alternative existences, all these different lives, played out to different ends, but in complimentary keys. The map to understanding the splendour of this actor's cinema becomes a ripped collage of moments echoing to one another across the planet-sized gulfs that separate one film from another. Some of these moments last only seconds, and sometimes a film will consist of practically nothing but these raffish smithereens and yet still, somehow, fail to be a Beautiful, canonised film in any regard other than its being a beautiful Mitchum film.

There are two Mitchum movies guaranteed to find their way with relative regularity on to film theatre circuits: *Out of the Past* and *The Night of the Hunter*. Both are utterly sublime. If you're lucky, a cinema near you might pick up a print of the original *Cape Fear,* or *Pursued,* or *The Lusty Men* or maybe even *The Friends of Eddie Coyle.* But that's about it, meaning you're only ever likely to see the bulk of Mitchum's movies on television,

unless you happen to live beside God's own video store, which in many cases still wouldn't help.

Where Danger Lives is one of those films, one you never really hear much about, except, perhaps, that it's not as good as *Out of the Past*, or that you should be alert to Nicholas Musuraca's gorgeous camera work (because he's the guy who did, like, *Cat People* and *Out of the Past*). The weird thing about *Where Danger Lives*, a characteristic it shares with that vast majority of Mitchum movies, is that it is the sort of film you are only ever likely to make the effort to see if you are already a Robert Mitchum fan; this is a hazy chicken and egg thing. It's hard to say just how and when exactly this transfiguration from regular Joe to Mitchum fan happens these days, but it continues to go on. He's a cult hiding in broad daylight, all the girls changin' to chicks, all the fellas changin' to cats. To put it another way: everybody you know knows who Robert Mitchum is, but relatively few could name more than a couple of the movies he's been in, if that many. Far less again could tell you where to find him wearing a rubber monkey mask,[2] and even fewer could understand why you'd want to.

For this reason *Where Danger Lives* is the sort of film that holds a special place for anyone whose relationship with Robert Mitchum has been worked out almost entirely on the small screen. You have to go a-lookin'. It's a film you discover for yourself, that you have to track down to 2.30 on a Wednesday afternoon or 2.30 on a Monday morning until you've captured it on videotape; one you come to alone, with a clean slate, and have to excavate for the silver moments scattered beneath the surface. For instance, I would argue that this is a great Mitchum film because it's one in which he gets arrested for not having a beard, down towards the border in some hot frustrated town of the night. This is a great thing, made even greater when viewed from the perspective time offers, with all the intervening layers of Mitchum pressing at once against it, filtering its colour.

By the time, anyway, I had clicked my way back down the channels, *Where Danger Lives*, if it had ever been there, had gone away, replaced by another splinter – maybe a tight early clinch with Ava Gardner in *My Forbidden Past*. Then, still in silence, this too abruptly jumped to another, probably some sad-eyed shadow from *Out of the Past* or weird scare from *The Night of the Hunter*, I can't remember. In the instant of that cut I worked out that this must be the final minutes of a news programme and I knew that Robert Mitchum was dead. Because this is how we learn these people die, towards the end of the late night news, in a collision of moments stitched together beneath a voiceover, resolving into some still, smiling portrait hanging above two dates separated by a dash.

A few hours later, less than twenty-four, after Mitchum's death, James Stewart had also died. The death of James Stewart, and the far more public structures erected around the event, knocked the death of Robert Mitchum into the shadows. This is perfectly fitting – it's where he belongs, his meaning is that shadowy kind of meaning. It's hard to say what he means, beyond the fact that he seems to mean something, even if it is very likely that what he means is he would much rather go fishing.

America was the fable of the West and Stewart was a repository of American reflections as much as John Wayne had come to serve as its violent wet dream. Even if sometimes, often, the mirrors Stewart and Wayne presented were fractured or had caught in their glass the wavering edge of some terrible chasm, there was always still an assurance, at least its memory, there somewhere, ingrained in the frame. The America Mitchum represented was a markedly different place, one where there was rarely anything that smacked of certainty or assurance. Patriotism was never a motive, even if it was being explicitly presented as such. Memories of Depression and war, and the desires and manias those memories gave rise to, ran as the vital stuff through the core of its populace. This was a country recognisable as America in surface detail, but which vibrated with a universal ache, hung over with a strange grey ambivalence. This world lay as the skin stretched taut over a deep resounding blankness, the drum its inhabitants marched to.

Here, the haunted cowboys were burdened and unsure. All the heroes – the cowboys and soldiers and doctors, the private eyes and policemen and drifters – moved without any real conviction, seemed to act only finally, reluctantly, with no great hopes for, nor particular interest in the outcome of their actions. If they went so far as to function according to some moral code, then that code was an obscure and personal one, running as a tangent to those circumscribing the rest of society. Occasionally these men were capable of looking slightly surprised at a turn of events; but theirs was a mild and weary sort of surprise, as though surprised more to find that, after all this, being surprised was still somehow possible.

The villains were all this and something else again. They had crawled somewhere unspeakable and back, and now stood changed and tall among the oblivious citizenry, carrying awful secrets. If they followed any kind of code at all, it was an utterly unrecognisable one, writ in a relentless alien hieroglyph.

Importantly, however, this was not a world of misery. If the Mitchum protagonist moved without hope, still he continued to move, and reacted always with a hip weird humour to whatever was thrown up, amused both by the tangled machinations of others and the fact that, of all people, he was supposed to care. He didn't run to meet his death exactly, but knew vaguely that it was waiting to meet up with him one of these times. In the meantime there was still nothing anyone had thought up to top it. There were jukeboxes and broads and beers.

Mitchum's other America, the other fable of another world, ran as counterpoint to that wholesome, busy daylight place of Manifest Destiny, as befitted a man who was, after all, one-quarter Blackfoot blood. It was a noir America, certainly, with all the levels such an elusive definition suggests, but it was also a swinging America, a beat America, a folk America, a punk America. There were other shades moving around in here.

A cosmos of swingers and mourners, killers and lovers, petty criminals and gamblers, fated hobo poets and nihilist ex-boxers, romantic boozers, factory workers, bootleggers, gun-runners, boat designers and ambulance drivers, preachers, schoolteachers, sheep-shearers, jailbirds, cowboys, doctors, artists, soldiers, private eyes and casual causeless revolutionaries, all swarmed slowly about, none of them caring too much, way down in the depths of Robert Mitchum. He contained multitudes. And, occasionally, on that calmest of surfaces, the tiniest of ripples would float up and break to betray their presence.

An interviewer, questioning Mitchum once about his years spent on the road and riding boxcar rails as a young teenager in the hardest days of the Depression, asked after the reasons behind the movement: what was he after, what was the purpose? His answer, after a fragment of a pause, allowed a brief glimpse into the heart of the country Mitchum came from:

> "Well, nothing, really. Just keep moving. No purpose. It was… no purpose at all, really. I supposed that if I kept walking long enough I'd lull across something. A warm body, or something usable." [3]

Nothing really. Just keep moving. No purpose. This is a book about Robert Mitchum written in something like that spirit. It is not a biography, although reference is here and there made to some of the events that went into making up his life. Then again, as the truth of any such event is welded within a whole caboodle of Mitchum mythology, a matrix where truth rests on a foundation of nurtured rumour, dummy leads, trap doors and misinformation, it's up to the individual reader to decide whether or not he or she chooses to buy any of it as having ever actually happened at all. As Mitchum once famously told an interviewer:

> "Booze, broads, all true. Make up some more if you want to." [4]

Although, with this in mind, it's worthwhile remembering that, early in his career, he also wrote:

> "Many of my statements have been smoke screen, designed to allow me to follow my own course without exposing it. I learned early in life that by telling a story far more colourful than the truth… one's truth is let alone. I like to be let alone." [5]

That this statement – a smoke screen in itself, the only difference being that in this case we glimpse the dry-ice machine warming up beyond the billows – is about the closest Robert Mitchum ever got to clearly saying anything publicly about himself speaks volumes. Saying a great deal without saying much of anything at all, the words turn back on themselves, swallow each other, and in fact go some way toward wholly eclipsing anything we think there is to know about the man. In its way, it's an equivalent to the credo of the protagonist of that famous conundrum, the man who tells you everything I say is a lie.

As if this were not enough, in the same piece he goes immediately on, opening up a further abyss with an indecipherable piece of self-definition:

> "I know what I am: I am a patient cynic." [6]

Already these words, from a lazy-lidded young studio hunk of the late 40s? From here there is no way back. This is a man with the smell of stale smoke in his hair, a man who expects, at best, to be disappointed.

Utterances like this, with their fusion of weary enigma on to flip everyday bluster, are a part of what this book is about. But not a biography. What this book is, in a sense, is an attempt at mapping the fleeting dimensions of the world Robert Mitchum brought about. This entails not a research trip to excavate the foundations of a fallen Hollywood, but a journey of a different sort, an interior stumble among the landscape made up of the half-a-century's worth of films and other recordings that constitute Mitchum's career: not a linear journey, because the geography folds back on itself, places and times, future and past intermingle. A guide book, then, tracing one particular path through an awkward and beguiling and frequently wonderful country. Following the litter. One particular path. There are others.

Chapter One

ChronoMitchology [1]

"A long, heavy westbound freight train was slowly pulling out when I got to the railroad yards.
A car of lumber, clean and white, piled halfway to the roof, the door invitingly open, came along.
Nimbly I swung up and in…" [2]

1917 – Robert Charles Durman Mitchum born, Bridgeport, Connecticut, on 6th August. A second child following the birth in 1914 of his sister, Annette Mitchum (later Julie Mitchum-Sater) to Norwegian immigrant Ann Harriet Gunderson and the quarter-Scottish, quarter-Irish and half-Blackfoot-Indian James Thomas Mitchum. **1919** – Mitchum's father dies in February. A railroad worker, he is killed in an accident at work, caught between two coupling trains. Seven months later, Mitchum's younger brother, John, is born. The family are living in Lane, South Carolina, but move back to Bridgeport, living for a while at the home of his maternal grandfather, Gustave Olaf Gunderson. **1923** – Mitchum's mother enters a short-lived marriage with a journalist, Bill Clancy. **1925** – Poetry the young Mitchum writes for his mother begins appearing in the local *Bridgeport Post-Telegram*, where she works as a Linotype operator and has met the man destined to become her third husband, English journalist and First World War veteran, Major Hugh Cunningham-Morris. **1926** – Mitchum and his brother sent to live on their grandfather's farm with their aunt Gertrude and uncle Bill Tetreault, in Woodside, Delaware. Mitchum begins attending the nearby Felton High School. **1927** – Aged 11, Mitchum decides to leave home and hits the road for the first time. Discovered in Connecticut and returned. **1928** – Mitchum is expelled from Felton High, accused of shitting in a girl's shower cap. **1929** – Wall Street crashes. The Mitchum brothers are sent to live with their sister and her husband in Philadelphia. Dashiell Hammett publishes the first noir story, *The Maltese Falcon*. **1930** – The Mitchum brothers arrive in Manhattan to live with their mother and her husband, Hugh Cunningham-Morris. Mitchum attends Haaren High School. **1932** – The Mitchum brothers return to the Delaware town of Rising Sun. On the eve of his

graduation, the re-instated Mitchum – named as Felton High's valedictorian – takes to the road again, failing to pick up his diploma. Arriving in Fall River, Massachusetts, he falsifies his age and works for a while as a deckhand on the salvage ship *The Sagamore*. **1933** – Mitchum embarks on his first transcontinental trip, planning to ride the boxcars from Delaware to California, there to meet with his sister and her husband at their new home in Long Beach. In Savannah, Georgia, he is arrested for vagrancy and sentenced to work repairing roads near the swamps as part of a chain gang of the Chatham County Camp No. 1. After a month, Mitchum escapes and makes his way back to Delaware, where he is found to have contracted gangrene from an ulcerated wound left on his leg by the chain gang shackle. In Delaware, he meets future wife Dorothy Spence. **1934** – Continues to hobo. Hops freight trains between Delaware and California. Works as dishwasher and truck driver. **1935–36** – Continues riding the rails and hitch-hiking across the country, working when the opportunity arises. His jobs in this period include working as a forest labourer in California, a coal miner in Pennsylvania, punch-press operator in a factory in Ohio, bouncer and fill-in prize-fighter in Nevada and California. Discovers marijuana. **1937** – Living in Long Beach, at his sister's urging Mitchum debuts as a stage actor in the theatre company she has joined, The Long Beach Players Guild, in their production of *Rebound*. Around this time he also begins writing and selling cabaret songs for night club entertainers and material for radio. He writes his unproduced play *Fellow Traveller*, about the real-life union organiser Harry Bridges. **1938** – For the Long Beach Player's Guild, appears in *Stage Door; Life Begins at Sixteen* and, playing Duke Mantee in *The Petrified Forest*. **1939** – Around this time, Mitchum works for a short spell as a junior writer at the Warner

Brothers studio. Writes the oratorio *Refugees*, performed by Benny Rubin in the Hollywood Bowl as part of the first Jewish Relief Fund show. His sister is working as a night club chanteuse in Hollywood. Mitchum writes material for her act and that of a female impersonator. Begins spending time hanging out with Hollywood fringe-dwellers on Sunset Boulevard. Works as an assistant for the astrologer Carroll Righter. In Louisiana during a lecture tour, Righter's car is caught in a storm and plunges into the bayou. Mitchum manages to free himself and the unconscious astrologer from the submerged vehicle. At Long Beach he writes and directs two children's plays for the company, *Smiler's Dragon* and *The Moss Green Bird* and appears in *Ghost Train*. The Second World War breaks out in Europe. **1940** – Mitchum and Dorothy Spence marry in the kitchen of a Methodist minister in Dover, Delaware. He takes a job in the famed Lockheed Aircraft plant in Burbank, California. Appears in LA in the stage play *Maid in the Ozarks* with Gloria Grahame. Continues trying to write for radio and night club acts. **1941** – Mitchum's son James is born. In LA, appears in the plays *The Lower Depths* and *I Die An American*. Japanese forces attack Pearl Harbour. **1942** – Mitchum works as a shoe salesman in a shop on Wilshire Boulevard. Brief screen debut as a model in the short *The Magic of Make-Up*. Hired by Harry 'Pops' Sherman, producer of the *Hopalong Cassidy* Western series as a heavy type. **1943** – Mitchum appears in the films *Hoppy Serves a Writ*, *Border Patrol*, *The Leather Burners*, *The Human Comedy*, *Aerial Gunner*, *Follow the Band*, *Colt Comrades*, *Bar 20*, *We've Never Been Licked*, *Corvette K-225*, *The Lone Star Trail*, *Cry Havoc*, *False Colours*, *Minesweeper*, *Beyond the Last Frontier*, *The Dancing Masters*, *Doughboys in Ireland*, *Riders of the Deadline* and *Gung-Ho!* His second son, Christopher, is born. **1944** – Gains his first star billing in the Zane Grey western *Nevada*. Also appears in *Mr Winkle Goes to War*, *The Girl Rush*, *Johnny Doesn't Live Here Anymore*, *When Strangers Marry* and *Thirty Seconds Over Tokyo*. During filming on the latter he causes an incident

Mitchum teaching his two sons, Christopher (left) and James, to tune in during the late 1940s.

by beating up an air force sergeant who had been riling the cast as 'Hollywood fags'. He signs a seven-year contract with RKO but refuses to change his name to 'John Mitchell'. **1945** – Gets top billing for the second time with another Zane Grey adaptation, *West of the Pecos* and co-stars in *The Story of GI Joe*. In April, he is drafted into the US Army, serving seven months of active duty, training at Camp Roberts and then transferred to Fort MacArthur, San Pedro, California, where he works as a medical examiner, examining fellow troops for haemorrhoids. The A-bomb is dropped on Hiroshima. The Hollywood anti-communist witch hunt kicks off with the House of Un-American Activities Committee being given permanent status. **1946** – Mitchum receives his only Academy Award nomination, for best supporting actor in *The Story of GI Joe*. He loses to James Dunn for *A Tree Grows In Brooklyn*. Appears in *The Locket, Till the End of Time, Undercurrent* and returns to the stage for the final time in the play *The Gentle Approach*, which he co-produced. **1947** – Appears in *Crossfire, Pursued, Desire Me, Out of the Past*. **1948** – Arrested on August 31 and charged with conspiracy to possess marijuana. Trial is postponed until the following January. Appears in *Rachel and the Stranger, Blood on the Moon*. **1949** – Sentenced on 9th February to 60 days in jail. Serves part of his sentence at Wayside Honour Farm, California. Released on 30th March. Appears in his first colour film, *The Red Pony* as well as *The Big Steal* and *Holiday Affair*. **1950** – Appears in *Where Danger Lives*. Fear, paranoia and anti-communist hysteria spreads throughout the picture business with the jailing of The Hollywood Ten, among them Edward Dmytryk, Mitchum's director on the movies *Till the End of Time*, the anti-fascist *Crossfire*, and later *Anzio* (1968). Mitchum is reported to have destroyed the set in a drunken brawl during the protracted filming of *His Kind of Woman*. **1951** – Mitchum's marijuana case is reinvestigated and expunged from the court records. In a bar in Colorado Springs, Mitchum gets into a fight with a soldier named Bernard Reynolds and knocks him out. Also a heavyweight boxer, Reynolds is ranked 10th in the world at the time. Appears in *His Kind of Woman, The Racket*. **1952** – Mitchum's daughter, Petrine, named for his maternal grandmother, is born. Appears in *Macao, One Minute to Zero, The Lusty Men, Angel Face*. **1953** – Mitchum is pulled

over for speeding and drives away from the motorcycle cop during questioning. A warrant is issued for his arrest, charging him with Escape From Lawful Custody, Resisting, Obstructing and Delaying a Public Officer in the Performance of his Duty, and doing 75mph in a 35mph zone. Eventually he is fined $200. Shooting in California, Mitchum is reported to have destroyed his dressing room when he found he was unable to get a dial tone on his phone. Appears in his first film in 3D, *Second Chance*. Also appears in *White Witch Doctor*. **1954** – Mitchum's contract with RKO expires and he begins working as a freelancer. At the Cannes Film Festival, aspiring British actress Simone Silva rushes topless at Mitchum and throws herself into his arms, to the delight of the assembled photographers of the world's press. Appears in *She Couldn't Say No, River of No Return, Track of the Cat*. **1955** – Mitchum is fired from the set of the John Wayne-produced *Blood Alley*, allegedly for throwing the transportation manager, George Coleman, off a pier during an argument. Wayne replaces him in the film. Mitchum sues the scandal-sheet *Confidential* for $1 million over a story alleging he had stripped naked at a dinner party in Charles Laughton's Malibu home, covered himself in ketchup and danced on the table declaring he was a hamburger. Forms his own production company, DRM productions, based out of an office at 9200 Sunset Boulevard. Makes his debut TV appearance hosting the variety show, *Stage Show*. Appears in *Not as a Stranger, The Night of the Hunter, Man With the Gun*. **1956** – Makes his dramatic TV debut, playing a cameo as himself in an episode of the show *Climax* based on the life of Hollywood columnist Louella Parsons. Appears in *Foreign Intrigue, Bandido*. **1957** – Having shot two films back to back in Tobago, where he became embroiled in a fight with three sailors, Mitchum falls in love with Calypso music and releases his own album, *Calypso Is Like So...!* Appears in *Heaven Knows, Mr Allison, Fire Down Below, The Enemy Below*. **1958** – Mitchum writes the original story and songs for the film *Thunder Road*, which he also stars in and produces. Later in the year, his own recording of the title track from the movie is released as a single. Also appears in *The Hunters*. **1959** – Mitchum buys a 300-acre farm in Maryland and moves his family there, 3000 miles from Hollywood. He begins breeding horses. Appears in *The Angry Hills, The Wonderful Country*. **1960** –

Appears in *Home From the Hill, The Night Fighters, The Grass is Greener, The Sundowners.* **1961** – Appears in *The Last Time I Saw Archie.* **1962** – Appears in *Cape Fear, The Longest Day, Two for the Seesaw.* **1963** – Appears in *The List of Adrian Messenger, Rampage.* **1964** – Appears in *Man in the Middle, What a Way to Go!* **1965** – Appears in *Mister Moses.* **1966** – Tours American bases and visits frontline soldiers in Vietnam. **1967** – Tours American bases and the front line in Vietnam for the second time. In total, Mitchum participates in 152 missions, spending the weeks following his return contacting the families of the soldiers he has met, to reassure parents and wives and communicate personal messages. During his second tour, Dorothy sells the farm and the family move into Cole Porter's old house in Brentwood, California. Mitchum releases his second album, *That Man.* Appears in *The Way West, El Dorado.* **1968** – The family move again, to Bel Air, California. Appears in *Anzio, Villa Rides, Five Card Stud, Secret Ceremony.* **1969** – Appears in *Young Billy Young, The Good Guys and the Bad Guys.* **1970** – Following a protracted shooting period, during which he lives in Dingle on the west coast of Ireland, appears in *Ryan's Daughter.* **1971** – Appears in *Going Home.* **1972** – Appears in *The Wrath of God.* William 'Hopalong' Cassidy Boyd dies in Ohio, aged 77. **1973** – Appears in *The Friends of Eddie Coyle.* **1974** – Mitchum's stallion Don Guerro wins Champion of Champions at the annual Quarter Horse world's championship. While filming on location in Corsica he is fired from/walks off the set of Otto Preminger's *Rosebud.* **1975** – Appears in *The Yakuza, Farewell, My Lovely.* **1976** – Mitchum's graduation diploma from Felton High is finally presented to him. Appears in *Midway, The Last Tycoon.* **1977** – Visits the Vortex, a short-lived punk club in London, where he watches Siouxsie and the Banshees perform. Appears in *The Amsterdam Kill.* **1978** – Appears in *The Big Sleep, Matilda, Breakthrough.* **1979** – Appears in *Agency.* **1980** – Appears in his debut TV movie, *NightKill.* **1982** – Appears in *That Championship Season* and the TV movie *One Shoe Makes It Murder.* **1983** –

In an interview with *Esquire* magazine, Mitchum discusses his role in *That Championship Season*, in which he played Coach Delaney, an ageing, right-wing high-school basketball coach. In the film, Delaney is given to spouting bigoted cant, and Mitchum lapses into the role, reciting such a speech. The remarks he makes are mistakenly interpreted and presented as his own and widely reported, causing a furore. Mitchum issues an apology and explanation, reading in part: '… I am truly sorry that this misunderstanding has upset so many people, especially since it is so foreign to my own principle. The attendant misfortune is that it has brought me a spate of mail from people and organisations who are encouraged to believe that I share their bigotry and discrimination…' Appears in the TV series *The Winds of War* and the TV movie *A Killer in the Family.* **1985** – Appears in *Maria's Lovers, The Ambassador*, the TV mini-series *North & South* and the TV movies *The Hearst and Davies Affair, Reunion at Fairborough, Promises to Keep.* **1986** – Appears in the TV movie *Thompson's Last Run.* **1987** – Fills in for an ailing Edward Woodward on the TV show *The Equalizer* for two episodes. Guest-hosts *Saturday Night Live.* **1988** – Sings on the soundtrack for *Broken Noses.* Appears in *Mr North, Scrooged* and the TV series *War and Remembrance.* **1989** – Appears in the TV movies *The Brotherhood of the Rose* and *Jake Spanner, Private Eye.* **1990** – Mitchum's mother dies, aged 96. Appears in *Believed Violent* and the TV pilot movie *A Family For Joe.* **1991** – Appears in *Cape Fear* and starts playing a cranky vagrant in the shortlived sitcom *A Family For Joe.* **1992** – Appears in *Midnight Ride.* **1993** – Narrates *Tombstone.* **1995** – Appears in *Dead Man, Backfire, Waiting for Sunset.* **1997** – Mitchum dies at his home in Montecito, California on 1st July. His ashes are scattered at sea. **1998** – Picking up his best actor award for *As Good As It Gets* at the Academy Awards ceremony in March, Jack Nicholson dedicates his Oscar to the memories of Mitchum and Miles Davis. Mitchum appears in *James Dean: Race With Destiny.* **1999** – Appears in the straight-to-video *Woman of Desire.*

Chapter Two
About a Photograph

"All these guys talk about is acting. I'm from the school
where all we talked about was overtime and screwing."[1]

When he was seven, Bruno Bernard's mother gave him a camera. Later, in the late 1930s, Bernard, a German Jew, fled the place his country had become with the intention of trying South America. Brazil, maybe. As things turned out, he got as far as seeing the movie *San Francisco* (1936) and, hypnotised by Clark Gable and Spencer Tracy moving around those precarious streets, plumped instead for the west coast of the US. Settling in California, Bernard attended Berkeley, completing a degree in Criminal Psychology. Thus armed he drifted into studying directing, under the tutelage of fellow countryman Max Reinhardt, the theatre legend and film-maker who, having arrived in the US some years before, had orchestrated the casting masterstroke of having James Cagney play Bottom alongside Mickey Rooney's Puck in *A Midsummer Night's Dream* (1935). Also appearing in Reinhardt's movie, as a toddler Changeling, was the little Kenneth Anger who would grow up to become an avowed occultist, write *Hollywood Babylon* – that peachy series of books devoted to cataloguing dark Tinseltown trash[2] – travel with the Avant Garde and conduct Satanic marriage ceremonies in public. Mickey Rooney would grow up to marry Ava Gardner, on her way to driving Frank Sinatra to the brink of suicide.

Bruno Bernard, though, had nothing to do with *A Midsummer Night's Dream*, and furthermore needed to eat. Finding it impossible to get work in movies, he started taking photographs, legend has it with that very camera his mother presented him with. Within five years, Walter Winchell was describing Bernard as 'The Rembrandt of Photography', Clark Gable would shut down filming to sit for him and, by the late 1940s, the re-christened Bernard of Hollywood had opened a studio on Sunset Strip, on the gangster Mickey Cohen's patch.

While he was being The Rembrandt of Photography, though, Bruno Bernard was also busy as King of the Pin-Up. In some versions of the story, it was this King Bruno who discovered a young Norma Jean Dougherty on the street outside his dentist's surgery, persuaded her to be caught in his lens and, around 1946, brought her to the distracted attention of 20th Century Fox's Darryl F Zanuck.

When he found he hadn't been absorbed into the dream factory, Bernard set to capturing fragments of other dreams, hitting on a flair for creating those weirdly wholesome fantasy X-rays detailing the lush swim-suit landscapes every red-blooded All-American Boy was encouraged to hope lay waiting beneath the apple cheeks and rosebud sweaters of the All-American Girl in next door's backyard. Bernard's Breathtaking Beauties hung half-forgotten in the lonely afternoon corners of a thousand neighbourhood garages, turned by smudging greasy fingers, radio dreaming lazy in the background. A thousand guys working in sloppy clothes beneath their coveralls with reasonless caps pushed back 'beats-me' high on top, watches ticking down the minutes till knocking-off.

Bernard of Hollywood took this picture of a 33-year-old Robert Mitchum in his Sunset Strip studio in 1950. By this point, Mitchum had been in movies for seven years and was the veteran of some 40 films, an impressive amount even then, when the production rate at the dream factory was phenomenal, somewhat explained by the fact that he appeared in 19 movies in 1943, his debut year,[3] alone. He has been Robert Mitchum for several years now: the consolidating drug-bust was two years ago, past midnight on the last night of August, the first morning of September 1948.

Hidden away among the thousands of photographs taken of any Hollywood star, this

picture of Mitchum is not particularly famous. It's not James Dean on Times Square in the beaten rainy go-home hours of the morning, nor Marilyn flowering in the night on a Lexington Avenue subway grate. It's not even the most famous photograph of Robert Mitchum. There are, however, a few hundred great things about it, about the way Mitchum has signed it. The fact that the orchestrating eye behind the camera belongs to The Rembrandt of Photography, snapper to the stars, places this as a glamour shot. Really it should be that kind of misty, exotic, yet almost within-reach beefcake milkshake icing designed to wet the eager imaginations of hungry-eyed post-war bobbysoxers. What is

presented, though, is something else: someone who not only looks just too easily reached but actually looks as though he might well be the one who'd be doing all the reaching.

Bernard's deceptive photograph demonstrates superbly Mitchum's facility, well established by this point, in negating a camera's existence while busy at his craft – which is performing for that camera. In this case the job is manifold. The first task is filling a couple of the Robert Mitchum roles Mitchum liked to project: those of the film star who doesn't care how he comes across, and his close relative, the regular unwashed Joe Schmo who, despite being "a movie actress", is exactly the sort of fella who might shell out a buck for Bernard

of Hollywood's latest portfolio of pin-ups (or more likely roll the thing up and cram it into his back pocket, sort of forgetting to give it back when he leaves the studio), and not particularly because this is the issue in which Bernard's famous camera technique is revealed for the first time.

He is the guy, of course, with dirty hands in the garage, or driving home at the end of a once-in-a-while-weekend with a happy sore head and a trunk full of fish fresh for gutting from some clean place upstate. Or come to fix the air-conditioning in this photo shop, idling some time in reception while the broad behind the desk has gone to get the guy to sign the chit and, hey-hey, what's this, picked up the glossy girlie mag from the lucky coffee table there.

Heel digging heedless into the tough fabric of the fancy chair buckling under his slouched weight, the man's slovenly presence calls attention to the tiny white triangle of a rent in the surface of the leather cushion near his thigh, as though it had sprouted there, cousin to the hole worn through the left arm of his sweatshirt. It's a coiled, easy acting job of a high elastic calibre, where costume, posture and body language are harmonised, intricately balanced. Mitchum is at work here in this photographer's studio, don't forget, clocking on just as much as he had back when he worked in factories and in bars and down mines and on the sets of those 40 films. The guy described in this picture is not one who gets his photo taken for kicks.

The photograph wraps itself around time. This 1950 Robert Mitchum, cap pushed back, feels close to how we imagine the unknown Robert Mitchum who went to work at Lockheed Aircraft 10 years earlier, in the summer of 1940, must have looked: regular working stiff, laughing it up with the boys lazy behind the foreman's back, digging the latest and checking his watch every half an hour, yokking it up over fan mags lifted from secretaries in the canteen.

Across in the Europe Bruno Bernard had escaped, a Second World War was raging and the American defence industry was happily up-scaling, hiring workers in droves. Lockheed needed men to turn out aircraft for the British forces to send up and the Axis to shoot down. Mitchum, recently married, needing a home and harbouring thoughts of a family, needed to find himself a regular pay packet. So he got himself a painted metal lunch-box and became a sheet-metal worker and drop-hammer operator at the aircraft plant.

In there, close by, working the terrifying metal-shaper Mitchum was himself sometimes required to queasily steer aluminium sheeting through, was a 19-year-old boy built like a brick called Jim Dougherty, who had recently started seeing the 15 year old Norma Jean Baker destined soon to become his wife; then, after The King of the Pin-Up had discovered her smiling in his viewfinder and pinned her on to garage and locker room walls, Arthur Miller's, then Jo DiMaggio's.

Robert Mitchum, who would in 1954 hook up with the fabulously blue-jeaned Marilyn Monroe, another natural splendour among the treacherous waterways of the Rocky Mountains, tumbling and fumbling around in CinemaScope for a film called *River of No Return*, knew her from all the way back then. He first clapped eyes on her when Jim Dougherty pulled her sweet-faced picture from a wallet for his perusal, while the machines howled around them. Clocking how Dougherty ate the same cold egg sandwiches every break time, Mitchum queried him:

"Your old lady makes you the same sandwich every day?"

"You ought to see my old lady."

"I hope she looks better than your egg sandwich."[4]

Although this is a phantom conversation that was perhaps only ever conducted along one path branching off inside one version of the story; by the time Dougherty took Norma Jean for his lawfully married 16-year-old egg-boiling old lady and set up house in May of 1942, Robert Mitchum had already left Lockheed behind him.

Contained within the reasons for Mitchum's quitting the aircraft plant are the restive seeds giving the partial lie to his regular guy routine. Before his marriage to Dorothy Spence on 16th March 1940, Mitchum had been attempting to carve out a career as a writer. Turning out risqué songs and jokes for night club acts and contributing dialogue to daytime radio shows brought in variable money when it paid at all, but it was all writing and what cash it

did bring in encouraged him in the work he took seriously: the short stories and poetry he'd written since childhood, the plays he was beginning to write for the local theatre group.

In 1937, the year Bruno Bernard caught his first sight of Ellis Island, Mitchum wrote a play called *Fellow Traveller*, a weird, funny-sounding fiction about union activity and cannibal islands, constructed around the real-life figure of Harry Bridges, a labour organiser the US attempted to deport between 1937 and 1955 on suspicion of Communism. The play was optioned by the Theatre Guild of America and subsequently somehow critiqued by no less than Eugene O'Neill: the playwright's notes, Mitchum liked to point out in years to come, 'were longer than the play.'[5]

In the summer of 1939 Mitchum wrote routines for ex-Vaudevillian Benny Rubin. Later that summer he composed the words and music for an oratorio, *Refugees*, themed around the plight of Jews in Hitler's Europe. Rubin performed this in the Hollywood Bowl at the first Jewish Relief Fund Benefit, an evening directed by the *wunderkind* of the American stage and, more recently, radio, Orson Welles; himself just arrived in Hollywood from New York, and trying to work out how to fit.

Considering that Mitchum had early in life rebelled along the solitary paths of writer and wanderer (his first poetry was published, against his will, in a local newspaper when he was eight; he ran away from home for the first time at aged 11, getting it all down on paper while Jack Kerouac was still a dreamy 6-year-old boy watching the gloomy shadows moving mysteriously around Pawtucketville), given that he'd had his words and music echoing around the glittery Hollywood Bowl all lit up with lights directed by a genius, it's hardly surprising Mitchum hated the routine, the monotony, the jerk foreman and constant machine danger of the aircraft factory.

Not long after starting at Lockheed, he was put into a world of constant night-shifts and insomnia took over. He spent his days writing, his evenings helping out with The Long Beach Players Guild with his sister, her urging him to try out acting, before going off to work another pounding graveyard shift at the plant, crawling home again come morning, trying to sleep, trying to write again.

No egg sandwich, this tomato: Mitchum and Norma Jean preparing for the *River of No Return* (1954).

New kid in Tinseltown:
Marlon Brando limbering up
for his part in *A Streetcar
Named Desire*.

Sleep would only sneak up when he didn't need it, at nights in the factory, when he was risking an arm to slice out metal shapes under the inadequate yellow lights, so to keep awake he hit his beloved black coffee by the gallon, chewed tobacco laced with stinging tabasco sauce and quaffed NoDose in quantities that would have had the manufacturers biting their lips. No use. The stuff didn't seem to ever kick in until the next morning, when he was trying to get to sleep and the blinding light and the sounds of kids playing in the street hammered through his window. And he kept right on hating the work.

Finally one morning, after about a year, on the way home from Lockheed his eyes started to go funny. Through the bus window, the passing streets grew blurrier and blurrier. By the time he fell into his house he couldn't see anything at all. A doctor came and looked him over, then told him there was nothing wrong with his eyes. Tests followed and it was concluded that his blindness was psychologically induced due to his hatred of his work. The physicians recommended that, you know, if he hated it that much, maybe he should think about quitting, before he went insane.

This is another of the early signs of Robert Mitchum's particular greatness, his otherness, and deserves consideration: he hated his job so intensely he drove himself blind.

He quit and went to work as a salesman in a shoe shop on Wilshire Boulevard, on his knees at women's ankles. He was regularly fired. One day, figuring he could do it at least as well as any of these other jokers – at least the Long Beach Players seemed to think so, since they kept upping his roles – he registered with a casting agency and started looking out for work as a film extra. It was a job. Wasn't it?

Back inside Bruno Bernard's frame, another job of the photograph, of course, is to advertise Bernard of Hollywood himself. It's a task that's intertwined with the previous one of establishing Mitchum simultaneously as a citizen of mythic Hollywood and common workaday grease-monkey type, but it's an assignment so expertly, completely carried out, right down to the delicate ballet Mitchum is choreographing with the magazine in his big-fingered grasp. In the world of the photograph he is actually, outrageously, unconsciously steering the magazine into a better angle in a better light, to gauge whatever, whoever it is in there that has caused his eyebrow to raise in mild, surprised appreciation, instigating the curl just starting out across his mouth. In the bigger place beyond the white edges of the picture's frame, the actor is conscious of the way he lifts the magazine exactly into the light, presenting its leggy cover page for us to register and later recognise, curious, on the stands. 'Poifect Bob, tha's it. Jes' great, tha's it.' Click.

Bruno Bernard's 1950 photograph of Robert Mitchum is the same photograph as this picture of Marlon Brando taken the same year by a studio stills photographer between takes as the actor makes *A Streetcar Named Desire* for Warner Brothers. Mitchum has been in movies for seven years, Brando for only a year, but Brando's has been a meteoric rise. Each caught as their initial wave of fame is cresting, both pictures are presented as informal, un-staged moments of a star–anti-star's captured reality, clad in thoughtless utilitarian off-screen outfits. But, clearly, both are perfect, structured little essays on the character of their subjects, largely authored by their subjects, and the stories they tell are revealing.

Weighing the two photographs from this vantage point, decades removed, what becomes clear is how the easy breezy Mitchum snap emerges as the more nonchalantly sophisticated of the two. Brando's choice of props and signs seems overstated, for one thing. Brando has only recently arrived in Hollywood – *Streetcar* is his second movie – and that punch bag, as well as insisting on his strength, his danger and his down-on-the-street masculinity, hangs there like the historical body of acting itself. Setting himself heroically, independently against it Brando, the new kid in town, is preparing to beat the shit out of it.

The Brando photograph is, perfectly, all drive, energy jabbing, jagging; tilting his head just so, weighed down, alert, angles flashing in his buzzing temple, brooding shadow sculpting veiled drama of his features. In contrast, with Mitchum everything seems smooth, rested, down to the softly curving outline of the amorphous sofa and the relaxed duck-bill rise of his cap's peak over that insolent hair. Still without even a cigarette in view, a comfortable history of trouble is gently inscribed. The light just catches it.

Brando, in short, looks conscious, trying for it while Mitchum doesn't, isn't. Stretching into the movie house, these are the qualities that account in part for what is so fascinating about each actor. Almost all the differences there are between Marlon Brando – the most famous graduate of the Stanislavskian Method school – and Robert Mitchum – 'The Rin Tin Tin method is good enough for me. That dog never worried about motivation or concepts and all that junk'[6] – can be found in these two photographs.

For all the talk about how Brando brought a new level of reality to cinema acting, his was a studied, heightened reality, a dizzying verisimilitude that called attention to itself against the placid fakery surrounding it. Brando rendered himself unreal through his very striving for reality. No one lived like Brando acted, a raw, accelerated charcoal cartoon with an itching crotch, all jagging angles, ticks and pauses and shrugs, eyes rolling heavenward in search of the right words, screams, sighs. Brando, with his dextrous trickery and arrogant beauty, picking at an ear, slurping a melon rind, at the outset of his cinema career specialised in constructing surfaces, truculent canvases marked with complex, carefully worked lattices of dents and rips, ostentatiously buckled from the blows of the things hammering to get up and out from depths they concealed. He drew the eyes of an audience like a fire in the screen's fabric, he couldn't help it.

Mitchum captured attention in exactly the opposite way – he drew attention to what he was doing by not drawing attention to it. Not a fire sparking on the surface of a movie, but one glowing at its heart. Pulling you in with a force as noticeable as gravity, without seeming to care. The magnetic north of a film.

When, at 48, Brando marshalled his forces and tempered them with maturity, he unleashed one of the screen's greatest, most human, raw and bleeding performances: the shredding monologue at his dead wife's side in 1972's *Last Tango in Paris* . This, above anything, felt real, painfully so. But even here, the towering nakedness of that performance – if 'performance' is a word that can be used, considering how Brando poured his own

histories, public myth and private grief into the role – the place it spoke from, was one that most people witnessing it would shy away from, could never allow themselves to enter, an abstract place of all consuming, unendurable drama recognisable, yet alien to the viewer: the place where the artists go for us. Mitchum never exposed so much of himself.

Brando's esoteric *Tango* sits in a perfect, uneasy balance with the more familiar human anguish subtly displayed by Mitchum in the following year's far less famous *The Friends of Eddie Coyle* – say in one of the scenes where he sits alone in the dim, beaten silence at the end of a sad afternoon bar, 56 years old with nothing but whisky and age and more afternoons of such realisation ahead of him, wrapped in a small life of quiet despair he's just about aware of, distractedly studying the backs of his weary, abused hands.

Importantly, however, differences are not all that emerge when comparing Bruno Bernard's

Mitchum and Brando's punch bag routine. In the messy clothes, in the confidence and arrogance it takes to turn up this way before us, and then, further, ignore our gaze and still not care, it's clear that Mitchum and Brando are, if not exactly brothers, then at least running as members of the same tiny, heedless slob cabal, and it's pretty much to hell with you, Charlie, if you have a problem with it. Although Brando moved into film following the footprints of Montgomery Clift, a lot of what he would become – what others would try to become in his wake – had been anticipated on the sly by Robert Mitchum.

"I don't even get in the tub. I just throw a gob of spit in the air and run under it."[7]

The quote is Brando's but it has echoes of the young Mitchum who chewed 'baccy between takes till it left a brown scum around his lips, wandered sockless through studio back lots with his hair sprouting like a well-nourished brown weed patch, and flipped out the powdered love interest in clinches with raw garlic and onion clinging to his post-lunch breath. It calls to mind the Mitchum who, protesting the fact he hadn't been given anywhere to get changed during the filming of *Nevada*, a Zane Grey B-Western he was starring in – the first time he carried a movie, graduating from unshaven heavies and faceless support – stood crusted in fake blood and real dirt in the central flower gardens of RKO wearing nothing but a towel. Carrying a bar of soap and a garden hose, he threatened loudly to wash himself there and then if some sort of dressing room wasn't forthcoming, while happy studio secretaries leaned from windows and eagerly watched the towel's knot at his hip.

When Brando brought bongo-beat nonconformity to the streets of Hollywood, slouching it in T-shirt and jeans and refusing to play publicity games and nice up the columnists, when he bad mouthed the acting caper and mooned his co-stars, the world sat up and wondered. Robert Mitchum, who had laid that path and grown tired of being the columnist's favourite rebel – the one they loved to cause a flutter so long as he didn't go so far as to upset them – sighed and watched them go, recognising a chance to relax and disappear. Let the other schmuck handle it. It'll be nice to have a drink in peace.

"This guy Brando, how I welcomed him on the scene. I knew he'd get a lot of the heat."[8]

These were mavericks who just missed each other. The long-distance camaraderie of the two can be heard ringing through statements that were often interchangeable, say, from the hundreds both laid down on the nature of their profession:

"I never will believe that there is such a thing as a great actor."[9]

"[To me it's] Just like slicing baloney. It's my favourite way of slicing baloney, the pay is better."[10]

"I like getting up at 5am and having my head painted for the cameras. What real man wouldn't?"[11]

"I have no respect for acting. Acting by and large is the expression of a neurotic impulse… Acting is a bum's life… You get paid for doing nothing, and it all adds up to nothing. Acting is fundamentally a childish thing to pursue. Quitting acting – that is the mark of maturity."[12]

"Acting is a ridiculous and humiliating profession."[13]

Again, however, there was something vaguely studied about Brando's nonconformity, something almost like the rebelliousness of a spoiled child, bored and testing the limits. Although the two shared a fundamental sense of absurdity, a weird hipster humour coupled with a fundamental baseline rejection, Brando came across like a perfectly, beautifully realised concept of The Maverick. He went to school, after all, to learn how to slice his baloney, from heavyweight New York butchers like Erwin Piscator and Stella Adler, with his parents paying for the lessons. Mitchum, whose father had died when he was two, had it in him, carried it around with him from the first time he ran away from home.

Where Brando sparred with stagehands on Broadway to keep in powerful-slobbish Stanley Kowalski shape when he was acting in *A Streetcar Named Desire*, and, later, when making the movie, toyed with his punchbag for a photographer in a well-paid Warner Brothers' basement, Mitchum had been a real, reluctant prize-fighter fighting to make ends meet as he travelled around America during the mid-1930s. Sometimes he was easily wrestling bums around the ring, sometimes he was beaten around the ring like a bum, making $35 per bout. That's where he earned the break in his nose.

There's a rough analogy, perhaps, with the way that, while Brando famously, passionately, loudly embraced the issue of Native American rights, Robert Mitchum actually was himself descended from Blackfoot Indian stock. His father was half-blackfoot and Mitchum had a parcel of Indian cousins roaming around.

In earlier times, although never actually at war against the US Government, the Blackfoot people were nevertheless generally hostile toward these new Americans. These were a plains people, dwelling in skin teepees, a nomadic tribe who moved regularly, were of no fixed habitation and had few possessions they cared about. Robert

Mitchum had it in him, quietly. Sometimes, the Blackfoot in him could be clearly seen in his features, gazing out on a distrustful world: when his eyes narrowed and their shadowed heaviness became more profound; when he drew deeply on a wary cigarette; as he got older and those eyes became fathomless hazel and the etched lines deepened while around them his face flattened into a passive, threatful place on which it was impossible to read the signs until he wanted you to, to tell whether he was putting you on or what, till cracking it open with a twinkle, an eyebrow hitch, violence, a tired sadness.

One other analogy: Brando, in the 1959 film adaptation of Tennessee Williams' *The Fugitive Kind*, played a weird angel guy with a guitar, a guy from somewhere else, wearing a snakeskin jacket, who had to get a job as a shoe salesman.[14] Robert Mitchum *was* a guy who had to get a job as a shoe salesman. And he didn't need any prop jackets.

If Mitchum was aware that, on some obscure level, there existed an affinity between him and Brando, he was not the only one. He mentioned the younger actor in interviews occasionally, in flip ways, managing to put them both down but nevertheless suggestive of a deep understanding of their fundamental difference, although the very fact he mentioned Brando at all is some kind of acknowledgement. In 1947, Mitchum was offered the role of Stanley Kowalski in Elia Kazan's original stage production of *A Streetcar Named Desire*, the part which, of course, eventually introduced Marlon Brando to the world. Perhaps it was this weird connection, seeing Brando filling out a body he might have filled, which lodged in Mitchum's mind: Tennessee Williams' original concept for Stanley called for a man of around 30 years old; Mitchum was then 29, Brando only 22.

By then under contract to RKO, Mitchum pitched this *Streetcar* stage idea to the studio. In the period 1946–47, he'd completed some nine films, what with RKO loaning him out to MGM and Warner Bros. at a healthy rate. At one point he'd spent an entire month without break working every day around the clock, filming three movies simultaneously, flying from one morning set in Hollywood to another set in Monterey every afternoon, then back to the RKO lot to work through the night, graveyard shifts again. He had

solid 'box-office appeal' and the studio had plenty in mind for him. So he was told that, if he really wanted, he could go do his play for a couple of months, maximum, and then, no matter what, whether the show bombed or soared, he'd have to come back and carry whatever the hell same pictures they'd had lined up in the first place. With this in mind, Mitchum passed on playing Kowalski and Brando became a sweating icon.

Streetcar's sold out New York opening on 3rd December 1947 followed hard on the heels of the premier of Mitchum's movie *Out of the Past*. Earlier, that summer, Mitchum had co-starred in *Crossfire*, a film that had attracted headlines due to its theme (the evils of anti-Semitism) and garnered five Academy Award nominations. Just before that, he'd made the great-granddaddy of all psychological westerns, *Pursued*. Having already given two of his most captivating, off-beam-haunting performances (*Out of the Past* and *Pursued*), as well as one of his most noticed (*Crossfire*) that year, and having been nominated for an Oscar the year before, it's tempting to speculate what Robert Mitchum would have become had he been granted a sabbatical and become Stanley Kowalski.

Almost certainly, for one thing, his marijuana bust and subsequent prison stretch, with all the association therein contained, wouldn't have occurred, or at least, not when it did. On the night of the arrest, 31st August 1948, Brando/Kowalski was still in the theatre, toiling through *Streetcar*'s mammoth run, a long way from the shady Hollywood suburb Mitchum was surprised in. But then, had Mitchum played the role, with the subtle fire he burned, with his different silence, Kowalski might never have lived so long. The chances are, had he gone on to play the role on film, we would have only just recently woke up to whatever he might have accomplished, such has been the case with so many of Mitchum's performances, *Out of the Past* and *Pursued* among them.

Although it should be noted that both often played men whose physicality provided them with no reassurance – indeed, the two actors authored long lines of beaten, powerful masochists – Mitchum and Brando shared a massive physical presence. Brando's, again however, was far more consciously, more sexually on display. He put it in your face, a beauty that was almost feminine, but overpoweringly, stinkingly muscled and male.

Kowalskiesque: *Cape Fear* (1962).

Having graduated from the heavy roles, Mitchum didn't again reveal his awful physicality until *Cape Fear* in 1962. The rest of the time it was just there: unequivocally masculine but felt, veiled, suggested by his sleepy panther grace. With his factory knowledge and real life, Mitchum's self-assurance and ability in generating that everyday Charlie stuff, seems so much closer to the tenement animal Kowalski that Williams originally nightmared up. Stanley, though, is now forever Brando's, that other, more exotic, fantastic brute creation.

It's difficult, also, to now imagine a Kowalski speaking in Mitchum's mellifluous baritone flow. Even when he played a man of less intelligence than he – which is to say, most of the men he played – his characters had an effortless articulation peculiar to themselves, a world away from the famed, ah, Mumble of Brando's portrayal. During the 1940s, Mitchum whiled away spare moments by sketching tunes with a saxophone and his diction purled with an easy, conversational syncopation (Mitchum's coming to maturity as an actor coincided with the birth of be-bop and its slide into cool). This was a low control that wasn't seen to try, it exploited the microphone and was close to Sinatra's method.

This is one of the reasons why Mitchum, even assuming he would never have burned Williams' Kowalski into the cultural fabric the way Brando did, would have been far more ideally cast than Brando was in the role of Sky Masterson in the Runyonesque musical *Guys and Dolls*, another part for which Mitchum had originally been considered. When it came to singing, Brando, especially with co-star Frank Sinatra smirking off camera, just couldn't get the words out. This is the Sinatra, who, as a real Hoboken kid, had so desperately wanted the part of Terry in *On The Waterfront*, and had been promised it, even, only for that crumb Brando to waltz in with his mumbling method shit and waltz out again with an Oscar. Eventually, Brando's songs in the film had to be assembled in editing, spliced together word by word from the tapes of countless fluffed takes, while Sinatra laughed up his sleeve.

In addition to already having a couple of films worth of experience in how best to get around Jean Simmons, Mitchum, without ever making a musical[14], sang easy whenever and wherever he got the chance: in films, on night club stages, on TV, and, calmly, wildly on a few records all his own. Sinatra once claimed 'he knows more about music, from Bach to Brubeck than any other man I've known.'[15] And this is deeply important. It's the one sure fact, the certain knowledge hovering between and around those two photographs, keeping them that crucial distance apart. Whatever else there is to say about Marlon Brando, true and beautiful hipster saint though he may be, when he showed up he couldn't sing for shit. Robert Mitchum could. Click…

Chapter Three
About a Drugs Bust

Pressing against Bernard of Hollywood's photograph of Robert Mitchum, informing it, is another photograph. This other picture had itself been anticipated by words in a film, spoken towards the centre of the hazy labyrinth of *Out of the Past,* when a taxi driver murmurs from the corner of his mouth to the Robert Mitchum he is ferrying through a San Franciscan night:

"Buddy, you look like you're in trouble."

"Why?"

"Because you don't act like it."

Two years and one month after shooting wrapped on that film – on 9th February 1949 at 9.40am by the Los Angeles County Courthouse clock – a flashbulb popped. The resultant picture has this sliver of dialogue echoing all around it: as the polished courtroom fills behind Mitchum, as his attorney stands staring grimly ahead, hands on hips, as the blonde to his right in the white gloves and black hat moves her rosy mouth in a pensive gasp and half the world waits to hear what sentence the judge will hand down. Robert Mitchum, hair drowsing, tie shining careless in his jacket, stands with a look on his face. The look, a fugitive caught in the camera's lucky instant says one thing: 'Oh, yeah – this really impresses me.'

Mitchum's bust, coming in a time of true reefer madness, a pre-history when a counter-culture had yet to be identified, formularised and

Mitchum in court:
9th February 1949.

commodified, could have, should have, wrecked his career. That it didn't, that the American public didn't allow it to, shows how deeply, perhaps unconsciously, they understood and responded to Mitchum's persona, his utterly detached cool-that-doesn't-bother-speak-its-name-ness. He got it right, took it right and took it quiet, rather than crawl through any 'but I didn't inhale' routines.

No matter that he may have been privately upset, frightened by what was most likely to come, when that courtroom bulb flared Mitchum was instinctively at work and, simply by not blowing it, he confirmed all the vague feelings his audience had about him. He consolidated his own image in that instant – whether he actually didn't give a damn or if he just looked like he didn't is immaterial. The difference is none.

That courtroom photograph is exactly what the balanced portion of America wanted to see: 'Hey, hear Mitchum got busted, smoking reefer with some broad.' 'Oh. Of course. Yeah.' This was something new: for once, for perhaps the first time, the exposed reality seemed to match the image. Even better than that, Mitchum's image – and therefore his reality – turned out to be ambiguity itself, unfathomable, way beyond any simple tough-guy tag. A real-life mystery thing.

Even the little girls, maybe especially the little girls, the ones who were supposed to want the beefcake romance, understood this, and understood it early. Interviewed in 1945 outside a screening of *The Story of GI Joe* – three years before his arrest and the subsequently attempted demonisation – a posse of the teenaged schoolgirl bobbysoxers (an inspired RKO publicist would fantastically dub such fans 'The Mitchum Droolettes') explained his attraction:

"He has the most immoral face I've ever seen."

"He's got sex appeal in an evil sort of way."

"He's got the mean kind of face I go for."[1]

Sex appeal in an evil sort of way? The Droolettes knew it. They never said these things about chorus boys like Van Johnson or Guy Madison. When the cops came drug-busting through the

door on the last August night of 1948, there was set in motion a ripple in the fabric, one of the rare folds pushed up when art and life rub edges. Martin Scorsese touched this when he said 'Mitchum *is* noir.' Perhaps it is why the novelist James Ellroy, whose own life became a noir narrative in the summer of 1958 with his mother's brutal murder, seems fascinated with Mitchum's arrest. Ellroy first brushes the bust in his 1988 novel *The Big Nowhere* and the same year's story, *Since I Don't Have You*; but it's with *LA Confidential* that he really embraces the thing, imagining his Jack Vincennes as the cop who collared Mitchum, carving out a reputation with carbon-copy arrests.

In reality, though, the men in the shadows outside what became known as the Reefer Resort on the night of 31st August 1948, were named McKinnon and Barr. Men moving in the eucalyptus shadows that move around the house at 8443 Ridpath Drive. Imagine an anonymous, funky little wood-framed, three-room shack built off the twisting white road on a hillside in the Laurel Canyon district of Los Angeles, where the party-set party, moon-painted behind the ubiquitous suburban cacti and waving dry shrubbery of Hollywood's satellite streets, that parched plant life vaguely glimpsed pressing dark on the peripheries of the writings of Chandler and Thompson and Cain and the black Los Angeles-set pictures of the period. Tugging at the roots of the fated, well-to-do house in Joseph Losey's *The Prowler* (1951), say, infecting chalky walls with swaying charcoal nets of shadow. Or whispering the chorus to the foul lover's final meeting in *Double Indemnity* (1944) beneath the sticky night-time lullaby of the radio dance-band down the street, the papery black leaves within which a fatally wounded Walter Neff hides himself on leaving the home of the already dead Phyllis Dietrichson.

Raymond Chandler, highest of the original cartographers of that hidden LA, seeing the shadows spreading with refined outsider's eyes, first found himself, bewildered, working as a screenwriter in Hollywood in 1943, the same year Mitchum first found himself on screen, in some desert place with Hopalong Cassidy to contend with. Mitchum ran into Chandler sometimes around town during the early 1940s; he'd encounter him in bookshops and while tending bar in a joint called Sullivan's and, noticing the gloves Chandler wore to hide a skin condition, figured he was a bit affected.

It was Chandler, along with director Billy Wilder, who took James M Cain's Walter Huff renamed him Neff and, in an ending wholly different to Cain's moonlit suicide original, hid him dying in those dry bushes, like some flip-rotted Moses, towards *Double Indemnity's* ending. Those bushes exist for hiding, Chandler recognised; they screen the fragile bleached houses from the eyes of the street and the neighbour, at the same time providing close, threatening cover for gut-shot insurance men and dubious, precipitous prowlers and policemen on narcotic stake-outs.

Sergeant JB McKinnon and Detective-Sergeant Alva M Barr were LAPD narcotics officers into the eighth month of a surveillance operation, feeling pressure from above and itchy for a famous head. At the top of the ladder they clung to, whipping public hysteria, sat Harry J Anslinger, Commissioner of the US Bureau of Narcotics all the way from 1930 to 1962, from Woody Guthrie through to Bob Dylan.

Anslinger obsessed on cannabis. In 1937 he penned the article *Marijuana: Assassin of Youth*, a catalogue of rapes and murders supposedly committed under the drug's influence:

"How many murders, suicides, robberies, criminal assaults, hold-ups, burglaries and deeds of maniacal insanity it causes each year, especially among the young, can be only conjectured… No one knows, when he places a marijuana cigarette to his lips, whether he will become a joyous reveller in a musical heaven, a mad insensate, a calm philosopher, or a murderer…"

When Mitchum was busted, only reprobates, itinerant sailors and jazz musicians were smoking dope. Harry, naturally, also hated jazz intensely – too loose, following its own complex logic, too black – and around the time of the Mitchum bust planned a round-up of names from his 'Musicians and Marijuana' file, from Louis Armstrong to Duke Ellington (whether he was concerned about Charlie Parker's smack habit remains hazy). The plan fell flat, primarily because the members of the Bureau were much too square to be able to infiltrate the coded jazz scene. Hollywood, however, was another matter.

Five years after the Mitchum bust, in 1953, Raymond Chandler, by now having long given up Hollywood – or having been given up by Hollywood – in disgust, save a brief return to work curiously on Hitchcock's *Strangers On A Train* (1951), got around to writing *The Long Good Bye*. For that book he would house his weary Philip Marlowe nearby, on Yucca Avenue, in the same Laurel Canyon district as the little hillside bungalow those two policemen watched from their prickly shadows that night. Marlowe lived there because the rent was low, the same reason Lila Leeds was living there in 1948, sharing her small hillside rent with another girl, Vicki Evans.

The place was furnished, had a steep flight of steps to its front door and belonged to a woman called Nanette Bordeaux, an unlikely name later to feature semi-regularly in Three

Sex appeal in an evil sort of way.

Stooges shorts. Cashing in shortly after the bust, Landlady Bordeaux advertised the furniture from her bungalow as being for sale with the line *Robert Mitchum Sat Here*, and brought suit against him, claiming drooling souvenir hunters had stolen and damaged her property. As Bruno Bernard's 1950 flashlight claims highlights in Mitchum's inattentive hair, Bordeaux's measly claim still rumbles on, a ridiculous buzz beneath the papery sigh of the pages he is gauging, another echo of the bust, eventually to be settled in 1951.

Lila Leeds was a 20-year-old platinum blonde, an echo descendent of that phrase coined in 1930 by Lincoln Quarberg, Howard Hughes's personal publicist, to describe Jean Harlow whom Hughes was briefly wooing as well as promoting furiously in an effort to ensure a return on his messy flyer's epic *Hell's Angels,* an investment of $4.2 million. At the time of the bust, Hughes, as head of RKO would have an investment of some $2 million tied up in unreleased Mitchum films. From Harlow, the term 'Platinum Blonde' oozed its burning way down into common currency, settling for a while on the dazzled head of Lana Turner, who believed for a moment in 1946 that Howard Hughes was going to marry her, then bled out into the gutters and hopeful acid hairdressing salons of a dreaming hinterland, passing Norma Jean Dougherty and a million other fan mag fans on the way.

Lila herself had an exact ersatz Lana Turner glow, a smudged glamorous patina still dimly perceivable in the photographs taken of her receiving sentencing in the Los Angeles County Courthouse. She was an aspiring actress recently dropped by Warner Brothers with an unexercised option at MGM already behind her. No one, not Howard Hughes, not anyone, had anything invested in her.

For her part in the bust, history rewards Lila Leeds with the prefix 'would-be'. As Vicki Evans answers the door of their funky little bungalow – it was Vicki who ushered the cops in, Vicki who later disappeared and was never convicted, Vicki whose real name wasn't Vicki Evans at all, but Florence Fedele – Lila has already become a *would-be* actress. Lila Leeds' low-rent door opens on to a night of eucalyptus and honeysuckle and men with flashing badges

and guns in their hands. Rushing up those steep steps comes for her a future of drunk driving charges, heroin addiction, more drugs busts, solicitation and nervous breakdown, a gradual fade. Low-rent glamour, tarnished, exactly the sort of burned butterfly those black films like pinned up as a backdrop: Lana Turner, but less so, washed-out, a nice girl who has given up trying. Eventually, she found God.[2]

In James Ellroy's Los Angeles, a Lila would maybe have wound up hooking for the Fleur De Lis escort agency, where the girls were 'cut to look like movie stars'. As it was, she made one more film, a silly, massively entertaining anti-pot exploitation flick featuring a young, crazy-eyed Jack Elam just to underline the point, called *She Shoulda Said No* (aka *Wild Weed* 1948). At one point in the movie, an improbably whacked-out Lila, whose junkiedom has caused her college-kid brother to hang himself in the garage, stares herself in the mirror and watches, transfixed, as her gorgeous face ages, crumbling away.

In fact though, even before her life tumbled into a cold three-dimensional shadow of the black films, before she came to live briefly in the paint-peeling Three Stooges cottage where Philip Marlowe would briefly live five years later, Lila Leeds had already inhabited a weird noir place, had already met Marlowe and moved through a studio lot in Chandler's wake. She's still pinned there. We can visit her. Released in 1947, MGM's production of *The Lady In The Lake* was Robert Montgomery's directorial debut and Lila's big chance. The film was initially to be adapted by Chandler from his own novel, although in the end he drifted off the project, having grown bored of reworking such a familiar narrative. His short story of that name had first appeared in *Dime Detective Magazine* in 1939 and the finished novel also included elements of the story *Bay City Blues*, which had been published in the same pulp the year before. Employing his usual guiltily self-cannibalising working method, then, Chandler had already worked on and off on the story between 1938 and the novel's eventual publication in 1943 and was reluctant to be doing so again. To keep up his interest, he took the plot off on an entirely new tangent, which was not what the studio, who had after all purchased the rights to the novel as written, had in mind. In the end, the screenplay was completed by a studio writer and a disgruntled Chandler refused any credit for his work.

For a spell there, though, Raymond Chandler worked on the MGM lot, measuring out the spaces between drinks and grumbling about the air-conditioning in an office on the fourth floor of the Thalberg building. Not long after he was gone, Lila would sashay around the place, hoping they'd pick up her option, looking about her to see if anyone noticed.

Robert Montgomery, with a stomach full of playing dapper-footed slicked-back smoothies – all that cosying up to Norma Shearer back in the 20s – had been hankering after a directing job for some time, becoming obsessed with the idea of making a film in which a subjective camera acts as the main character. As Chandler grouched in his letter to Alex Barris of *New Liberty* magazine, this was old stuff:

"…The camera eye technique of *The Lady In The Lake* is old stuff in Hollywood. Every young writer or director has wanted to try it. 'Let's make the camera a character'…"[3]

The most famous example of a young writer/director wanting to attempt the style is Orson Welles, who signing to RKO in 1939 – the same year he produced Mitchum's *Refugees* oratorio in the Hollywood Bowl – determined to adapt Joseph Conrad's *Heart of Darkness* in precisely this manner. The attendant budgetary problems – along perhaps with a studio antsy about such an untested project being the first fruit of their loudly trumpeted deal with the young genius – scuppered Welles' *Heart of Darkness*, and he turned to what would become *Citizen Kane* (1941), but his subjective camera would emerge again, among the ruins of *The Magnificent Ambersons* (1942), moving through the softly howling rooms of the dead Amberson mansion toward the close of the film.

Around the same time as RKO released their destitute, glowing reworking of *Ambersons*, the studio fired Welles, ordered his Mercury staff from the lot, and came up with both a secret company motto – *All's Well That Ends Welles* – and a wonderfully inane new slogan to plaster across the top of all their stationary: *Showmanship Instead of Genius*. By the end of

the decade, though, a changed RKO would still be breathing genius cheaply without realising it and Robert Mitchum would somehow have assumed Welles' one-time role of representing the studio's finest – RKO's own trademark lion, or as Mitchum would have it, horse shit salesman – involved in a fathomless, subversive economy, spinning a buried black genius all his own.

Old-stuff or not, though, Robert Montgomery was determined his subjective camera idea was a goer, and Chandler's first-person narrative seemed ideally suited to the treatment. So it was that MGM came to make *The Lady In The Lake* starring, as the posters had it, 'YOU and Robert Montgomery' as Philip Marlowe.

YOU accept an invitation to a blonde's apartment!

YOU get socked in the jaw by a murder suspect!

YOU slug the crooked cop who tries to frame you!

YOU look into the gun of a fear-maddened killer!

Suspenseful! Unusual!

An MGM mystery in which everything that happens to Robert Montgomery seems to happen to YOU![4]

A bizarre slice of Hollyweird, *The Lady In The Lake* is an awkward, fascinating experience, one of the dollar-eyed dream factory's most unwittingly experimental projects. Rather than forcing an audience to experience its world in a certain way, to empathise, rather than submerging us in some mass subjective delirium, the first-person camera works as a strained, prolonged gimmick as we become infinitely more conscious of the mechanics involved. The attempted embrace triggers a distancing effect. Perhaps Welles could have pulled it off.[5]

However, although the whole thing feels as comfortable as a pair of 3D glasses, there is something peculiarly watchable about it. It is all about an ungainly, unwieldy camera creature that looks like Robert Montgomery whenever it catches sight of itself in a mirror – like an ancestor of Harvey Keitel, playing the TV network employee with a miniature camera filming through his eyes, in Bertrand Travernier's *Death Watch* (1979).

Marlowe–Camera–YOU bob along corridors whistling, smoking cigarettes, getting beaten up, while the rest of the cast are all gazing, talking, swinging directly at YOU in the way that Oliver Hardy sometimes would. Early in the film, YOU bob into an office of a pulp-publishing house – to supplement his–YOUR private dick earnings, YOU–Marlowe–Camera creature writes dime crime stories – settle into a chair at the desk of the woman who sent for YOU, and light up a smoke. And while YOU wait, in sashays her platinum bombshell of a receptionist, Lila Leeds.

YOU stalk her with your eyes, all around the room. Lila Leeds, caressed by YOUR lascivious stare. YOU have no choice, YOUR eyes claim her up and down, asking questions. And her responding in her turn, Lila Leeds claiming her moment, smelling contracted opportunity through the ammonia, simmering, pouting stiltedly back into YOUR one flat big cyclops eye, a brief unworded, awkward seduction, a whole unspoken thing built up then burned in the air.

Then, out the door she flirts, glancing back, hopeful '*Did I do it right Mr Montgomery?*' out of the film, off the lot, gone away somewhere else. Lila's moment. That whole huge screen to herself, leching after her. Her big chance.

Back in *Out of the Past*, the conversation in the taxi whispers on. Robert Mitchum turns to the cabbie:

"I think I'm in a frame,"

"Don't sound like you."

"I dunno. All I can see is the frame. I'm going in there to have a look at the picture."

If *The Lady in the Lake* was Lila Leeds' big chance, it was back at home the night of 31st August 1948 that she played her biggest role.

The story went that Mitchum and his would-be-real-estate-agent friend Robin 'Danny the Moat' Ford rolled up around midnight to be greeted by Leeds and her wide-eyed house-mate, the fortuitous cops beneath the window caught sight of Mitchum lighting up a print-free cigarette and came through the door without bothering to knock. Mitchum and Leeds were charged with conspiracy to possess, the first 60 days of the sentence to be served in the County jail.

The part no one remembers is that in 1950 – the same year Bruno Bernard snapped his shutter at Mitchum – another judge reviewed the affair, changed Mitchum's plea to 'not guilty' and removed the case from the records. The details surrounding this twist were never fully explained; Mitchum himself rarely bothered to remind anyone. However, evidence unearthed by the LA District Attorney's office pointed to a stitch-up: for one thing, Leeds' bungalow had been lousy with concealed microphones; for another, the press had been tipped off to the arrest almost before it happened.

Reportedly a sycophantic character who had attached himself to Mitchum, Robin Ford was working at the time as a bar tender, but trying to break into the real estate racket. Mitchum, then looking to sell his house and move, figured on doing a guy a favour and let Ford handle the transaction. The day of the bust, the two had been driving around viewing properties, and Ford had divided his time between attempting to persuade Mitchum to go with him to a party at Leeds' cottage and placing phone call after phone call to Leeds and parties unknown, reporting in. Eventually, after Mitchum had decided he'd rather stay home and read a script that night, Ford suggested they stop by a chilli restaurant for food, and just kind of detoured over to the Laurel Canyon shindig on the way.

"I think I'm in a frame."

Links later were rumoured to have emerged with the figure of Paul Behrmann, previously Mitchum's business manager and 'best friend'. Oh, and previously also Lila Leeds' agent, come to think of it. Mitchum and Behrmann could often be seen sharing a table at Slapsie Maxie's Cafe, the night club where Mickey Cohen sat in a backroom office with the county sheriff in his pocket and able to obtain whatever you desired.

Making movies: Shooting on location during *The Sundowners* (1960).

In 1947 Behrmann had been unable to account for around $50,000 of Mitchum's savings that had vanished. Although the stung actor declined to press charges, he and his wife Dorothy were later called to testify against Behrmann in another, similar case, and Behrmann – rumoured to be connected to an extortion racket linked to Cohen – supposedly swore revenge. James Ellroy makes notes.

At the police station the night he was arrested, Mitchum gave his occupation as 'former actor' and amused himself by toying with a police psychiatrist who asked questions just like psychiatrists in the movies:

"Do you like pretty women?"

"Yeah."

"Do you go out with them?"

"No."

"Why not?"

"Because my wife won't let me"

Mitchum served his time without complaining. He'd encountered marijuana, 'poor man's whisky,' early on during his days along the Depression road, and as he later stated was 'morally guilty, factually innocent.' Unlike Leeds and the Hollywood party-set, for him this wasn't the latest stop on some freak highway of new kicks. He'd smoked joints when working the punch-press in a Toledo factory in 1936, just as he had shaping steel at Lockheed, just as, according to the movie's writer, Daniel Mainwaring, he had on set while filming *Out of the Past*.

Anyway, LA County Jail was easier than when, at 15, he'd been sentenced to a chain-gang in the Savannah swamplands. Occasionally someone inside would try to fit him up, plant weed in his cell, but he was hip to that. Howard Hughes came to visit in a blaze of secrecy, smuggling chocolate. Photographs emerged from the joint prefiguring, negating, *Jailhouse Rock*: prisoner 91234 mopping sad concrete floors in jailhouse denims, buying milk and cigarettes, quiff drooping over patient eyes. He spent some of his sentence on Wayside Honour Farm, mixing cement and milking cows in the open air, and described the experience as being 'like Palm Springs. Without the riffraff.' He got fit, got a tan and lost some weight. And he got himself plenty of sleep. Later, after he got out, he donated vending machines to the place for the prisoners to use, bubble gum and candy.

The fabric ripples. *Out of the Past* was the last Mitchum film released before his arrest. Almost three decades passed before he played another private eye: just as flip and melancholy as Philip Marlowe in an amber 1975 adaptation of Chandler's *Farewell My Lovely*.

In the original 1940 novel, Chandler had written about a grass-smoker a passage that fits:

> …a man who looked as if any touch of the exotic would appeal to him. On the other hand lots of tough guys smoked marijuana, also lots of band musicians and high-school kids, and nice girls who had given up trying.

The novelist Jim Thompson, who followed Chandler and whose diseased stories of darkness and lonely ruin laid the foundations James Ellroy built upon, played a cameo in that movie, as the ageing judge whose young wife plays footsie with Mitchum's Marlowe. At the time the film was made, the world had forgotten Thompson, who died two years later, then was rediscovered. But Mitchum, who fetched Thompson coffee and sandwiches on set, knew who he was: the two first met inside LA County Jail in 1949, when Thompson was an elegant-looking reporter interviewing the Mitchum jailbird for the *LA Mirror*. They are together onscreen only briefly in the film – but the first time they meet, they shake hands. And their touch completes a circle. And their touch sets off another ripple.

The press Jim Thompson represented back in 1948, meanwhile, frenzied around Hollywood Babylon. A nervy RKO released a shelved Mitchum movie, *Rachel and the Stranger* (1948) to test public opinion. Mitchum was the first person sighted on screen, coming over a rise, leading a horse through the sort of idealised bucolic American landscape dreamed deeply of in youth: just another part of the tall straight trees and the wide blue skies and scudding clouds. He played a loner, an anarchistic, 'wild and woodsy' hobo spirit with a vague touch of trouble in his kindly eyes, wandering in and out of the movie singing to himself over the burble of tumbling, icy fresh rivers, a knife in his belt. Audiences flocked to the picture, applauded and cheered whenever he appeared on screen.

Well, not all. After Mitchum's bust, Dwight D Eisenhower, who would become President in 1953, would refuse to watch anything with him in it. While in office, Eisenhower, a movie buff, had films screened regularly at the White House, at least one a week during his eight-year tenure. If Mitchum turned up, Dwight would walk out of the screening room.

Finally, in Bernard of Hollywood's studio photograph of Robert Mitchum (1950), all of this, casually, is what we see. The man with the immoral face, working at relaxing for our pleasure. Ridiculous with self-assurance, needing nothing, let alone a President's approval. The man who came to Hollywood riding a freight train boxcar and who always figured that, sooner or later, he'd leave the same way. The worst – all the worst – has already happened, and he endured. It didn't kill him, it made him stronger. He's moved into the place that comes after The Worst, intact, and all by himself. He's collapsed the distance between life and art, between who he is and who he appears to be. But at the same time he's also suggested enough of a mystery void – dropped clues enough as to the existence of a sad, solitary poetry – that a dim awareness of difference, of some haunted distance wraps around him, and we, watching, begin to doubt we could ever know him at all.

Furthermore, he's emerged some kind of star, without giving it all away to do so, without begging. Without becoming one of them. Look back into Bernard's studio, see where his finger is pointing on that magazine cover, that phrase there. This is what he has accomplished, what he has become.

A Step Beyond, it says.

Chapter Four
Mitchum In Pictures

Noir Movies, War Movies, Weird Movies and Westerns

To hear him tell it, Robert Mitchum's long career in pictures, spanning over half a century, had nothing much to do with him. It just kind of happened, while he was waiting.

That span is itself worth considering. In his time, Mitchum worked with figures rooted in the dawn of the movie industry – silent-schooled directors like Raoul Walsh, who gave up cow-boying to become a stunt rider for DW Griffith in 1912, and Rudolph Mate, who, long before coming to Hollywood, spun ghostly expressionism as cameraman for Karl Freund and Carl Dreyer; actors like Lillian Gish, synonymous with Griffith; Laurel and Hardy, as unlikely as that seems; and William Boyd who, before becoming Hopalong Cassidy, had been a favourite lead of Cecil B DeMille's – through to directors like Martin Scorsese and Jim Jarmusch, actors like Jack Nicholson, Robert DeNiro and Johnny Depp.

The most remarkable aspect of Mitchum's journey, however, is not the long, varied line of people he brushed against on his way, but the fact that he always travelled alone, tramping along off to the side. He sometimes cited Spencer Tracy's gruff repose as an early influence, and credited Humphrey Bogart for clearing the way by inaugurating 'the era of the ugly leading man'; but, Mitchum was never a Spencer Tracy type and the amused, resigned melancholy he maintained was far removed from Bogart's nutsy, urgent ferocity.

Ready to rebel without making a show of it, Mitchum brought his own new agenda, a darkness, monumentally bored with all the shiny straight stuff on offer, and profoundly unhopeful about what was coming to replace it – but, still, on the look out for a good time if there was one to be had. There were no actors who foreshadowed his particular sensibility.

Unlike Bogart with John Huston; John Wayne with John Ford; Jimmy Stewart with Frank Capra, Anthony Mann and Alfred Hitchcock; or Cary Grant with Hitchcock, Howard Hawks and George Cukor, Mitchum never hooked up with a particular director for an extended collaboration, an exploration of his persona. It's almost as if he arrived fully formed. From the first, he ploughed his own straight furrow, counting purely on his own strengths, not bothering to look up.

He brought nothing to movies but himself, and that was more than enough. In Mitchum a unique combination of experience, intelligence, talent and attitude occurred; even in his earliest films, his Mitchumness – a very natural stillness, a graceful, jaded insolence, the suggestion of observation, thought and spontaneity, and the confidence to hold a lot in reserve – is recognisably in place. Movies eventually caught up to what he was doing, to an extent; for his part though, whether he was acting with Katherine Hepburn, Marilyn Monroe, Cary Grant, Bruce Dern, Harry Dean Stanton, Bill Murray or Michael Wincott, he continued just doing it. As he put it, across those 53 years, he didn't change 'anything but my underwear.'[1]

And all the way, he continued to put the business down at every opportunity. His professed attitude toward being 'a movie actress', chimed very closely with that of one of his contemporaries, Sterling Hayden, an actor who had a stillness, a sleepy stoicism, a buried mania, and a hint of dreaming poetry not the same as, but parallel to Mitchum's own.

Always one for healthy self-loathing, Hayden had experienced life before Hollywood and, like Mitchum, decided pretty soon into his career that wearing make-up and standing in front of a camera was no damned way for a man

No damned way for a man to earn a living: braving the *River of No Return* with Marilyn Monroe and Tommy Rettig.

to earn a living. An entirely more tortured soul than Mitchum ever allowed himself appear, however, Hayden lacked Mitchum's bottomless self-confidence in his ability to simply draw upon himself and do the job. As a volunteer Commando during the Second World War, Hayden had run guns to partisans in the Yugoslavian mountains under the noses of the Nazi blockade, and parachuted into Croatia to fight side by side with the anti-Axis guerrillas, but the prospect of stepping before a movie camera continued to petrify him.

Still, unlike Mitchum, who always carried around the half-open secret that he'd really wanted to be a writer, Hayden, who had always wanted to write, too, finally bit the bullet and published. His autobiography, *Wanderer*, written after walking out on a movie contract and defying a court custody ruling by sailing from San Francisco to Tahiti with his children on a tall ship, is wild and dense, the sort of thing Herman Melville might have turned out had he been born into the hard-boiled school. Hayden is hard on himself throughout, but in one passage in particular, he rounds savagely, taking himself to task over acting and writing. And, because of parallels in their disposition and ambition, it's tempting to believe that Hayden's excoriating self-interrogation could almost be an X-ray of Mitchum's own attitude, that this might be the small voice gnawing away at him some nights – say the night before he had to turn up on the Twentieth Century Fox soundstage ready to wrestle a man in a gorilla costume for *White Witch Doctor* (1953):

"Why did you never write? Why, instead, did you grovel along through the endless months and years, as a motion-picture actor? What held you to it, to something you so vehemently professed to despise? Could it be that you secretly liked it – that the big dough and the big house and the high life meant more than the aura you spun for those around you to see? ...Sure you liked it, part of it at least. The latitude this life gave you, the opportunity to pose perhaps... Maybe what kept you from writing was that you knew it was tough. Maybe what held you to acting was the fact that you couldn't lose – not really lose, because you could not be considered a

failure if you had not set out to succeed... and you made it quite plain that you didn't give a damn..."[2]

Against this, though, should be balanced the equally plausible notion that Mitchum continued to disparage the motion picture business because it was ridiculous and peopled with idiots, and kept acting because he had experienced the sweating alternative and was smart enough not to want to go back to that. His eternal rationale for continuing working in movies was the simple, honest summation that 'it beats working.'

There is one other possibility. That passage of Hayden's touches on it; the chance that all that not giving a damn was a case of protesting too much, a cover story. Because for all Mitchum's aspersion of his work, his veneer of not caring is dented by scattered hints that he cared very deeply. He knew he was good – when Henry Hathaway, directing that *White Witch Doctor* confection, expressed amazement at Mitchum's ability to, seemingly from memory, run through a six-page scene, including passages in Swahili, in one shaded, impromptu take, Mitchum's response was: 'what'd he expect at these prices, a bum?'

Among all the quotes of his deriding the business, the most telling, and most poignant, is this:

"I always thought I could do better. But you don't get to do better. You get to do more."[3]

Maybe that hope continued to plague him. He talked about retiring often, but he never did.

In a sense, his acting became a surrogate form of writing. Across his career, even as he wandered without plan and often without discrimination from one job to the next, turning up in films great, good, bad and worse, Mitchum developed both a subject and a style.

In terms of style, he perfected an acting language of incredibly dense economy. In the way that Sinatra understood the whole dynamics of singing into a microphone, Mitchum seemed possessed of an innate sense of the less-is-more nature of acting for a movie camera, a fundamental understanding of what the minute scrutiny of that close camera and the

magnification of that big screen could do. He knew how much, or how little, was required to make a moment, a gesture, look real. As a result, his acting – with perhaps the exception of *The Night Of The Hunter*, in which he stylised himself so as to fit a stylised universe – became invisible.

Like certain of the writers of his time working to bring the rhythms of everyday language to their novels, Mitchum, through a process of simplification, a cutting away, developed an American vernacular style of picture acting, concentrating on rhythms of speech and posture that had more to do with the street, the range and the bar room than the stage or the studio set. He kept his movements minimal, fluidly to the point; vitally, though, he often weighted his performance with the suggestion of chasms of meaning and unexpressed feeling beneath the surface. There are parallels with the quivering, tight-lipped qualities of Hemingway, the lyricism of Raymond Chandler describing the loneliness of a road leading out of a city at night.

Once, when writing about Roberto Rossellini, Martin Scorsese came up with a summation that could just as easily, just as perfectly, fit Mitchum:

"Very few artists, in film or any other medium, had the confidence, the nerve or the genius to keep things as simple." [4]

Take those words, type them on a small white card, and mount it in a museum beside a video monitor playing an endless, looped, slow-motion montage: Mitchum moving, listening, observing in the landscapes of *Pursued* (1947), *Out of the Past* (1947), *The Lusty Men* (1952), *Heaven Knows, Mr Allison* (1957), cutting up the bright main street of *Cape Fear* (1962), wandering the lonely Brooklyn Bridge in *Two for the Seasaw* (1962), coming out of the city darkness in *The Friends of Eddie Coyle* (1973), fading back into it in *Farewell, My Lovely* (1975), sadly kissing Natassja Kinski in *Maria's Lovers* (1985), talking to a stuffed bear in *Dead Man* (1995).

His great theme, meanwhile, in all those films and in many more, was an exploration of

the varieties of aloneness, of being eternally outside. In part this was down to the sorts of roles he was offered, and in part it was due to the way his playing, his presence affected those roles. Eventually, the two merged, and the films he was in began changing purely because he was in them.

The cast of characters he animated were distracted mavericks, outcasts, misfits. Distantly anguished men, but electing to appear comfortable in that anguish, simultaneously alienated and perfectly at home in it all. Mitchum took the independent-laconic-lonesome-stranger archetype familiar in American's cultural tradition from cowboys to cops, and infected it with diseases of uncertainty, fatigue and ambiguity, suggesting the possibility of a different kind of American, a different kind of America. He started out in movies as a heavy, a peripheral bad guy, a big ugly unshaven mug up to no damn good, and he carried the traces of that character throughout his career, corrupting the DNA structures of all the other men he played. Even playing a hero, Mitchum embodies precisely what the critic Robert Warshow once defined as:

"that part of the American psyche that rejects the qualities and the demands of modern life, which rejects 'Americanism' itself." [5]

In noir movies, war movies, weird movies and Westerns, his characters were united in that they were all inscribed with the calm acceptance that, no matter how tough they were, they would never get out of this world alive. They seemed intimate with that knowledge, and carried it as the filter through which they viewed everything else, leading to their resignation, their melancholia, and their insolent, amused irony, no matter how good the good time or how bad the bad fix.

What follows is not just a list of all the movies Mitchum ever made. Rather, it's a consideration of the key works in which he articulated and examined this condition – the biography of a persona through its various levels of reincarnation, flitting intact from one genre to another, starting in the unstable, unlit region of the pictures where it was first allowed to escape.

Chapter Five
Noir Movies

Film noir is… well, what? Neither a genre nor a style, it's more like a thread, a drift, a mood, a strain of thought. Or a stain. Noir can be triggered by sex or money, or sex and money, or by a mysterious metal suitcase full of shining nuclear apocalypse. It has something bitter and pessimistic and neurotic at heart. It said the world is not a place to trust. It said look out… what's the point?

Noir takes in movies about laconic private eyes and neurotic cops and treacherous killer women, about boxers and truck drivers and farmers and psychopaths, about Hollywood scriptwriters, newspaper reporters, sick old rich men and poor sad teenagers. About soldiers staggering mechanically back from war not knowing the fighting's over. About doctors and ambulance drivers who couldn't care less about saving lives. Even about cowboys. It unfolds in dim smoky city worlds, in dingy border town dives, in suburbs and in bright little rural communities. And when it was happening, all these places looked as though they were perched on the edge of an abyss. It's hard to say what noir is, except that you recognise it when you see it.

The French were the first to see it, in 1946. Since the country had fallen to the Nazis in 1940, no American films had been imported, but in the years after the Second World War, the embargo dam finally burst and the Hollywood-starved country was awash with a backlog glut of American movies. Watching five years' worth of the dream factory product in such a concentrated rush, French critics noticed that a lot of these films had their roots in a new kind of nightmare, an awkward, jazzy anxiety.

Many of the movies looked as though they'd been filmed in cities at the bottom of an ocean of oil, pierced occasionally by stark, sudden shafts of moonlight revealing pained, grotesque faces close-up in the murk. The uneasiness wasn't confined solely to cop movies or gangster movies or mystery movies; the stain spread. These were films swarming with blackness, so they called them black films.

Noir was conceived in the Depression, but born with the war. For one thing, a host of film-makers and movie technicians fled Europe for Hollywood. Many of the most influential noirists arrived on the sunny west coast from the darkness of Germany – directors like Fritz Lang, Robert Siodmak, Billy Wilder, Edgar G Ulmer – bringing with them some of the old country's Expressionist tradition, memories of the stylised, visually dark and jagged silent movies of the early 1920s, pictures of psychologically tortured, even lunatic worlds.

In Hollywood, this tradition meshed with the pulpier, grittier look of the gangster genre, always more inclined toward action and documentary than art. A new dark celluloid kingdom was born.

Noir festered in its most interesting colours in the basement of the B-Movie – where cash was always tight, but particularly during the war – and that darkness was eagerly embraced down there for reasons as much rooted in economics as psychology: if you keep the scene blanketed in darkness, there's no need to go spending money building and dressing sets.

The inspiration for the stories to be told in these places, tales of bad things happening at night, cities at night, dark streets, dark corners, sprung from the black ink wells of a quartet of Dashiell Hammett, James M Cain, Cornel Woolrich and Raymond Chandler, high cartographers of a hidden America, a hidden world. Children of the doomed, melancholic, gothic perversion of Edgar Allen Poe and the tersely romantic, near-neurotic toughness of Ernest Hemingway, fathers to the sanguine hopelessness of Albert Camus, in their writing – variously labelled pulp, hard-boiled, crime, mystery, detective – they laid the

foundations for what would become the noir world along America's Pacific coast.

The war had another influence. As noir was born, the generation that had staggered, bowed down with apprehension but nursing high hopes through the uncertainties of the Depression found themselves confronted with undeniable evidence that the world awaiting them was a charnel house.

Atrocities were being committed on an industrial scale across the globe. Boys who had been playing ball games 10 years previously were turned into serial killers, doing things to each other with flame throwers and bayonets and machine guns and bombs. Concentration camps were operating in Europe, holding camps were set up in America. Cities were burning. Atomic bombs were dropped on the citizens of oblivious cities. And back home, they found the girls they dreamed were

waiting for them had changed, bust out of domesticity and in no hurry to go back.

Studios set their A-talent to producing a deluge of morale-boosting movies and propaganda to take audience's minds off of all the blood and dirt in the air: more bright, busy musicals than ever before; teary-eyed escapist soldier-boy romances; Bing Crosby and Bob Hope stuck eternally together and tussling with casual rancour over Dorothy Lamour someplace exotic. Blithe and inspirational, sunny movies from a sunny world, ambassadors, propaganda, even weapons for America.

Such was the day-lit Yankee front. Honest noir came leaking out from the backroom, though, a nightsweat reaction to all of that sunny stuff. Movies like the terrified, nauseated id throwing up.

Robert Mitchum arrived just in time to catch the first wave of the convulsion. His own flip

Cities at the bottom of an ocean of oil: *Out of the Past* (1947).

fatalism chimed extremely closely with that of the lonesome Chandleresque anti-heroes and the horny sons of Cain that the noir movies demanded. Mitchum seemed to recognise this black planet for what it was, knew it held danger and sickness and disappointment – but that was no more than he seemed to expect. He sashayed through the nightmare, comfortable in it.

The scepticism and disenchantment Mitchum exuded, the dreamy, uncertain pessimism that could sometimes be glimpsed in his eyes, coupled with his front of cocksure, street-savvy toughness, made him a natural. He looked like he had nothing to lose, like he was born to lose, like noir in a bottle. In these movies, Mitchum found the subject he would explore across his career: the outsider. Over and over these movies would present him as a misfit, an outcast, condemned to wander. He wouldn't fit, and he wouldn't care about it, but you could see it gnawing at his soul all the same. He projected an alert, if melancholy intelligence, but gave himself over to laziness, to lust, to stupidity with alarming readiness, as if for the sake of having something to do.

In these films he nailed down and articulated his loner sensibility, crafting an expression of being neither one thing nor the other, an independent state, floating between society and its underworld, occasionally interacting, but ultimately rejected by and rejecting both. Above all, in noir he became a man with a past, a past he had to escape, and sometimes a past so strong that it came close to using his future all up. A man on a black elevator going down. In the noir world to come, Mitchum would often be punished for his past, and for the way he didn't care whether he was punished. Sometimes he survived, sometimes not. He wasn't being punished for renouncing the straight life, so much as for sticking quietly to his own meandering path. Walking like a winner along the slowest, most strangely scenic routes to defeat.

When Strangers Marry

Director: William Castle. Monogram Pictures, 1944. (aka *Betrayed*)

Synopsis

In Philadelphia, visiting businessman Sam Prescott (Dick Elliot) drunkenly flashes cash around a nearly empty bar. Overhearing that a stranger can't find a hotel room, he offers to share his own, and the two leave. The next morning, Prescott is found strangled with a silk stocking, his money gone. Meanwhile, the recently married Millie Baxter (Kim Hunter), travels to New York to join her travelling salesman husband, Paul (Dean Jagger), but at the hotel where they've arranged to meet, discovers he hasn't arrived. In the foyer, Millie encounters her ex-boyfriend Fred Graham (Robert Mitchum), himself a travelling salesman. Millie spends an anxious night alone. The next morning, at Fred's urging, Millie reports Paul's absence to the police. It emerges she married Paul knowing very little about him. Later, Fred hears from the desk clerk that Millie has checked out. She meets Paul in a run-down apartment. He acts shifty and orders her not to see Fred again. Suspicions already aroused, Millie discovers Paul was in Prescott's hotel the night of the murder and becomes convinced he is the killer. Nevertheless, she remains in love with him and the two attempt to escape the police dragnet out to catch him. Paul admits to Millie he shared Prescott's room, but maintains he is not the killer. The police capture the couple in a flophouse hotel, and Paul is charged with murder. Speaking with Fred, Millie realises that he, in fact, is The Silk-stocking Strangler. She reports to the police, who arrive to search Fred's room for Prescott's money. As he talks to the police lieutenant in the hotel corridor, Fred breaks down, and is caught attempting to slip a self-addressed envelope filled with the incriminating cash into a mail-slot.

If you've seen both, it's impossible to watch the sweet, easily broken Kim Hunter thrown headlong into the black paranoid mass of the fake city in William Castle's *When Strangers Marry* without thinking of the same girl making the same journey a year earlier in her debut movie, *The Seventh Victim*, one of the peaks in producer Val Lewton's intensely personal cycle of melancholic, minimalist B-horrors for RKO[1]. Both cities are the same city: a studio-bound, claustrophobic maze of shadow, conjured as an abstract facsimile of some half-remembered nightmare New York. In both you sense vaguely that, out of sight around that corner there, behind the linear facades of these one-way streets, the city simply stops, hanging abruptly alone as the only overcrowded outpost in a vast blank expanse.

In *The Seventh Victim*, Hunter travels to this New York to discover what has happened to her elder sister. She finds no trace of her, but meets a brother-in-law she didn't know she had, and falls in love. It emerges the exotically mournful sister has fallen afoul of a prissy group of Greenwich Village Satanists, who are trying to persuade her to kill herself over an infringement of their adolescent code, without realising she has already long wearied and decided to be done with life anyway.

Alongside Hunter and the oppressive city, there is also in both films the anxious sideline presence of a perfect, rarely-glimpsed character actor, Lou Lubin. In *The Seventh Victim*, Lubin, with creased, slicked-back crummy hawk features, nervously animates an unlikely little private eye who soon gets murdered. His death is Hunter's fault: she pushes this stick-like little guy toward his fate, stabbed with a pair of scissors along an empty black corridor in a deserted cosmetics factory, his corpse later fetched up aboard a mundanely terrifying evening subway car Hunter finds herself aboard.

In *When Strangers Marry*, Lubin is Jack Hauser, trembling Philadelphian barman, chewing his lip, bony fingers pounding out nervous jazz on a policeman's desktop as he tries to remember the face of the strangler he served, the name of the New York hotel that strangler was headed for. So extremely nervous is Lubin here – face collapsing, mind crowding with the image of the fat, lecherously happy features of the dead man, the memory that it was Lubin himself who suggested murderer and victim could share their death room – it's as though some recollection of his own previous-life murder in that perfumed corridor dark is dimly re-emerging, terror and confusion flooding his face.

Both movies, too, feature a visit to the busy, lonely hopelessness of a Missing Persons bureau. In these films Kim plays a tentative Hunter, an uneasy searcher entering the labyrinth to locate someone with whom she should be extremely close – a sister, a husband – but, as she comes to recognise, does not know at all. In both cases, this person is not to be found where they should – a weird, austere cosmetics parlour in *The Seventh Victim,* a tall lonesome hotel filled with travelling salesmen in *When Strangers Marry* – and in fact seems at first not merely to have gone missing, but to have entirely ceased to exist; slipped off around one of those corners into the white. And in both films the missing person is caught up in something weary, dark and desperate. Indeed, they may have lost their souls.

Tiny Kim from the clean-air sticks, at the opening of *When Strangers Marry,* caught inside the smoking iron of a rushing train, clattering into a long dark tunnel, the threshold to this other New York. Where Castle's film and Lewton's diverge is soon after Hunter finds herself alone and lost here. In Lewton's movie, although Satan sits in banal afternoon clubs and brushes the steamy curtains of dripping showers in friendly Italian bathrooms, although there are dying women coughing along bereft hallways, although there are empty rooms with abandoned, still-smoking cigarettes and patient hanging nooses, and although the film has the most incredibly hopeless ending of all time – despite all this, the city at least offers some little warmth, exemplified by the earthy momma-poppa proprietary team of Dante's restaurant who shelter Hunter.

In Castle's film, however, although the hanging despair is less cosmic, the city is comprehensively hopeless; not a single friendly face in sight. When Hunter's Millie thinks she has finally found her husband, played by Dean Jagger, instead of love and security she discovers some kind of seedy shape-shifter. Summoned to a street-corner restaurant she spies Jagger through a window; when she looks again, he has been replaced by a threatening fat man. When she goes to his basement room for the first time – a barren place the wind blows through – she finds another name on the post box and a bizarre, framed photograph

of some other sinister man on the mantle. Jagger even baffles Hugo the Great, the rough, cigar-chewing mental marvel the two visit at a night time carnival during their honeymoon tour of the city, who comes up blank when trying to guess what Jagger does, is: 'first time I've ever missed.'

Jagger is an actor who can win an audience's sympathies easily, with his look of decent, harried nobility on the verge of crumbling (think of his limping grey General in 1954's *White Christmas*), but here, Castle finds the dead, black spots in his eyes, a smug ugly pettiness, quick to panic, deceit and recrimination.

A small-minded conglomeration of weary misery, this New York decays around Hunter's hopes into a place of shadows and damp rented rooms, shouts in the night and lights that flick on and off. Things go wrong, children's cries go unanswered and transport is undependable. In a beautiful sliver of cheap detail, the window of Jagger's apartment looks onto a narrow cardboard alleyway where kids squabble over dirty marbles in the dust; in the wall opposite, another window frames a view into a room where a withering blind man in dark glasses is read loud newspaper accounts of murder by his nurse, figures dressed by Samuel Beckett, sketched in charcoal by Edward Hopper.

Castle summarises his universe of weighted dread with a single, extremely weird shot towards the movie's end, when they are on the run and Jagger has sent Hunter to rent a room in an unfriendly flophouse hotel in the tenebrous part of town: from an infernally low angle, the camera gazes up at a black door hanging in a grey angle of light, encroached on by gloom. Out from the black surrounding muck, Hunter's gloved hand creeps to ring the doorbell. Then, agonisingly slowly, the door opens to reveal the pale, puffy face of a curious little pig-tailed girl floating small there in the crack of blackness behind, her mother's voice sounding harshly from somewhere out of sight as the girl clutches a fearful rag doll to her chin.

No hope. There's a newspaper-vendor in this city, for instance. Now, anyone who has seen any film, ever, that features a news-stand man will understand these sweetheart guys are the salt of the earth on which any city is built. Grouchy, maybe, or a little punchy from a failed career in the ring, but good guys; like the newspaper guy played by Jimmy Archer, himself a former middleweight fighter, with whom Mitchum's Philip Marlowe trades chummy punches and DiMaggio baseball banter in *Farewell, My Lovely* (1975), who provides Mitchum with a no-questions sanctuary to hole-up in while sleeping off an armful of drugs he's been shot-up with, exactly the sort of fella you'd like to turn up when things looked bleak.

In *When Strangers Marry,* having discovered that, contrary to his assurances, her husband had in fact stayed in the murder hotel the night of the killing, Kim Hunter flees into the night. Jostled by faceless citizens all pouring along the sidewalk in the other direction, she soon comes across a fabulous news stand tended by the most surly, dog-faced vendor ever to have pulled a cap across his head. A poochy cartoon grouch of a guy with a thick, hairy brow, staring intently at a sandwich painstakingly grasped between his huge paw-like hands, as though it might drop to the concrete if he devoted anything less than full concentration to the task of keeping his mitts around it, this is The Anti-News-stand Guy, unreasonableness personified.

Does he have a Philadelphia paper, Hunter asks, looking for a report on the killing.

Without looking up, Nah.

Is he sure?

Yeah, he's pretty sure.

Couldn't he at least look?

What date is she after?

August 8.

Still without looking up, No, we don't got none of those.

Couldn't he at least look?

Finally, the guy turns just a fraction of an inch and pulls a single paper exactly from a pile: Whaddaya know, Philadelphia, August 8.

He had it all the time! He just, absolutely, couldn't be bothered getting it for her! Only on the outlying precincts of hell could there be such unremarked, lethargic spite. Strangely, the actor playing this newspaper vendor, Dewey Robinson, had also turned up in *The Seventh Victim,* as the can't-be-bothered subway cop Hunter runs into on her nightmare train, unconcerned by her frantic reports of Lou Lubin's corpse in the next carriage. Robinson looked like the foul-tempered dog Droopy always got the better of in the Tex Avery cartoons; his crabby demeanour in part explained by the fact that, although he showed

up on the margins of over 140 films between 1931 and his death in Las Vegas in 1950, he as often as not went uncredited.

In *The Seventh Victim,* Hunter finds herself surrounded by vaguely predatory men, teeming with half-glimpsed sexual motives, centring on this convent schoolgirl like sharks (how beautifully quickly her missing sister's colossally bland husband decides to give up his weird lost spouse and opt for the ample attractions of his nun-schooled kid sister-in-law), but they are finally all fairly decent types, and, for all their strange manias, willing to help her sort it all out. In *When Strangers Marry,* Hunter runs into something much, much worse. She runs into…

Robert Mitchum, guising as Fred Graham. Fred Graham! From back home! An enormous small-town boy at large in the city. Fred Graham: a solid, symmetrical name, two first names, belt and braces. Fred is announced by the weird scampering waddle entrance of Junior the dog, across the shiny floor of a hotel lobby; this is great stuff: the guy calls his dog Junior. Mitchum and Junior make a fantastic double act, the palm-sized, funny, funky little dog coming on like his familiar. Junior is a tiny dog, black and eerie, with a chain around his neck. Junior is a ridiculous dog, his littleness pointing up just how huge Mitchum is.

When he first spies Kim Hunter, all lost and lonely in the foyer of the Hotel Sherman, Mitchum's reaction is superb: cued by his eyebrows, his hat actually rises up and stands briefly to attention on his head in delight. He absolutely glides across the floor to her; meanwhile, at his feet, Junior too stands erect, up on hind legs at Hunter's ankles.

As Fred, Mitchum smokes a cigarette with his coffee for breakfast, but also smokes a grown-up pipe, that juts out in a black cartoon geometry, slashing from his mouth at an absurd angle, almost Tati-esque. If this were *The Seventh Victim,* this young Mitchum, clean-cut and 27, and just nicer-seeming than the shifty, 41-year-old Jagger, would be helping Kim Hunter out-and-out and up-and-up. And, indeed, he makes all the moves here, takes matters protectively in hand – making phone calls, arranging the visit to the Missing Person's Bureau that somehow ends up in the Homicide office – but his true motives, of steering the police away from himself in the direction of Jagger, are slowly revealed.

Fred, the travelling salesman from back home: this solitary, charming big guy with his little-boy dog, plodding an endless circuit around all these confusing places and empty hotel rooms, the same room in so many different cities. Fred the killer. Has city life infected him, has his mind simply spasmed, unable to take in all the noise and dirty air? Or was he always this way, waiting? He knows the city, many cities, all with the same eternal hotel at their centre. And he knows the town he's left behind, a suffocating place filled with frustrating girls like Hunter. He carries that place and that frustration around inside him, a cosy, rotting locale he can return to when he clicks the bedside hotel lamps off at nights and the big-city party lights from across the way flash parallelograms on and off across the ceiling, punctuating his rhythmic thoughts about the package of silk stockings he's got waiting for her.

Mitchum plays a precious little scene that exactly paints Fred and Junior's purgatory life: cutting to his room as Hunter calls him from a pay phone, the camera finds Mitchum alone save for his dog, just waiting, vacant, for the next workday to dawn. He sits in silence on the edge of his transient bed, with his pipe and his dog and his robe, slowly untying his shoes. Nowhere else to go, face emptied. At first sight it's a scene of quiet content. On subsequent viewings it becomes a scream of total absence.

Those first nights, with her husband missing, Mitchum comes to visit Hunter and offer comfort in her high hotel. Drowsing huge and heavy-lidded in an armchair with a look of serene square content on his face, a huge, many-bulbed sign flicks off and on through the window in the dark enticing metropolis out there behind his head, like a glittery thought bubble spelling out buried desires: DANCE – DANCE – DANCE.

Pipe jutting, that ridiculous Freud-dog cradled in his lap while he strokes its little black head with a big hand and nods and yawns along with the syrupy music seeping from the radio, Mitchum sighs a sleepy murmur toward his ex-girlfriend, who sits rigidly facing him from another armchair: 'This is like old times in Grantsville.'

What exactly is he remembering here? Is it the stifling frustration of their dating that he recalls? Because, beneath the comfortable, dozey surface, the tension screams. Is this the existence he had offered when he proposed – a twisted domestic tableau, nights spent staring at each other in silence, a sick light pressing feverishly behind the curtains of their life?

They talk a little, Mitchum moving closer to the edge of sleep. Perhaps dreamy memories of the man he strangled are starting to emerge and become tangled with his conscious thoughts, for finally, somnolently he mutters from within his reverie: 'Places are all alike, Millie. You can't run away from yourself.'

Mitchum hangs out for a while with the police Lieutenant out to catch the killer, played by Neil Hamilton. They first meet in Hamilton's office, but later the policeman seeks him out at his hotel, discovers him basking in Turkish baths among the bowels of the building. With Hamilton smaller, almost demure beside him, Mitchum sits flagrantly massive in the steam room, a towel around his waist, another draped ridiculously over his head, giving him the passing look of an ancient Egyptian labourer. In the margins of this improbable scene, Mitchum has fun sketching all sorts of calmly scratchy physical stuff – he pours a bucket of ice-water over his head and shivers like a wet cartoon, he does a thing with a finger in his eye, itching it, poking around in there, before digging something infinitesimal out he then peers at, he wipes at his nose with his hand. When the possibility of going with the cop and catching a nearby ball-game swings into his head he seems genuinely, mildly eager to go – it doesn't matter to this salesman whether he does any work that day, any day, he sincerely, serenely doesn't care.

Instead of the ball-game, Hamilton takes Mitchum back to his precinct where he shows him slides, mundane mug-shots of the cast of a particularly grizzly murder similar to this current Silk-Stocking Strangler affair: killer, accomplice and victims with dreary faces caught in mundanely odd photographic moments, like heads clipped from Weegee. Mitchum watches the slideshow, listening to the grim killing tale, sucking a cigarette, and seems genuinely satisfied at its end, offering an amused hipster's blasé appraisal: 'You tell a good story, Lieutenant.' Just before he leaves, the cop throws a comment 'A man who murders once for money will go on murdering for money.' Catching it, Mitchum turns the idea over, before letting slip a small,

inner-directed reflective murmur: 'Yes, I suppose so.' Not so bad, really. He can accept that.

Near the end of the film, after Jagger has been arrested and charged with murder, Hunter goes to find Mitchum and ask his help. He is discovered alone with pipe and dog up on the chessboard roof garden of the hotel, gazing out into the oblivious city moving blackly all around, sitting in the same blank stillness with which he waits out nights in his room. Hunter has just received a forwarded letter that Mitchum, knowing nothing of her marriage, had sent from Philadelphia the morning after he'd choked the porky life from the laughing businessman, in which he lets slip the clue to his guilt. He tries to prevent her, but she opens the envelope.

As Hunter, standing at the roof's edge with her back to Mitchum, reads his words and begins to understand, behind her the calm killer inside

suddenly steps to the front. Mitchum makes something extraordinary happen here – it's as though something, some part of life, simply falls from his face. His eyebrows lift, practically imperceptibly and, all at once, he is changed, become cold, seeming almost distantly curious as he moves in toward Hunter and sets himself to push her over the parapet, gets ready to watch her fall down into the slight dark wind.

As Mitchum moves, Junior starts to bark, alerting her to the danger, and he snatches his hands away; he's betrayed by his dog, his one true companion, his familiar. The UK title of *When Strangers Marry* was *Betrayed*, but this in fact is the most prominent instance of betrayal in the whole movie.

Soon after comes Mitchum's final, incredible, sweating collapse. Hamilton and his cops have arrived to search his rooms for the dead man's money, but he has already sealed it inside a self-addressed envelope stowed in his jacket pocket. As the busy policemen go through his hotel room, he steps nonchalantly into the hotel corridor to shoot the breeze with the Lieutenant, inching closer and closer to the mail-slot in the wall to send the cash safely away, one eye on the minute-hand of his watch, all the time creeping closer to 10pm, the final postal collection.

As they wait for the search to conclude, Hamilton, constantly tossing keys in the air, starts telling more of his party stories about murderers and how they get caught. As they talk, Mitchum manages anxiously to slip the envelope into the slot, but Hamilton notices he isn't listening and, to distract the policeman's attention away from the mail cascading down the mail-chute behind him, Mitchum launches into an extraordinary, nonsensical monologue, his voice starting down in the depleted, slumberous register he has employed throughout the film, but all the time raising towards frenzied breakdown, gaining speed, the words tumbling faster and faster toward a fractured, wild hollering peak, like a desperately improvised chorus of paranoid jazz riffing, a definitive blowing of cool:

Mitchum: "Say, do you remember that woman who poisoned six husbands for their insurance? What was her name? Goldsmith, Emma Goldsmith. And the man in the case the… chauffeur wasn't it? They collected over a hundred thousand dollars. They would've got away with it too, if it hadn't been for Emma Goldsmith's…"

Hamilton: "Borden. You mean Emma Borden."

Mitchum: "No, No. This was Gol – you're thinking about somebody else, this, this was Goldsmith, I remember distinctly, I know a buyer in Miami named Goldsmith, Herbert Goldsmith, I thought about him as soon as I heard about the case. He took me out to his house one time, he's got a beautiful house in the hills overlookin' the ocean…"

[right here, sweat beading his forehead, Mitchum smiles, as though proud of what he's proven, happy, like a child out to convince].

Hamilton: "There are no hills in Miami."

Mitchum: "No, that's right, he didn't live in Miami, he lived just outside. You oughta see that house, it's the most beautiful thing you've ever seen. Fifty rooms and a golf course!"

By now, Mitchum is frantically grabbing the cop's lapels, screaming into his face about Herbert's beautiful house and its fabulous golf, the veneer cracked and lying in pieces on the floor. It's the last we see of him. They find his envelope, burst open at the bottom of the mail-chute, dollar bills leaking like paper guts. In a coda, Jagger and Hunter find themselves happy aboard another train, like the one Hunter took into this film, where they meet another young bride en route to meet her new husband, somewhere in the city.

At the time of its release, only the most perceptive eyes recognised *When Strangers Marry* which is today often declared The Finest B-Movie Ever Made. Among the film's original champions was Orson Welles, who, in his column for *The New York Post* in 1945, urged his readers to go and see the movie on two separate occasions. Likewise, Manny Farber, who, writing in *The New Republic* commented on the way Castle's film captured 'the solemn melancholia of being troubled and lonely in a strange city,' and Mitchum's 'sardonic, cold-faced' turn.

William Castle, the picture's director, subsequently worked with Welles as associate producer on *The Lady From Shanghai* (1948), and would become infamous as a horror showman, notorious for such incredible works as *The Tingler* (1959), eventually becoming the producer responsible for bringing *Rosemary's Baby* (1968) – another tale of a fearful young bride in a new city – to the screen. His direction here is exceptional, like a cheap American Hitchcock, squeezing more than would seem possible from 67 minutes and a budget of $50,000, creating a film at once incredibly economical, but crammed with layers of dirty detail, a weird New York that breathes, with its own busy Harlem and boxing champions, its own idle motorcycle cops, weary coast-to-coast car-ride stations and lonely haunted walkways.

This was the 21st movie Robert Mitchum had appeared in since debuting a year before as a dusty peripheral rustler in *Hoppy Serves A Writ*, and was the second and last picture he completed for

Monogram, the tiny studio through which producers Frank and Maurice King released their films (early in the movie, a hotel page boy wanders past, calling beyond the edge of the film: 'Mr King! Mr King!'). Fantastically smudgy, straight-ahead cinema, when Jean Luc Godard directed his dead-eyed-murder-punk-on-the-run debut, *A Bout de Souffle* (1959), he dedicated the picture to Monogram.

In Mitchum's first Monogram picture, *Johnny Doesn't Live Here Anymore* (1944), a comedy, or so it claims, he'd turned up in uniform in the last reel as an army officer looking for a quiet place to spend quality time with his wife, only to find the room he has inherited keys to occupied by a bizarre invisible gremlin and the recently cursed Simone Simon, the mischievously feline actress best remembered for her performance in Val Lewton and Jacques Tourneur's *Cat People* (1943).

When Mitchum's career threatened to take off at RKO, with whom he signed a seven-year contract in 1944, the King Brothers, known for their association with gangland figures, contacted the larger studio, claiming they still had rights over the actor, a claim RKO's lawyers blew out of the water. The Kings supposedly wanted Mitchum to lead in their hoodlum biopic *Dillinger* (1945), a role which eventually, memorably, went to an itchy, fit-to-bust Lawrence Tierney. To give them their credit, though, the thought of the easily charming young Mitchum as John Dillinger, the mythic Midwestern Robin Hood of the Depression, crashing out of jail and roaring along under the leaves of rural backroads in Model Ts, fake wooden gun in his jacket, like some pistol-totin' psycho precursor to *Thunder Road* (1958), remains a frustratingly enticing one.

Importantly, *When Strangers Marry* was the first noir Mitchum participated in, a genre he would come to personify through his performance in *Out of the Past*. The film marked his first truly sizeable role, receiving third billing after Hunter and Jagger, giving him time to stretch out and relax into his signature lazy-panther sashay, as when he first zeros in on Hunter and sails across that hotel lobby. Having played soldiers and cowboys almost exclusively, this was the first time Mitchum could really be seen moving among the sidewalks of a city dressed as a civilian. Plotting his own course away from the demands of the range and the uniform, he breezes easily through the film as though he has all the time in the world and is vaguely looking out for ways to kill it.

Although way out west Mitchum had played his share of transient sideline baddies and, the previous year – in one of those unlikely meetings history sometimes leaves as a gift – in Laurel and Hardy's *The Dancing Masters* (1943) he had played an ugly urban customer called Mickey, pulling on his first raincoat and soft dark hat (a premonition of his iconic *Out of the Past* manifestation) to visit a ballet school and briefly menace Stan and Ollie, this was Mitchum's first real, fully (mal)formed villain. The moment when he finally cracked open his lacquered hep and watched, gibbering, his own sicko insides spill out, was the initial sweating clue to the various flavours of acting he had access to but would only rarely be called on to employ, the first visible display from the grotesques swimming his mind. A decade would pass before he would be again required to pull on bad man's rags and let another beast escape, playing a maniacal pioneer, isolated among the snow drifts of the Nevada mountains in *Track of the Cat* (1954).

For the time being, though, back in the city, from *When Strangers Marry* Mitchum headed further into the new gloom. New York the borough was called again, sometimes San Francisco or Los Angeles, Boston, Mexico City, Acapulco, Cuernavaca, Macao, even, but always the same place, the roads that seemed to promise ways out leading only deeper into the pit. He'd wandered in off the prairie, come home on leave, found this shifting city full of dim, undependable surfaces and flashing danger, and gone AWOL. Relaxing into it, he saw it held a darkness. Only rarely again, however, would he be the one who saw what was really going on.

Noir Movies
Out of the Past

Director: Jacques Tourneur. RKO Radio Pictures, 1947 (aka *Build My Gallows High*)

Synopsis

A stranger arrives at a gas station in the small town of Bridgeport, telling the deaf-mute kid working there (Dickie Moore) he's looking for the owner, Jeff Bailey (Robert Mitchum). The stranger tells Jeff a man wants to see him at Lake Tahoe. Driving there with Ann (Virginia Huston), a local woman he's dating, Jeff relates his past. His real name is Markham. Working as a private detective in New York alongside a man named Fisher (Steve Brodie), he was hired by racketeer Whit Sterling (Kirk Douglas), the man he's going to see, to find his mistress, Kathie Moffett (Jane Greer), who'd shot the mobster and absconded with $40,000. Jeff tracked Kathie to Mexico. She claimed she hadn't stolen from Sterling and Jeff fell for her. They ran from Sterling, until Fisher, working for Sterling, found them. Kathie killed Fisher and disappeared, leaving evidence she'd stolen the $40,000 after all. After burying Fisher, Jeff moved to Bridgeport. Arriving at Lake Tahoe, Jeff sends Ann home. Meeting Sterling, he's shocked to find Kathie back with him. Sterling wants Jeff to travel to San Francisco and retrieve documents his accountant, Eels, is blackmailing him with. In San Francisco, Jeff realises he's the fall guy in a plan to murder Eels and discovers Kathie has named him as Fisher's killer. Two murders pinned to his name, Jeff flees a police manhunt; however, he has Sterling's documents and, confronting him, persuades the gangster to surrender Kathie to the police for Fisher's murder — but Kathie kills Sterling. She tells Jeff they can start afresh together and he seems to submit; secretly, however, he telephones the police. When Kathie realises Jeff's betrayal she shoots him dead, killed herself by police bullets. In Bridgeport, Ann asks the kid if Jeff was really leaving with Kathie. He nods.

Skimming sadly across shadowy American continents, New York to Mexico City, Acapulco to San Francisco, but opening and closing in a little town called Bridgeport, *Out of the Past* whispers of the hinterland darkness surrounding the emphatic metropolitan loci of the US. Many of the small places scattered there steadfastly take the same name for their shouts of identity; a handful of Bridgeports litter the map, sea to shining sea, the ubiquity of the name, like blurring generic branding, reflecting the thoughtless size of the country, the flattening distances, how safely, how dreadfully easily you could disappear.

Metaphor hovers about the parish. 'Every time I look up at the sky, I think of all the places I've never been,' murmurs Virginia Huston, as local despondent sweetheart Ann, to Mitchum's Jeff Bailey when first we see them, fishing on the outskirts of town. 'Yes,' he replies, 'and every time you look up, they're all the same' – a line echoing his sleepy murderer's throwaway in *When Strangers Mary*: 'Places are all alike… You can't run away from yourself,' a lesson Mitchum will learn intimately in this film.

Mitchum's presence heightens the hazy quality of the place: 30 years before Tourneur's movie, he was born in another Bridgeport far away, a bustling little harbour community hugging the US's eastern shore. Just as that town witnessed his actual birth, Tourneur's picture has come to be seen as the site for the celluloid genesis of Robert Mitchum, the birthplace of his particular cool. Much of what now hangs around Mitchum is rooted in his sad, snotty, soft gumshoe through this film: in the way Miles Davis' album forever fixed him in many minds, this is Mitchum's own *Kind of Blue*, a defining artefact, his unhurried playing filled with melancholic blue notes, pauses, and scurrying flashes of flip hipster wit with which he would always be associated.

At the core of the Mitchum persona is stamped this calm knowledge: *You can never win, but you can choose how you go about being defeated. If you can be bothered.* Here, he finds the rhythm of that wisdom, spells it out, over a roulette table, to Jane Greer, the agent of his destruction. 'I didn't know there was a way to win,' she says. He responds with philosophy: 'There's a way to lose more slowly.'

White buildings clustered beneath enormous skies, this Bridgeport has an ambiguous nature. There's old, good, poetic American beauty surrounding the place Mitchum has chosen to

hide in, maybe responding to the frontier call of the cowboys he used to be, but the town is filled with small minds, squares, suspicious of the jazzy city ways he also understands, the worldly mystery and relaxed misery. This is a limbo town, where he waits to see whether the judgment he knows must someday be passed on his life – a life of willingly crooked blind-eye work, easy betrayal, damning sex and bodies buried shallow in obscure forests damp with night – will allow him access to the heaven he glimpses when he speaks about building a home on that bright lakeside, or condemn him back into dark hells he's already tasted.

Yet, much as it is an allegorical anywhere, the town is a defined, geographically specific locale – Bridgeport, California – and its reality bears on the movie. The Bridgeport scenes were filmed on location, in crystalline winter light, weather crisp enough to make the actors' breath transpire; by contrast, although Tourneur sent second units across the country to capture exteriors, the cities

in the film, marked by damnation, were created on the RKO lot: fake, airless, and all within the postcode of the abiding unlit city noir described.

During the titles, landscape shots spell out the lonely radiance of the region. Dark and snowy Ansel Adams mountains. Dim stretching plains. Bare trees and trees with pines bending slightly in the wind, everything laid out deserted beneath immense wintry skies. Between two sets of titles, the camera finds a busy sign, cheerily butting an emptied road to interrupt lonely nature with reports of civilisation:

Bridgeport	⇨	1
Bishop	⇨	76
Los Angeles	⇨	349
Lake Tahoe	⇦	78
Reno	⇦	98

The sign summarises the movie. Reno and Lake Tahoe, the two locales associated with Whit Sterling, the pernicious gangster that Mitchum

On the beach: Mitchum succumbs to the spider-girl, Jane Greer.

once crossed, lie back in the road's memory. Mitchum's past has solidified, the tarmac cutting the countryside is a two-way strip of time snaking from there to his futureless Bridgeport present. Along it, one of the minions of the past has been dispatched to fetch him back.

At our first sight of Bridgeport, against a lowering horizon, an open-topped black car moves into frame, aimed at the town. Now we're in the back seat, looking over the driver's shoulder as he drives the main street. We feel the decent space of the town, see matchstick figures away ahead, about their oblivious business. Our driver wears a black hat and topcoat and he stinks of the city. Gripping the steering wheel, his black leather gloves look decadent.

Slowing, the car swoops on a gas-station on the sinister side of the street. A sign along the roof reads JEFF BAILEY, huge letters against a clouded sky. In the cluttered forecourt, the stranger dragging the past to town, Joe Stefanos – Whit Sterling's right-hand, played with low-rung malevolence and primping self-satisfaction by Paul Valentine – encounters the most uncanny element in the film, a deaf-mute boy known only as The Kid.

The Kid, who notices how Valentine tenses up when a police car passes, is Mitchum's conscience, a clammed-up Jimminy Cricket. He's played by Dickie Moore, with an unprotected, doe-eyed look, like a juvenile outcast imagined by Disney, starring in his own silent movie: *I Was a Teenage Haunted Melancholic.* By the time Paul Valentine found him mending a tyre here and asked him where Robert Mitchum was, Moore, an ex-child star, had already been acting 20 years. He started by playing John Barrymore as a baby in the lusty *The Beloved Rogue* (1927), and scribbled a footnote in pop history by giving Shirley Temple her first on-screen kiss in *Miss Annie Rooney* (1942), signalling the beginning of the end for the Shirley phenomenon. Moore later wrote a book *Twinkle, Twinkle, Little Star (But Don't Have Sex or Take the Car),* the first to speak about the ordeals of being a kid amid Hollywood's galaxy.

This Kid can't speak and he can't hear, pointing up how untrustworthy most of the words traded between people in *Out of the Past* are. He goes to find Mitchum.

Throwing off sunlight, the lake is huge, a mirror full of sky, ringed by far mountains. A tiny figure moves along its shore, our first sight of Mitchum, walking in heaven. Following his first brush with noir in *When Strangers Marry*, he'd ventured near its edges again, in a couple of pseudo-noir women's pictures: Vincente Minnelli's *Undercurrent* (1946), during which he incurred the snippy wrath of Katharine Hepburn by imitating her between takes; and the voguish Freudian flashback bonanza *The Locket* (1946), for which, playing a sensitive, semi-surrealist painter, he'd committed suicide by leaping from a skyscraper. Mostly, though, he'd played soldiers and cowboys. Once as a cowboy, and once as a soldier, however, noir had still found him – first among the dark prairies of Raoul Walsh's *Pursued*, then in Edward Dmytryk's *Crossfire* (1947).

The source novel for Dmytryk's inky movie was *The Brick Foxhole,* about the killing of a gay man by a homophobe. Such subject matter was still beyond Hollywood, so, in a timely piece of adaptation, the victim became Jewish, and the murderer a ranting anti-Semite. Suspicion falls on a missing young GI, just returned from war with his platoon; Robert Young is the pipe-puffing policeman on the case, Mitchum a cynical zen-hipster army sergeant helping and hindering him.

An impassioned pulp-liberal low-budget tract, Dmytryk's film is also, however, just as much a quick, nightmare thriller about seedy city streets after dark and trained killers sent home with war still buzzing in their heads. First glimpsed playing cards, wearing his stripes like he'd fit the gang-hut scammery of Sgt Bilko's barracks, Mitchum finds beats of aware, half-interested apathy. Late in the film, he summarises the noir universe and his whole ambiguous career there: 'The snakes are loose. Anyone can get 'em. I get 'em myself. But they're friends of mine.' He carried this disposition into Tourneur's film.

Back at the lake, Virginia Huston lounges against a tree. Stolen time wraps the scene. 'It's clouding up,' she says, accurately describing what's happening to the film. Then she says this: 'They say the day you die your name is written on a cloud.'

An average enough throwaway in the pensive cosmos Jacques Tourneur conjured.

Tourneur's father, the French director Maurice Tourneur, had a reputation as a film-maker partial to fantasy; in Jacques that predilection mutated into a civilised, graceful pre-occupation with half-caught grey worlds of super-nature, shimmering behind the fabric of the everyday, impregnating the air with apprehension. Like his former creative partner, writer–producer Val Lewton, Tourneur favoured sombre, foreboding universes, peopled by sorrowful murmurers. The inhabitants of *Out of the Past* speak so very quietly: taken one way, it sounds the way real people talk; taken another, it sounds as though they're exhausted from the weight of melancholy; taken another, it's like they're trying not to wake something, either out there, or within themselves. Mitchum's special stillness found its perfect home.

Bent over his fishing box, he catches Huston's doomily romantic cloud comment and seeks to dispel it; attentive viewers, however,

are thinking about that gas-station sign, shot so it looked like his name was already among the clouds. The lovers nuzzle. She talks about places she's never been; he tells her he's been one place too many. Beside the lake, Huston tries a more tentative kind of angling, trying to catch things he hasn't told her (fishing features strangely throughout the movie: the names Fisher and Eels; abandoned fishing nets; a man who suffers death by fishing line).

Mitchum, head pressed into her hair, the big world wheeling around, does incredibly subtle, naturalistic work as he listens, reacting with small, relieved amusement when she asks was he ever married before. This stuff is all minimalist. While *Out of the Past* is marked by the mesmerising resonance of Mitchum's voice, the amount of watching and *listening* he does in the film, a deeper, brush-stroke form of acting, is significant. As Huston speaks, he glances off screen, catching sight of something with a cat's-hair facility for suggesting and using off screen

Cynical zen-hipster, caught in the *Crossfire* between Roberts Ryan and Young.

space. An almost imperceptible change crosses his face, like a cloud brushing the horizon's edge. A cut and we see that the Kid has been holding off, but now approaches with news of the past.

There comes the most lyrical and haunting shot: the Kid, alone in the long grass, silently flashing out trouble on his fingers. In front of him, black branches form arthritic fingers of their own, snagging stark, white light. The music catches a thrill of horror. 'We'd better go,' Mitchum sighs, knowing what's ending.

As they move off, Huston lights him a cigarette, his first in this chain smoke film. Her first match dies in the breeze. Almost every cigarette he lights announces something bad: this one prefaces his meeting with Valentine, a warily easy conversation in which meaning skates around their words, and he accepts he must return to see Kirk Douglas again, face the music.

It's night, and he's come to meet Huston at her little edge of town house, to ask her to drive to Lake Tahoe with him. His small-town garage clothes are gone, replaced by raincoat and hat, his old urban armour. As he waits on the wrong side of the fence, he hears her parents inside, berating her for seeing him. Snow on distant peaks catches a line of moonlight.

As he drives, Mitchum begins telling his story, the car becomes a confessional, and the film becomes his. Dashboard lights hit his face from beneath, faint fires from a deep pit. He's talking about a cold winter in New York, back when he was a detective with another name, a vague, unspecified age '…three years ago, maybe more...' The time scale codes Bailey, Fisher and Whit Sterling as men who were not off serving in the war, but stayed home to prosper from disreputable work.

As Mitchum speaks, his words, like his clothes, revert to old patterns. Speaking casually about the arcane subjects of guns and dames, there's a hint of his rubbing her face, and his own, in it, to see whether she can take the revelation. Whether he can take making it. His casualness contains a brittle tang of self-disgust. Something passes on the road, headlights briefly illuminating him; even though, lost in listening, she doesn't look up, this is Huston's first sight of his true face. He doesn't look at her either, telling his story to the road falling beneath the car. As he lights a cigarette, the camera dives into his memory.

The flashback sequence is the central joy of *Out of the Past*. Entering Mitchum's mind, where cities, beaches and forests are described from artificial light and half-remembered shadows, Tourneur and his cinematographer, Nicholas Musuraca, conspire to make the film increasingly more darkly beautiful. Musuraca photographed Mitchum in five movies: this, *The Girl Rush (1944)*, *The Locket*, *Blood on the Moon* (1948) and *Where Danger Lives*. Although he shot a bewildering variety of films, Musuraca is among the chief architects of the noir vision. Between the 1930s and the mid-1950s, he refined his low-key virtuosity at RKO, crucible of the black flicks, where darkness was originally spread around to cover the cheapness of the sets. In 1940, a year before *The Maltese Falcon* and *Citizen Kane* – routinely cited as the genre's twin seeds – he shot *The Stranger on the Third Floor*, a jagged mystery which now looks like the first full-blown noir. Like Tourneur, an integral element of Val Lewton's B-unit, bringing old horror into city streets with *Cat People* and *The Seventh Victim*, Musuraca's noir was a calm, diseased baroque, made from silver and white and the deepest shadows the American screen had seen.

Mitchum is remembering Kirk Douglas' opulent New York pad, besieged by night. Tourneur and Musuraca light the place with low table lamps in odd places, casting capering shadows high across the walls. Douglas, in silken robe, nursing the wound the girl who absconded left him as a reminder, is asking Mitchum to find her, bring her back, he doesn't care about the money, just bring her back. Mitchum asks what happens if he does – some sense of decency rousing, or a formality he has to go through? – then, kidding himself he's satisfied that, at least, she won't be killed, lights a cigarette, agrees. Finally, he asks her name. 'Kathie,' Douglas spits it like the taste of ruin. 'Kathie Moffett.' Kirk Douglas, in his second movie role and sizing up Mitchum as competition in every scene they play, motors through the film like a dapper, ecstatically spiteful iron-fed blond shark.

There's a clue: Kathie Moffett, a beat from Little Miss Muffit. The whisper of spider legs, but Mitchum will find too late that this miss hasn't been scared away at all; she's eaten the spiders and adopted their logic. Daniel

Mainwaring adapted the movie from his own novel, *Build My Gallows High*, written under his pseudonym Geoffrey Homes. The script went through many drafts; the not-inconsiderable work of RKO staff writer Frank Fenton went uncredited, as did contributions from James M Cain. Percolating through these minds, there were many changes from page to screen – among the most merciful was the re-christening of the Kathie Moffett character; in Mainwaring's original, she lumped along under the name Mumsie McGonigle.

As Mitchum leaves to pick up her trail, the film is disrupted by a shock cut; suddenly, in extreme close-up, the gaping, blaring horn of a trumpet fills the screen. We're in a Harlem night club, filled with jazz. Mitchum is moving happily relaxed through the room. We discover he's 'an old friend' of the proprietor. Given the still largely unselfconsciously racist period of its creation, what is remarkable about this juke joint is the fact it is not imagined as some exotic den of primal iniquity. It's relaxed, a Friday night aroma in the air, and it's full of folk, humans, individuals, people – there's no sense of this being an alien environment, no sense of massing threat or difference. Maybe it was the Paris in him, but Tourneur had a track record of avoiding stereotype when portraying black characters, and here Mitchum's unremarked hipster vibe chimes with it.

He's here to quiz the missing Miss Moffett's maid, Eunice, who is wearing her hat like a Billie Holiday flower, and relaxing with her partner. Eunice is played by Theresa Harris, who by then had appeared in some 40-odd movies. Practically uncredited through a career lasting three decades, she'd later appear in Mitchum's universe again, as the nurse fussing around the traumatised murderess Jean Simmons in the psyche-ward of the prison hospital in *Angel Face* (1952). The scene they play here is short and delightful; there's nothing patronising about the way in which Mitchum speaks with her, nothing deferential about the way in which she answers. They *banter*. From the cutesy misdirection she offers, he works out Kathie's gone to Mexico.

The movie melts into views of stately Mexican thoroughfares and vacated street corner hotels as Mitchum follows the trail south to Acapulco. This was the first time the Mitchum protagonist headed into Mexico, but by no means the last. The US is a country capable of, even founded on, the most virulent racism, and much of that feeling has been focused on its neighbour through the border fence. Mitchum, though, came to embody an American in flight from that US; soon, it would seem as though he was always for Mexico, chased by ghosts, or the guns or laws of other men, perpetually trying to escape across the unstable borderline, into the imagined, unsettled, dangerously wild freedoms that start where the bankrupt States end, into the land of hope and disappointment.

Feeling like another person's sun-dazed dream, far from Bridgeport's winter, the film drowses around hazy, empty streets, shady stalls no one visits. Mitchum finds a dim afternoon cantina across from a movie house where music trickles from speakers on the marquee. An ancient-looking woman sits black-wrapped outside, selling something from pots that send steam into the air. A man in white lounges against the doorway, like a sentinel. Inside, Mitchum sets to waiting. For a blissful lull, the movie waits with him. All this time, the words he's speaking to Virginia Huston murmur on the soundtrack; and, although the section is so good-looking, it is the way the film *sounds* so good, Mitchum's narration, cosying into memories that warm and disgust him, that raises this flashback.

With a fluent, musical burr, the way he handles the good pulp poetry he's given to speak rests squarely on his own facility with crafting words – this is a *writerly* narration, his inflections and phrasing adding subtly to the lines. He takes the monologue and wraps it around his character. Take this, floated tranquil across the image of him sitting at that table, nursing time:

"I sat there in the afternoon and drank beer. I used to sit there half asleep, with the beer and the darkness."

Note that comma, that pause. Mitchum doesn't play the lines the obvious way, doesn't say: 'I used to sit there, half-asleep with the beer and the darkness' – that is, he doesn't say he's half-asleep *because* of the beer and the darkness. He says he's *with* the beer and the darkness, as if they were companions. As he continues speaking, something important happens: 'And then I saw her. Coming out of the sun.'

Kathie enters, wrapped in white and the image of Jane Greer. Coming out of the sun. Every time he meets her in this memory vision, she appears from light, moonlight mostly because, soon, as he says, exhaling slow existentialist paperback be-bop: 'We seemed to live by night. What was left of the day went away, like a pack of cigarettes you smoked.'

Mitchum gets talking with her, already aware he's lost. Her glinting eyes are wide and jet. Her face has a beauty death-mask still. Her voice is strange, low, thick-sharp.

The voice has its own music; then 23, Bette Jane Greer, who'd started modelling at 12, quit high school to sing with a night club band. Eventually, Howard Hughes laid eyes on a photo-shoot she did aged 18, modelling the WAC's new uniform in a bid to boost recruitment, and had her signed to his production company as a potential lover. Instead, to his dismay, she started seeing Rudy Vallee, who let her sing with his band some nights. They married, but soon split, and Greer started seeing Hughes – and saw him begin to disintegrate: she was in place to witness the onset of his increasingly bizarre obsessive–compulsive behaviour, and quickly disentangled herself.

Although made before Hughes bought RKO, *Out of the Past* establishes another precedent in that, after Hughes took over, Mitchum appeared to be employed solely as his double, moving through fun worlds of danger, wooing women Hughes wanted, usually revealed to be rotten; in life, Hughes' women usually deserted him for other men. When Hughes bought RKO in 1948, Greer was by then under contract with the studio, and married to her second husband Edward Lasker. When she refused to start seeing Hughes again, he had her kept under contract, but made sure she was given no film work, more or less killing her career, until she went to work briefly for MGM in the early 1950s. Since the mid-50s, concentrating on raising a family, she worked from a state of semi-retirement. When *Out of the Past* was remade as *Against All Odds* (1984), Greer was there again, playing the mother of the pale-shadow Kathie character. Taking the Jeff Bailey role in that film was Jeff Bridges, one of the most self-contained, Mitchum-ish actors of his generation. Greer had been present at the very birth of Bridges' movie career, when, playing an ex-con-trying-to-go-straight, she had carried him as a four-month-old baby bundle into the John Cromwell picture *The Company She Keeps* (1950), also photographed by Nick Musuraca. Later, she turned up in David Lynch's noir-soaked magical mystery *Twin Peaks* (1989), doing great, sharp, nasty-loving chiding as another mother, her daughter a sad-eyed diner owner in the titular town, a chilly, far away Bridgeport of a place, wrapped in forests.

Mitchum and the spider girl, talking. She plays it cold, but throws a line as she leaves: there's a local place where you can slip the guy a dollar and he'll play American music and you can sip bourbon and shut your eyes and imagine you're on 56th Street. She goes there some nights. Mitchum, kidding himself with the meagre excuse fate offers not to report to Douglas – when he goes to telegraph the message, the office is shut for siesta – goes there the next night, even though he knows she won't, sits drinking as the piano ripples, 'grinding it out.' The next night, she walks in, out of the moonlight.

She leads him around town. In an upstairs casino he explains his philosophy of losing. Nights later, he's alone on a silvery beach beside a pitch-black sea, waiting. Fishermen's nets hang everywhere, soft, semi-obscuring veils, stoking up the sensual charge, but also like traps drawing around Mitchum, spider's webs. She appears, walking through the moonlight. Sitting against an upturned boat, she's admitting she knows who he is, he's the one sent to fetch her, the one from out of her past. She's talking about the money nobody cares about. 'I didn't take anything…' she's saying while he looks at her, small words sounding small against the sea '…won't you believe me.' In response, falling into a deep kiss, Mitchum signs away his soul, uttering the line that sounds like everything in Robert Mitchum distilled into a single drop: 'Baby, I don't care.'

The scene ends with nets, the dark sea stained with moon.

They go to her place, lit again by one low-burning lamp. They run in from a torrential rain storm. Mitchum's drying her hair, then he throws the towel away as they collapse together. The towel knocks out the lamp, the room flooding with darkness. The door blows open, the tempest entering as the demure camera leaves. It's an obvious metaphor, but has fluid poetry, the sublimated message nevertheless clear – these two stir up a black storm in the sack, something that consumes all the light that's left.

Back in the car, Mitchum goes on, telling Huston how he and Greer took a steamer to San Francisco, flying from Douglas' shadow. The city appears – movie theatres, crowded racetracks where they look happy pressed against the wire fence. He talks about the 'cheap little rathole' office he took, the shabby jobs. 'It was the bottom of the barrel, and I scraped it... I didn't care. I had her.'

Then, one bad luck chance in a million: Brodie, now working for Douglas, appears from nowhere and spots Mitchum. How did he find them, all the way across the continent from his Manhattan stamping ground? Maybe he read Oscar Wilde, followed a clue from *The Picture of Dorian Gray* : 'Everyone who disappears is said to be seen at San Francisco...'

Certainly, Tourneur's San Francisco has that troubled charge. It looks a place of exile, where people with no memory turn up, unsure or unwilling to remember how they got there, where they're going, stuck, but always passing through. After a convoluted goose chase along lonesome west coast highways, the confrontation comes in a witchy cabin in a gloomy forest. Brodie and Mitchum fight. The place is infernal, lit by a fire in the hearth. As they careen around, Greer retreats against a wall, watching them with eager serenity, bathing in their lurching shadow. A shot rings out, Brodie falls and Mitchum turns to see her holding the gun, excited by the killing.

As he whips around, Mitchum has his face fall through a number of registers. It's a look of... what? Astonishment? Shock? Something else, something numb. Weighing up unwanted new factors, maybe. He looks her down and up, cold new realisation flickering: this is what she is. He knew it all the time, of course, there's no surprise. He puts a cigarette between his lips and she's gone, leaving the bankbook that shows $40,000 in her account.

He finishes telling Huston the story as they arrive in the daylight of Lake Tahoe. Standing with his back to the gates to Douglas' house, he

sends her home, Tourneur filming him low, from behind, through the gates; another strange, striking shot, a condemned man taking a last look at the bright world before going down to damnation. As he turns, he lights another cigarette.

Inside, a sick reunion – first with Douglas, delighted to see him, then, as they sit to breakfast, Greer, unexpectedly appearing, stiff at Douglas' side. As the air solidifies around the table, Douglas talks over what he wants Mitchum to do, go to San Francisco, retrieve the documents his accountant, Eels, is blackmailing him with. First, though, Mitchum needs rest. In his little room, Greer appears in the doorway, to tell him how Douglas forced her back. Mitchum's muttered response: 'You're like a leaf that blows from one gutter to another... Get out, will you? I have to sleep in here.'

Mitchum enters the Frisco fug, knowing he's walking into trap, but sashaying on in anyway, pulling his resources around him like the raincoat he belts against the city, knowing there's nothing now except losing slowly and with wit. His only friend here will be the cabbie, Petey, played by the veteran bit player Wallace Scott, who, performing a ballet with a toothpick, will ferry him around lightless sites of murder and betrayal like an upbeat Styx boatman.

Most of his time here, it's a place forsaken by daylight, by the people who live in daylight, and by all logic, save the disjointed, repetitious snake logic of nightmares. During the disorientating, convoluted confusion of this double-triple-crossing Frisco section, it's as if the knack for storytelling had deserted the film-makers, everything unravelling. It takes several viewings before you get what's happening as Mitchum, seeing traps, but never quickly enough, starts playing all ends against the middle.

This groggy perplexity seems to be generated for the sole reason of generating perplexity, the crushing atmosphere of a world conspiring blankly against the protagonist. The clue lies in the character of the second-run femme fatale Mitchum's instructed to liase with when he arrives in town, going to meet her at her little apartment, sitting on a daylit, back-projected street that could be close to Jimmy Stewart's *Vertigo* abode. Going under the Latin-loaded name Meta, she's the fated accountant's unfaithful secretary, and she's played, fantastically, by Rhonda Fleming.

Fleming had turned up in the Mitchum universe once before – she was glimpsed at the very end of *When Strangers Marry* as the hopeful, sweet-faced, vulnerable young bride taking a train into the treacherous city, seemingly about to repeat the nightmare journey Kim Hunter had just completed. Found here in San Francisco, it's as if in the intervening years the city has taught her secret lessons, rotted her insides and turned her stony. Her Meta is like a cheaper version of Greer's Kathie, more blatant. When Mitchum first meets her, she goes through catty, affected patter, which he bats back like a man tired of going through the motions, before getting down to talking over the cold business of stealing the documents from Eels. Knowing she's setting him up as much as the accountant, Mitchum grabs hold of her, and she purrs an invitation to an afternoon of icy perversion at him: 'Do you always go around leaving your fingerprints on a girl's shoulder? Not that I mind, particularly. You've got nice strong hands.'

Eels himself is played by Ken Niles, a one-time radio-announcer who, in his short film career, almost always played radio-announcers. Niles has a well-groomed, fatigued appearance; while Mitchum small talks absurdly with him, trying to warn him he's targeted to be killed, he already looks dead. A few scenes later, despite Mitchum's efforts, Niles is dead and Mitchum hides his dapper cadaver.

The film appears to be free-falling through the abandoned city, an increasingly incoherent place of mysterious office buildings deserted for the night, lonely tobacconists' kiosks, threatening elevators and empty apartments deserted by decorators who've left ladders that throw Constructivist patterns across the walls. The characters move in obscurely motivated, repetitive patterns. We're unsure where they are or what they're doing; then, when the tangle is at its thickest, comes the moment when it becomes clear all this bewildering discord is intentional. Mitchum has travelled to Rhonda Fleming's chintzy pad on Telegraph Hill. Going through derelict backyards, the sounds from a party he'll never join sparkling nearby, he breaks in casually. In the dark apartment, he's interrupted as the door opens and in she comes – it's

Fleming's apartment, and it looks like Fleming coming in, in silhouette, her hair pushed up the way Fleming's is, but suddenly, with surprise and confusion, Mitchum sees, we see, that it's actually Jane Greer, appeared somehow from nowhere, almost as though Fleming, the Meta-girl, had been a skin she'd been wearing all along. All of the confusion of Frisco points toward this single brief, warping, moment of misidentification. All these dark-city women are the same woman.

Mitchum watches her make a call, betraying him some more, then steps out. He discovers that, somewhere, there's an affidavit she's signed, naming him Brodie's killer. 'I don't want to die,' she says, a plea as much as an excuse. He explains his philosophy again, bluntly: 'Neither do I baby, but if I have to, I'm gonna die last.'

With the incriminating tax documents as security, Mitchum escapes the city, hides out, smoking cigarettes beside the river that runs past Bridgeport, where he watches Dickie Moore kill Paul Valentine with a fishing rod, then makes his way to Lake Tahoe. Douglas and Greer are there, and Mitchum makes demands: money, and the murders taken care of – Valentine can take the wrap for Niles; Greer can swing for Brodie. Douglas, holding back with difficulty considers making a move, and Mitchum stops him with a line that would trickle down to echo in *Get Carter* (1971): 'I wouldn't try it, Whit. You're out of shape.'

He's feeling pleased with himself, maybe lucked on to a way to win slowly; but then he sees Douglas, dead on the floor. This time, Greer didn't miss. Wrapped in severe grey, something like a vengeful Satanic nun, she stands revealed. All the softness of Mexico gone, she's become hard, frigid death. She points out there's only her left to deal with, and, in response, Mitchum leans into his most feverishly calm chorus, breathing sunset life into ungainly dialogue: 'Then build my gallows high, baby.'

Greer goes on, how they can run back to Acapulco. It's as if she'd been eavesdropping on his conversation with Virginia Huston: 'I want to walk in out of the sun again and find you waiting.' Here, his words in her mouth, maybe he feels the twinge of symbiosis, realises he's condemned to be with her. She goes to pack, and, while she's gone, he sits, drinks whiskey, looks at Kirk Douglas' corpse, and calls the cops, sealing their fate. She comes back, saying they deserve a break. Rising to walk into doom, Mitchum smashes his glass in the hearth – 'We deserve each other' – a symbol of their hellish marriage, the sound of last hope shattering.

Or maybe not the last hope: the station wagon death-wagon initially refuses to start, and there's a second when another possibility seems to offer itself, fate having one last snigger. Then the engine starts. Cops are ahead, moving in the headlights. Realising what he's done, Greer fumbles for her gun. She shoots him in the crotch – *of course, in the crotch* – and she's torn apart by police-issue bullets. Cops pull at his door, and out he tumbles, face-down on the road like dropped laundry.

Back in Bridgeport, Huston asks Dickie Moore: was he really going away with Greer? Freeing her from the past, he nods. He looks at the sign, Mitchum's name on clouds and flips a salute. Then he wanders off, swinging a stick, one hand in his pocket.

Mitchum wasn't the first choice for *Out of the Past,* the film that came close to defining him and the whole noir style. The script had been offered to Bogart, who was keen, but Warners wouldn't loan him to RKO. Next announced was RKO's own great Marlowe, Dick Powell – but the acclaim which greeted Mitchum's performance in *The Story of GI Joe* pushed the younger actor into the frame. With a force like Bogart at its centre, Tourneur's film would have been very different: Bogart was quite capable of operating in worlds of aching sadness, as he would prove with Nicholas Ray in *In a Lonely Place* (1950), but for all his anguish and control, he had a nasty storm of madness waiting to get out. Where Mitchum moves forward with the weary cat-grace of reticence, it's easy to imagine Bogart tearing into the cheats, failings and curve balls life throws at Jeff Bailey with the bitter, spitting relish of a Tasmanian devil.

Bogart, with his amused, but unsurprised Camus-looks, and Mitchum, with his low expectations and appetite for resignation, both wandered the boundaries of the same philosophy of independence, plugging into modern aloneness, kicking around a happy cynicism.

But Bogart was an angrier existentialist, the rage warping up from some deep-rooted, almost buried, conviction that there should still be room for hope in the world he'd almost turned his back on. He couldn't quite abandon older reflexes, couldn't give up the call to action. Tourneur's lowering world wasn't designed to contain this sort of an itch – here, the hard-boiled wisecracks a Bogart would send out like spit-flecked machine-gun fire were intended to crackle only faintly instead, like intermittent lightning, flashing dimly somewhere beyond a dark horizon, far away.

Mitchum's dreamily sassy stoicism represented disenchantment raised to the abstract level of music. Action is something he finds easy to resist. He knows he's turned his back completely on the world; but there's a *frisson,* because he can remember what it was like back there, and is encumbered, slightly, by the guilt and the hope in the memories.

Mitchum got the part after dying in *GI Joe,* and in Tourneur's film he would die again. Earlier, he'd died a few times in cowboy shoot-outs and, in *The Locket,* had jumped from a skyscraper. He'd never died quite the way he had in *Out of the Past,* though. Another precedent; soon, almost uniquely for a leading man, he'd be dying with a fair regularity.

The film set other formulae in place, too: on a surface level, many of Mitchum's subsequent RKO movies would see him similarly off pursuing women in vaguely exotic foreign climes. Deeper down, a particular set of ignoble character traits became ingrained, those of a regular, capable, itinerant floater guy, a rovin' gambler who, although wise to the world, was all too happy to kid himself, give his feet, fists and brains a rest when opportunities for lust and inertia presented themselves. A guy who was never quite as smart as he cracked on – to himself as much as those around him. Or, rather, too indolent and cocksure to get smart quick enough.

The Mitchum loser-hero always carried himself as though he was in control of events, either because, for all his wit, he was just dumb enough to believe that he was. Or maybe because he was smart enough to realise that it didn't really make any difference what he did, or what happened to him. Not in the long run.

Noir Movies
The Big Steal

Director: Don Siegel. RKO Radio Pictures, 1949

Synopsis

At the harbour in Vera Cruz, Mexico, US Army Captain Vincent Blake (William Bendix) boards a recently docked liner, finds passenger Duke Halliday (Robert Mitchum) in his cabin and pulls a gun on him. They fight and Duke escapes with Blake's identification papers. He encounters fellow passenger Joan Graham (Jane Greer), who's come to Mexico in pursuit of her fiancé, Jack Fiske (Patric Knowles), who disappeared with $2,000 of her money. At Fiske's hotel, she interrupts him as he's about to leave on a mysterious trip. She demands he take her along so she can get her money back but he makes off while she showers. Duke shows up claiming to be Captain Blake and searches the room, telling Joan he's looking for money Fiske stole from the Army. In the street, an altercation with Fiske, who escapes by car, leads to Duke, still claiming to be Blake, and Joan being questioned by Police Inspector General Ortega (Ramon Navarro). After this, Duke and Joan take off after Fiske, chased themselves by Blake, with the policeman following all of them. As they drive, Duke tells Joan who he is: an Army payroll officer, he was ambushed by Fiske, who stole $300,000. Now he's AWOL attempting to clear his name, fleeing a court martial which believes he stole the money himself. After a long car chase across the country, they track Fiske to the remote lair of a money launderer, Julius Seaton (John Qualen). Captured, they discover Blake and Fiske had been partners in the payroll heist all along. Blake kills Fiske, but is distracted before he can turn his gun on Duke and Joan, who manage to overpower the villains, before calling for Ortega. Back in Vera Cruz, Duke and Joan sit necking, discussing local courting customs.

Back into Mexico. A ha-ha/nasty featherweight chase thriller, *The Big Steal* isn't noir, not really, but feels like it should be. The pairing of Mitchum and Jane Greer, trailing their iconic *Out of the Past* vibration through Mexican streets, real Mexican streets this time, establishes this. The bullet-headed, brain-plated presence of William Bendix, one of noir's part-time key actors, bolsters the feeling. All bright light, Don Siegel's film resembles a daylit mirror held to *Out of the Past*. Details reverberate: this time, Greer's former lover has absconded south with money stolen from her; Mitchum's going under a false name, relating his past to a girl in a car as they drive. Maybe the movie

is Jeff Bailey's dying fantasy, as he expires quickly back in that other, out-of-control car, of how it could have been for him and Kathie if they'd stayed beneath the border and got involved in rattling jalopy adventures.

The same writer, Daniel Mainwaring, adapted the script, and, in common with the murkiest sections of Jacques Tourneur's movie, a lot of it makes little sense, but keeps moving. The bewildering opening minutes describe an almost incoherent cycle of repeated action, as if Siegel were staging a technical exercise, lining up a reasonless, tongue-in-cheek series of variations on one stock thriller image: a man in a hat, standing at a door, producing a gun from his jacket.

Rather than the perplexing gloom of Tourneur, though, the rapid senselessness of *The Big Steal* feels like a gutter relative to the daffy befuddlement of Howard Hawks' *The Big Sleep* (1946), a film that looks noir, but tastes of champagne comedy. In Hawks' film, plot and logic fade as, dispensing with anything as mundane as narrative concerns, he creates the sharp light of a rainy screwball heaven. Mounted around the flowering reality of Humphrey Bogart and Lauren Bacall, Hawk's movie is concerned mainly with the business of enjoying itself; *The Big Steal*, which tastes of tequila and beer, is similarly concerned, but the pace, the humour, the ridiculous cars after cars after cars thing, the foul-mouthed parrots, the girlish old spinsters and the comfortable 'mmm-hmmm' wisecracking between Mitchum and Greer, are all built around a different sort of reality: Mitchum's jailhouse vacation.

As it shoots down Mexican country highways, throwing off ramshackle energy, the film is noteworthy for a number of reasons: the clean line of the action, flowing forward from the first shot; the awkward shifts, particularly in the final section, between brutality and parody; the rhythm

of those endlessly repeated shots of stretching, snaking, dusty bare highways, shifting between the hectic, pedal-to-the-floor modernist pace of cars careening headlong with tyres screeching and engines droning like plummeting bombers, and the imperturbable country paces of goats and ox-drawn carts; and the happy tension between the hefty amount of ropey back-projection and the fine location photography of Harry J Wild. Siegel colludes with Wild to give this Mexico atmospheric, never quite postcard life – by far the wisest cats in the film, after all, are the two Mexican cops keeping an eye on all the gringo to-ing-and-fro-ing.

Perhaps the most remarkable thing about the film, though, is the fact that this picture is the film RKO rushed into production to persuade the court not to send Mitchum to jail after his marijuana bust. This picture presents him staging his own nonchalant, single-handed revolt against the massed forces of Uncle Sam – as represented by the edgily suppressed mania of Bendix, the only American authority figure in sight, finally revealed as murderously corrupt. A film about an AWOL soldier, who beats up his captain in the first minute. Fleeing to rebel Mexico, where most of the pot smoked on the west coast of the US – not to say the idea for smoking it – originated (the movie was filmed, according to Don Siegel, 'in the heart of the marijuana district in Mexico, halfway between Vera Cruz and Mexico City'[1]).

After his arrest on 31st August 1948, Mitchum had been bailed, returning to court to enter a plea late the following month. When his attorney, Jerry Giesler, was injured in a car smash, the trial itself was postponed until 10th January 1949. Pulling out a long-dusty script based on Richard Wormser's story *The Road to Carmichael's*, Howard Hughes hired Siegel, a former second-unit director and editor at Warners, who had handled the montage sequence in *Casablanca* (1942) among others, to get the picture shooting as quickly as possible. The reasoning was, if Mitchum was at work on a movie, any movie, by the time he went to court, perhaps the judge could be swayed toward leniency. If he went to jail, after all, the entire cast and crew would be unemployed.

With Mainwaring, as appalled at the script as everyone else, turning out new pages as fast as he could, and no one taking the thing seriously, the cast assembled in Mexico. Siegel finally began shooting on 4th January, trying to get as much of Mitchum in the can before the judge put him in a different sort of can for an unknown length of time. When Mitchum was found guilty, a date of 9th February was set for sentencing, and Hughes prevailed on Siegel to rush the film ahead as quickly as possible in the month they had left.

During Mitchum's spell in jail, Siegel shot around him, using a double in long shots. Occasionally, the director visited the honour camp, bringing new script pages and smuggled bars of chocolate to the actor, who was spending his time in there sleeping, drinking milk and making concrete blocks in the sunshine. After his release, Mitchum and the minder–watchdog Hughes had assigned to bird-dog him travelled to Tehuacan to rejoin the shoot; according to Siegel's account, both men were raging drunk on arrival, having opened two bottles of tequila en route.

Maybe, if you ran the film frame by frame, you could penetrate the calm, blasé defences of Mitchum's performance, and find glimpses here, somewhere, of a man working under the knowledge he's about to be sent down, sent away from his wife and his kids. Maybe elsewhere it's just possible to sense the light step of a man coming out the other side, giddy with release and enjoying how goofily stupid the work that's waiting for him is. And, while you're being so eagle-eyed, watch closely when Mitchum and Greer interrupt their frantic chase for a brief respite at a resort hotel – where Mitchum eyes up every passing bathing-suited chiquita – and you might just notice Dorothy Mitchum among the tarrying tourists, down in Mexico, sitting by the poolside, happily watching her husband back at work and liberty.

Cheap and quick and assembled like a cover story by artists goofing off, *The Big Steal* found itself being moulded by, and in the image of the Mitchum persona. The film tells the story of a man who doesn't and doesn't want to fit, a soldier, who didn't do his duty because, quite rightly, he valued his own neck more than $300,000 of the Army's money, and who is now casually breaking more Army laws by roving off along his own renegade track, trying to get the cash back, not because of some late-rousing sense of responsibility, but, again, simply to save his own neck.

However, he's not in so much of a rush, not so bothered by the weight of the Government forces coming down on him, that he won't take the time to shoot the breeze, kid and try his chances with the first good-looking girl he encounters – and also take time to check out any other good-looking women who pass by, just in case. Even when it looks as though she might be in cahoots with the villain he's chasing, and particularly when, having discovered her showering in another man's hotel room, he still decides that, despite her snippy exterior, there's every chance she might just be an easy lay.

Here again, Mitchum sketches a man of incredibly reluctant action, who looks as tough, capable and cocksure as a movie hero should, but who, when he puts his body to work, discovers as often as not he's neither as tough nor as capable as he thought. When Patric Knowles first flees Vera Cruz in his car, for example, Mitchum tries to stop him with a tried and tested movie manoeuvre: leaping on to the escaping vehicle's running-board. The car approaches. He sets himself. He runs. He jumps… He bounces uselessly off the side of the roaring vehicle, rolls around in the street and is left lying there with a bunch of kids and old women looking at him. Later, when Knowles, looking to create a diversion, throws what might be a case containing the missing money at two Mexican no-goodniks, Mitchum dives on them, all action. In the scuffle, he manages to achieve nothing more than to run face-first into a stone wall and ends up driving quickly away, chased by an angry woman whose table he's smashed, with Greer holding tissues to his nose, trying to catch the blood.

Before the trial, filming had already suffered delays because RKO couldn't find a leading lady willing to risk her career by appearing in a movie opposite the degenerate dope-fiend. First among those turning down the movie came Lizabeth Scott – 'Cinderella with a husky voice' as Bogart observed in *Dead Reckoning* (1947) – who would later be happy to work with Mitchum in *The Racket* (1951). With Joan Bennett turning the role down, too, and time running out, Hughes had no choice but to break his own embargo and call Jane Greer, who'd just discovered she was pregnant, back to work.

Later, Siegel, trying to piece the picture together, had other problems. In the fill-in shots Mitchum filmed after his release, he looked more lean and tanned, due to his wall-building days at Honour Camp. Meanwhile, the previously bare branches of the Mexican roadside trees behind Mitchum in those shots had started growing leaves. And, just to get in on the blossoming act, Greer looked a couple of months more pregnant. A staunch and outspoken friend of Mitchum's, she was more than glad to stand by him where other femmes had made dust. When she holds that tissue to his bloodied nose in this film, and he looks at her with something close to love, it's probably about the furthest from acting he ever got on screen.

Noir Movies
Where Danger Lives

Director: John Farrow. RKO Radio Pictures, 1950

Synopsis

In a hospital in San Franciso, Dr Jeff Cameron (Robert Mitchum) is prevented from going out with his nurse girlfriend, Julie (Maureen O'Sullivan), when he's called to tend to Margo (Faith Domergue), a young woman who's attempted suicide. The next morning, having given a false name, Margo flees the hospital, but later contacts Jeff, inviting him to her lavish house in the hills to explain her behaviour. Ditching Julie, Jeff begins seeing Margo regularly. One night, she tells him they have to break it off, because her elderly millionaire father, Frederick Lannington (Claude Rains), objects to their affair. Getting drunk, Jeff confronts Lannington — but is shocked to discover he's not Margo's father at all, but her husband. As he's about to leave, Jeff gets into a fight with Lannington, during which he knocks the older man out, but not before he has himself been hit around the head with a fire-poker. Groggily fetching water to bring Lannington around, Jeff returns to find him dead. Bewildered, he agrees with Margo that they must escape before the body is discovered and they start driving to Mexico. Slipping between clarity and confusion, Jeff diagnoses he has a concussion, which will eventually paralyse him. Mistakenly believing police are hunting them, they switch cars and take the backroads south. Arriving at the town of Nogales, they arrange to be smuggled across the border. Waiting to leave, Jeff, by now half-paralysed, finally realises it was Margo who killed Lannington and that she is insane. She tries to kill him and go into Mexico, but Jeff manages to drag himself after her. When she tries to shoot him, border police kill her. The dying woman contemptuously announces how Jeff had no part in the Lannington's murder. Recovering in hospital, Jeff finds Julie waiting for him.

In a sterile hospital ward, a little girl lies within an iron lung, a devouring contraption of the late 1940s. Her big-eyed head, sticking tiny from the thing, looks all the more vulnerable for the ponderous shell about the rest of her. We hear the machine breathing, but over this comes a soft, less mechanically rhythmic sound, a man's voice speaking in a low hypnotic purr, improvising a story that is lulling the girl gently toward sleep, because his voice is very close to being the sound of some narcotic kind of sleep itself. This is what he's saying, slowly now:

"So there was little Elmer the Elephant, with all these wild men chasing him through the jungle — guns booming, tanks rumbling after him…"

As the story goes on, filled with rain storms and adventure, his voice winds down, then drains completely away as he sees the child is asleep. In mask and gown, we recognise the man as a doctor. Then, though, the mask is removed and, turning from her, he says something else, and there's something in the way he says it, some infinite weariness, that stands him in contrast to all other clean-shaven, hair-ruffling young doctors patrolling the cinema hospitals of the 1950s. He says this:

"So much for Elmer the Elephant. He'd have probably been drowned anyway."

Quiff-tousled and jaded after unwilling nights on the sleepless ward, the doctor is Mitchum, knowing that he himself is Elmer, caught up in an another implausible, elephantine chase adventure, probably due to be drowned, back again in the foggy borough of San Francisco, but hoping for Mexico.

Mitchum's generous, gently responsive way of acting with children, first established in *Rachel and The Stranger* and the John Steinbeck adaptation, *The Red Pony* (1949), is one of the throwaway delights of his cinema, an element that, curdled all to hell, would eventually be stretched to unimaginable limits in *The Night of the Hunter*. Before the film found him doing the rounds of these sickly kids, the title sequence mounted a tour of the city's nightscapes: the glittering bay, the shrouded Golden Gate bridge, strung softly with bulbs, a busy downtown street with an ambulance tearing along it. We don't realise it but the screaming vehicle carries Faith Domergue, a black-eyed trouble-demon in soft-focus, bearing down on the static Kildare-existence Mitchum has reluctantly been maintaining, on the look out for something better, to offer him the excuse to tear it apart.

In the opening minutes of John Farrow's odd, under-rated Oedipal road-noir, Mitchum's Mitchum-ness already chafes against the role of the goodly doctor he's assigned. As he moves through these hospital corridors, more interested in chatting with nurses than working – 'Good morning, gorgeous,' he tosses at one; 'Thank you, doll,' he winks toward the elderly receptionist – there's a restiveness to his motion. Padding the wards with a beatnik roll, he looks bored, clock-watching, searching for an exit. A line of dialogue has mentioned how he's planning to get out of the place to go into practice for himself, but most of this disaffection bubbles purely from the actor himself: when he's about to leave for a night club date and is told he can't because there's an emergency to attend to, rather than jumping into selfless healing action with the sort of eagerness the doctors of *ER* still exhibit, he looks simply pissed off, wondering why some other fella can't do it.

The picture was built around that emergency patient, Faith Domergue, once one of Howard Hughes' most personal projects. Hughes first saw her during a party on his yacht, in 1941, when he was 36 and she was a 15-year-old Warner Brothers starlet. He'd soon gotten engaged to her, bought her contract and, keeping her in lonesome semi-imprisonment, was grooming her as a lover, wife and future star. By 1946, their relationship had fallen apart, helped along by Hughes' dalliance with Ava Gardner. Still, that year he'd set about trying to make a far-off dark star of Domergue, the kind of alchemical sex-creature he'd previously found in Jean Harlow and obsessively engineered from the geography of Jane Russell in *The Outlaw* (1941).

Hughes threw money at an intense promotional campaign for Domergue. The first movie he created for her was an overblown bodice-ripper, *Vendetta*. Four messy years in the making, that film passed through directors Preston Sturges, Max Ophuls and Stuart Heisler, with Hughes himself even shooting some, before eventually opening, to a poor reception, in 1950, credited to its final shepherd, Mel Ferrer. *Vendetta*'s stop–start production meant it was released after *Where*

Danger Lives, so, after all Hughes' build-up, Farrow's movie became Domergue's showcase.

The posters showed her writhing revealingly in Mitchum's grip, promising:

"She's tempting in a penthouse and dangerous in a border town dive!"

Blithely ignoring the fact there were no penthouses anywhere in the movie. The plan failed. Perhaps because of Hughes' heavy hyping, critics were not kind to Domergue's performance as the deranged Margo Lannington; then again, perhaps it was because she was no great shakes as an actress. She faded from sight, her career reviving briefly in 1955 for a trio of cultish flicks: brainy in *This Island Earth*; turning into an ardent snake in *Cult of the Cobra,* a part-stupid, part-great noir monster movie that sneaks in a surprising sketch of beat boho existence in the Greenwich Village of the 1950s; menaced in *It Came From Beneath the Sea* by Ray Harryhausen's five-tentacled octopus.

Despite the critical carping, there's something about the quality of Domergue's playing of the psychotic, pathological liar in *Where Danger Lives* that fits. She was 24 when the film was made. Sometimes you glimpse the sultry angel Hughes was aiming for. Often, she looks just... odd. Occasionally, you can still see the child in her, a sulking quality that's perfect because money-eyed Margo is among the most monstrously selfish characters ever put on screen. At the end of the film, Mitchum, still imagining he's her rescuer, sits glumly half-paralysed, facing imminent coma and death; Domergue, watching for the trucks that will smuggle her to safety, asks him what the time is, and, when he mutters sadly about his left side being numb, she cuts him off – 'I SAID WHAT TIME IS IT!?!'

Going from moments of curious distance into warmed-over hysteria that sometimes overheats into wild, head-shaking animalistic-thing freak-out shrieking, Domergue all the time moves with the self-consciousness of someone who knows she's being watched trying not to care she's being watched, and, to emphasise how much she doesn't care, throwing herself into her actions with abandon. This seems right enough for an insane murderess trying not to let on she's sick, but tortured by the paranoid suspicion that everyone knows anyway.

With its bolt for the border and chump-hero tempted from wholesome society by a spidery femme, *Where Danger Lives* is tenaciously formulaic. Raised by the unfussy glories of Nicholas Musuraca's cinematography – which, in places such as Mitchum's concussed-cat stagger through the darkened mansion after having had his brains knocked in by Claude Rains' fire-poker, stirs up weird urbane horror – Farrow's film nevertheless spins low poetry from cars flying south in the dry long light of desert highways. What makes the film jump with life, though, is the way the margins around its straight-ahead plot, scripted by Charles Bennet, who provided the screenplay for Alfred Hitchcock's archetypal couple-on-the-run flick, *The 39 Steps* (1935), are covered in detailed, offbeat graffiti.

Here comes Claude Rains, relishing the heartlessness of his part. Rains, then aged 61, fills his fleeting role as Domergue's acidly sadistic father–lover with inconceivable nuances. Employing a delicate catalogue of brittle movements, pauses, smiles that never reach his eyes and precise, cold rushes of words, he gets truckloads of depravity into his lines: 'Margo married me for my money. I married her for her… youth. We both got what we wanted. After a fashion.' When Mitchum, still thinking Rains is Domergue's father, meets him, Rains bites off a comment that could simply be the advice of a priggish older man to an eager young Lothario, but, flicking his eyes toward his sick young wife, hints a history of bodies strapped screaming to gurneys and electroshock therapy: 'People sometimes get carried away, come to their senses again with a jolt.'

Hung with gloomy oil paintings, Rains' well-appointed house in the hills is a mansion of perversity. When Mitchum first goes there, eager to check on his glitteringly befrocked, attention-seeking para-suicidal patient, Domergue pleads loneliness, hints she might try killing herself again and he starts making a phone call. She imagines he's calling a nurse to watch her; in fact, using the excuse of her illness, Mitchum, almost relieved, is breaking a date with his ultra-square girlfriend, Julie, played by Maureen O'Sullivan, once the sweetest Jane ever found by *Tarzan the Ape Man* (1932).

As Mitchum talks with O'Sullivan, Domergue tries snatching the phone from him, and he clamps one hand around her wrist: 'You're hurting me,' she states, with a slight, delicious surprise, as if she'd made a happy discovery, recognition and delight flooding the air between them. They share a look. Mitchum keeps squeezing her wrist. As they explore the potential bedroom repercussions of this revelation, on the other end of the line O'Sullivan is photographed like a prim mother-superior; she's shot in surprisingly unflattering ways throughout, more surprising because she was the director's wife. Later, when Mitchum and Domergue dance at their special Hawaiian-themed night club, he will continue to hold her wrist in that tight, secret, vice-grip of theirs.

This offbeat, everyday kinkyness permeates the movie. Farrow, was something an intellectual – a devout Catholic, a biography of Sir Thomas More counted prominently among his non-movie work – and there's a kind of amused, near-grotesque quality to proceedings. When Mitchum first starts seeing Domergue, he catches helter-skelter rides from the hospital to their trysting place in an ambulance driven by an unconcerned two-man crew. When we see them, they're glimpsed loading what could well be a corpse in the back of the thing, and take off with siren screaming; Mitchum asks if they're headed to an emergency, from around a wet cigar stub, the stubby driver replies, hell, no, he's off to get halibut for his wife.

Peering through growing concussion on his flight south with Domergue, Mitchum sees this careless noir disease has spread from the city to afflict the entire country. Farrow, an Australian immigrant, presents the remains of a pure folksy America eaten alive by laziness and corruption. Stowing Domergue in an out of sight junk-strewn back yard that looks like the derelict subconscious of suburbia, Mitchum meets 'Honest Hal,' a cheery, cackling used-car salesman in a busy, clean lot who, quickly realising Mitchum's running from the law, suddenly gets cold and slippery and makes a fast, cheerfully dead-eyed buck by trading him a beat-up, rust bucket dustbowl truck for Domergue's swish, conspicuous new Cadillac, roaring with laughter and waving at the traffic cops as he does.

Further along the road, Mitchum enters a sleepy small town, which seems to be a Norman Rockwell dream, but turns out to be a place where money buys silence, rules are disregarded and ethics have atrophied. Semiconscious in main

Knocked out by Faith Domergue, a black-eyed psychotic angel.

street, Mitchum ploughs his car into another, driven by a drunk Mexican, Pablo. Among the half-interested onlookers gathering to gawp are the local doctor and the sheriff. Pablo is happy to forget the accident for the few bucks Mitchum slips him, but the lawman is keen on making a big official paperwork deal out of the smash; mainly, because he's been wanting to throw the Mexican in jail for years. In the doctor's house, though, the sheriff gets excitedly distracted by radio reports that the glitzy big-city murderers Mitchum and Domergue are in the area – so concerned with grabbing glory he doesn't see what's standing right before him – and the doctor

sneaks the pair out, because Pablo's a friend of his and he wants to get him off the hook. As he ushers them to their car, the doctor notices how very bad Mitchum's eyes are looking by now, but, instead of trying to treat him, accepts Mitchum's insistence that he's fine and packs them hurriedly on their way, keen to save himself any trouble.

This unknown, run-to-seed America finds its demented apotheosis in the deranged night-time town of Postville, where, stopping to buy newspapers, Mitchum is confounded to find himself, Domergue behind him, hauled in front of the local sheriff *because he doesn't have beard*. In Postville, the citizens are celebrating 'Wild West

Whiskers Week' as part of some ongoing hellish frontier carnival, and it has been declared a crime to be seen clean-shaven in public. Some minor excuse about money raised from the hefty fines going to help a local hospital is floated, but unconvincingly. Rather, it looks as if the whole town is a raft of madness waiting to waylay strangers in the night, funding its eternal boozy orgy on the proceeds, an alcoholic forerunner to the town in *The Cars That Ate Paris* (1973).

Every single person in Postville seems blind, giggling drunk, so much so that when a photograph of hunted-murderess Domergue comes down the wire to the sheriff's office, one of his stupefied, whiskers-obsessed deputies sits happily defacing the picture by scrawling a beard over it, even though she's standing beside him. When Mitchum objects he can't pay any fine, the men have none of it. Domergue pleads they need the little money they have left to get married, and so the two of them suddenly find themselves being hitched by the chortling, filthy-jawed Justice of the Peace, played by Billy House, a bald, chubby bit-player who, as a checker-playing drugstore owner turned lynch mobster, previously brought similar jovially sinister small town touches to Orson Welles' *The Stranger* (1946).

Stranded here in their infernal honeymoon suite, while Mitchum, sicker by the minute, gazes abjectly at a tiny plastic bride and groom suffocating under a bell jar and Domergue slips further off the rails behind him, the carousing voices of loaded Postville revellers holler a stumbling serenade from the streets beneath their window, one tune fading into another. Mitchum gets to whimper aloud to himself, as if this small, majestic question holds the key to understanding his entire confounding plight. 'How many songs do those maniacs know?'

From here, there's nowhere to go but the border town. The place they find at the end of the road is Nogales, and it looks like the only place this forsaken road could end. Huddled in on itself around a chewed-up main street, the black night splashed white with the neon from chop suey joints and pawn shops, this Nogales – like the real Nogales – is a town split right in two by the borderline, Mexico to the South, America to the North. The foetid, desperate place Farrow creates resembles a smaller, seedier version of the nightmare Los Robles Orson Welles would conjure

for *Touch of Evil* (1958), a focus for all the anti-immigrant paranoia of a country. The people who inhabit the American side of these noir towns tend to act as though they've come to the very end of the world, casting aside all hope and human propriety. Anything goes because there are no more tomorrows.

In the pawn shop, beneath long-abandoned guitars hanging by their necks from the ceiling, the broker agrees that the necklace Domergue is pawning is worth at least $9,000 before offering her $750 for it. Watching how quickly the couple agree to be ripped off, the way they stumble around the street, keeping to the shadows, he arranges a meeting with the guy who can get them across the border at a price. The pawnbroker leaves Mitchum and Domergue to wait in the back row of a hot, shabby little theatre, where Farrow lets more gamy eccentricity spill across his film: an enormous bottle-blonde crammed into a tiny, mini-skirted tartan suit, feathered tam-o'-shanter on her head, prances the stage, twirling a handbag and shouting a raucous barrelhouse number while a ratty, weedy little guy hammers happily at the piano and a listless audience stare. Insanely, the show is called 'International Follies of Guadalupe'.

Then Mitchum finds himself in the backroom of the theatre, where the spivvy manager of the show agrees to stow them among his props and carry them across the border in return for all the money they have, regularly digressing from the matter at hand to discuss the accordion that sits strangely on his desk. They wait until 4am in the room of a chintzy hotel behind the theatre. A slow-flashing neon sign across the alley strobes a tic toc pulse at the corner of the room. Here, at the end of the film, Farrow mounts a discreetly extraordinary scene: as Mitchum and Domergue wait tensely in this trashy, too-hot border town hotel room, where even the battered iron of the bed frame seems to have gone bad, for the trucks that will smuggle them finally into Mexico, Farrow forces us to wait there, too, by shooting the entire sequence in one extremely long take.

The scene begins with a close-up of Domergue, regarding her reflection in a grimy mirror, then she sets to pacing, smoking as Mitchum sits numbly on the bed; for the next eight minutes, moving the camera subtly around to reframe and rephrase, close-up to two-shot to mid-shot, and so on, effectively editing with the camera, Farrow explores the crummy space of the room and the shifting emotional space between Domergue and Mitchum, who finally sees just how murderously mad she is. Eventually, almost completely paralysed, he drops out of sight to the floor behind the bed as she starts smothering him with a pillow, the way she did Rains back in that plush mansion in San Francisco, talking to herself as she does. Thinking she's killed him, she goes to the window to wave to the waiting truck and skips through the door. The camera waits, resting on the bed and regarding the emptied room until, like a vampire's talon in the crack of a coffin, Mitchum's hand appears, grabbing weakly the worn bedding, and he somehow drags himself up and out after her, the rotted wood of the hotel banister coming apart in his hands as he stumbles down the stairs.

In the sticky street, he watches her shoot at him, sees her get shot down, two steps across the border, clinging to the chain-link fence as she dies. Later he wakes, recovering in a hospital bed. Outside his door, like prissy punishment, Maureen O'Sullivan is waiting to drag him back to suburbia.

The noir protagonist's sense of cosmic disorientation is one of his defining characteristics; in *Where Danger Lives,* this is given a mundanely literal, but baroque expression. During Mitchum's confrontation with Claude Rains, he sublimely, simultaneously juggles a three-pronged fuggy perplexity that never quite lifts for the rest of the movie:

- He's drunk on coconut-cocktails from Pogo Pete's night spot, consumed as Dutch courage for his meeting with Domergue's 'father'
- He's trying to get his cotton-wool mind around Rains' confounding news that Domergue 'happens to be my wife'. This revelation is the movie's great slap and Mitchum builds his underplayed reaction on the atomic scale. Beneath his drunken fringe, his eyes focus confusedly on Domergue then briefly close as he pulls his chin in about a half millimetre, as if, with the late-firing synapses of a punchy boxer, trying to avoid the facts
- He's just been battered severely about the head and neck with an iron bar.

Somehow, without pitching over into slurry stumblebum manoeuvres, Mitchum manages to get these shifting layers of foggy bewilderment working in his every movement. You see him forming the shapes of thoughts in his head, then trying to keep a hold of them while he gets to fitting his mouth around their articulation. At one point, when their car has stopped along the desert road and the mists in his head suddenly, briefly lift, the film strangely hushed around him, he feels his way through these words as though they were the most important he'd ever had to say, his voice strange and precise in the stillness: 'Everything's quiet. Too quiet. I can hear the crickets.'

Mitchum's way-out/way-in performance is a main factor in the enjoyable bizarreness of Farrow's movie. The grotesqueness of his role, as a man who's had his brains scrambled, moving through an increasingly concussed state toward outright coma, progressive paralysis claiming his body so he ends the film with his entire left-hand side, even his lips, completely lifeless, could almost be a carefully constructed joke at the expense of pundits who had already long been criticising what they decried as the somnambulant nature of his performing style. In fact, the whole performance recalls an episode from his own childhood, when, aged eight, he was hit by a car and a passing doctor, aghast at the boy's distant, drowsy gaze, diagnosed a severe concussion, only to be reassured by Mitchum's mother that his eyes always looked like that.

The doctor he plays here is called Jeff Cameron. This Jeff is extremely eager to breezily throw away his life for a squeeze of Domergue – who, from the first, is plainly a bad-news nutbag – the same way that, as another Jeff in *Out of the Past*, Mitchum was lazily enthusiastic to get led around by the clearly degenerate Jane Greer. Unlike Jeff Bailey, though, Dr Cameron doesn't see this fatal femme for what she it until the very end of the picture. And, also unlike Bailey, he's lucky enough to survive her – although this is through no action of his own. Why the Mitchum guy was so keen to embrace chaos remains, as ever, magnificently unclear. Indeed, in *Where Danger Lives,* while explaining how his creeping concussion will progress and manifest itself, he mutters another line that could serve as an epitaph for his noir persona:

"I may talk rationally. But my decisions may not make much sense."

Noir Movies
His Kind of Woman

Director: John Farrow. RKO Radio Pictures, 1951

Synopsis

In Naples, Nick Ferraro (Raymond Burr), a notorious mobster deported from the US, is determined to return, and hatches a plan to assume the identity of a US citizen. In Los Angeles, having been beat up for reasons unclear to him, drifting gambler Dan Milner (Robert Mitchum) receives a mysterious offer: $50,000 to leave the country for one year. He accepts. Given an advance, he follows instructions and travels to the border town of Nogales. Waiting in a cafe for further instructions, he encounters night club singer Liz Brady (Jane Russell), passing herself off as an heiress called Lenore Brent, travelling to exclusive Mexican coastal resort Morro's Lodge to rekindle her affair with movie star Mark Cardigan (Vincent Price). Learning he is also to go to the resort, Dan shares Liz's flight. Wandering the hotel trying to work out why he's been sent there, Dan finds himself threatened by Thompson (Charles McGraw), who reveals he's there to make sure Dan doesn't leave. Dan and Liz are increasingly attracted — he also gets friendly with Cardigan, who's shocked when his wife arrives. Dan still has no idea why he's at the resort when Bill Lusk (Tim Holt), a US immigration agent posing as a drunken tourist arrives, and tells him Ferraro plans stealing his identity with the aid of another guest, Krafft (John Mylong), an ex-Nazi doctor who specialises in plastic surgery. Dan ignores the warning, until he finds Lusk murdered. Thompson and his men take Dan to Ferraro, whose boat has anchored offshore; seeing Dan led away at gunpoint, Liz alerts Cardigan. Escaping, Dan swims to shore, followed by Thompson and his men. On the beach, Dan finds Cardigan waiting with his hunting guns. Arming himself, Dan returns to the boat to attempt to capture Ferraro, while Cardigan keeps Thompson busy. Aboard ship, Dan is captured again, and subjected to a prolonged beating, until Cardigan arrives with a hastily assembled rescue party. In the ensuing fight, Dan kills Ferraro. Back at Morro's Lodge, while Cardigan boasts to the press, Dan and Liz get together.

One of the impressions Mitchum liked to foster, or maybe one of the things he liked to pretend to himself, was that he didn't do too much thinking about his career. He did, however, pay enough attention to formulate the opinion he'd made the same movie '103 times'. He propounded his own abstract synopsis for this archetypal Mitchum Picture:

Pounded to Death by Gorillas

We open-up with our hero, standing straight and forthright in the middle of the stage. Suddenly, behind him upending looms a great giant gorilla, and he hits our hero – duhnn – on the top of the head. And the hero just goes 'Uhn'. And he hits him again, and the hero goes 'Grumhmn'. And, finally, they fade out, with the gorilla pounding the hero on the top of the head. Now, we cut to a maiden dancing through a field of daises, near a wood. And she wanders into the forest and she taps on the door of a cabin, and a voice says 'Who is it?' – and the writers haven't thought of that yet, so we cut back to – POUND – and on and on and on. Finally, at the end, the girl appears from stage left. The gorilla has collapsed in exhaustion over his victim, all you can see is a spread-out rug on the deck. And the girl says 'I know he's around here someplace. I can smell 'im' because he hasn't bathed or shaved or anything, he's a real hero. And she sniffs away, and finally, peels the gorilla back and lifts the hero up, and he's bloody and filthy, and she turns straight into the camera and says: 'I don't care what you say, I like him.'[1]

His Kind of Woman, in which Mitchum spends his time being placidly pounded by goon armies, stripped, tied and whipped with belts, locked inside iron-walled chambers filling with boiling steam, held down and threatened by a Nazi scientist wielding a hypodermic of brain-destroying potion, before ending the picture in a clinch with a gal who's been undulating around far from the action, is the generic paradigm, the 'ur-gorilla' picture. It's also one of the most radically perverse, wrong-footing movies ever to come out of a studio, almost post-modern in its breezy self-regard and blithe disregard for plot, like *The Big Steal* before except multiplied.

Mitchum with gorillas.

Stopping off and forgetting gangsters and dark thrills and thuggery when it feels like it, to play instead a game of poker with a shoe on the table, or hear a curvy lady sing, or watch men sink slowly in a slapstick boat while declaiming Shakespeare, the movie is littered with red-herrings, riddled with side-alleys, taking any excuse to abandon generic duties and have fun. Two moments sum it up. First, Mitchum, in his role as perpetual drifting causeless rebel, is roaming an exotic, lazy modernist Mexican resort, not knowing why he's there, waiting for something to happen. He finds himself surrounded by vaguely weird characters, unsure whether any have anything to do with him. One, a lecherous investment broker, played by Jim Backus, future voice of Mr Magoo, approaches, all puffed-up square hep, to proffer a prime slice of exposition: 'You're probably wondering,' Backus offers from the corner of his mouth, 'what a man like myself is doing in an odd place like this.' And, mining the question to excavate his most honest response, Mitchum replies: 'No.'

The second movie-in-a-nutshell fragment comes as he and his kind of woman herself, Jane Russell, wander a beach. She begins singing,

Mitchum chimes in with a syncopated whistling counterpoint, and it's sublime in its backroom way, the two of them walking the studio-built shore, dueting for no reason – until all of a sudden they stumble over a corpse, half buried in the sand. You practically hear the film sigh to itself: *oh, yeah, that, we'd better get on with that.*

The movie is so demented exactly because it was another Howard Hughes hybrid special. Hughes tinkered and fooled with *His Kind of Woman*, adding suggestions for new costumes (special attention paid to Jane Russell's neckline, of course, and her fantastic pointy hat), new scenery, new dialogue, until, if not quite losing all shape, it assumed bizarre contours no one could recognise but him, assembled with the same toy box logic a kid might apply to filling a plastic rocket ship with cowboys and dinosaurs.

This insane thing reacquainted Mitchum with director John Farrow, whose cheery sadism he'd noted while filming *Where Danger Lives*, when Farrow asked him to fall down a flight of stairs. During *His Kind of Woman*'s drawn-out climactic torture, when Mitchum is held half-naked prisoner aboard Raymond Burr's yacht, there comes a point when he's been rendered unconscious by his diverse, ongoing beatings; the hulking gangster, though, anxious to shoot him in the face, tries to bring him around, by banging his head off an iron pipe, crooning 'Wake up, little boy. Wake up. I want you to see it coming.' As they filmed, Burr actually did crack Mitchum's head on the pipe, knocking him out. When he came to, Farrow ordered the scene re-shot because it didn't look authentic.

Filming stretched on. Another director, Richard Fleischer, was drafted in, uncredited, to handle re-shooting. A year in, Vincent Price threw an on set party, marking the anniversary – there are reports that Mitchum, reaching the end of his tether at the endless formlessness, tied one on during the party, then, thus fuelled, started to film a fight scene and halfway through decided to make a real fight of it, laying out stuntmen, going on to rip the set apart, screaming about directors, studios and Howard Hughes, too, as he went.[2]

Price himself was an unwitting cause of the protraction; he'd thrown himself with relish into the part of the hammy movie star on the sidelines of Mitchum's escapade. Hughes liked what Price was doing, and ordered rewriting, more shooting to beef up the role. Suddenly, Farrow's grim, hard-edged nocturnal noir (Mitchum's final beatings are extraordinarily brutal, their violence contemporised by the way that, due to restricted space in the torture ship's tiny engine room corridors, Farrow films scenes there with a free-swinging, hand-held camera) was intercut with broad, almost slapstick, comedy, courtesy Price's exquisite, hyper-camp performance. The bizarre tonal shifts between Price's on shore pantomime and Mitchum's on ship punishment are abrupt and unsettling; rather than undercut Mitchum's suffering, Price's distant capering sharpens its cruelty.

Hughes had always wanted there to be some fun, envisioning the film as a vehicle purely for pairing Mitchum, his favourite leading man, with Russell, his favourite leading lady, another woman he'd engineered on screen to fit the dimensions of fantasy, and who, when he pursued her off screen, routinely told him where to go.

This silvery meeting between Russell and Mitchum, it is now obvious, was inevitable; irresistible force languidly encountering immovable object, the collision resulting not in a bang, but a kind of stretching atomic purr. Hughes was consciously thinking of the leave-the-plot-behind, self-reflexive wonders made by Bogart and Bacall. Mitchum and Russell, each as physically impressive and amusedly laconic as the other, were a long way from Humphrey and Lauren. Equally, though, while a more primal coupling, they were just as knowing as Bogie and Baby, just as able to negotiate the heads of pins and together looked as if they'd fallen from another part of the same heaven, a neighbourhood with more dime stores and fewer cocktails. Mitchum's playing slotted into Russell's like he'd come home. They made only two films together but they fit so well it feels as if they made more. They, also, became lifelong friends and, finally, close neighbours. Mitchum strangely, reverently, dubbed her 'Hard John'.

He first lays eyes on her in Nogales. Where Farrow previously imagined the town as a fevered rat trap for *Where Danger Lives*, here, it's more salubrious, presented almost abstractly, consisting solely of borderline, airstrip and a deserted café that seems built right on the runway. In here, while awaiting a bowl of chilli, Mitchum hears music from around a corner and wanders over to witness the magisterial spectacle of Russell, flanked in a darkened alcove by piano player and guitarist like some voluptuous altar piece, singing out blunt and low the cartoon boop-bop tune, *Five Little Miles From San Berdoo.*

In mid-shot, Mitchum reacts to the sight with what can only be termed a silent whistle. Cut to her, looking him down and up, factoring odds. Back to a close-up of Mitchum, a tickled poker-face giving little away, except for his eyebrows, which are raised like appreciative drawbridges.

As he wanders across the Morro's Lodge compound, vaguely wondering why he's there, half-interested as to what might happen next, there's little for him to do, little that makes sense, except hang out with Russell, who lets him rub oil on her back in the sunlight, complimenting him on his good hands, aware of his slight you're-kidding-me look. Both casual creatures, they recognise each other amid all the busy, merely square mortals and gravitate accordingly. If Mitchum wasn't so entangled in the remaining tatters of the long-shredded plot, he'd clearly be off with her somewhere, following more constructive adventures in his afternoon room or along under the palm trees that stand in the wind-machine-tossed night at the end of the fake beach.

Russell herself certainly has no time for the little boy gangster story Raymond Burr has been left to try to hold together on his own. Maybe this is why Burr is so terribly angry – no one seems bothered about all his big hoodlum planning, and, like a kid trying to do a party piece when the adults have long since become bored and are chatting over drinks, he's left stamping his feet on the carpet. Russell floats around untouched, little to do. Finally, while Mitchum has to go put himself through the business of being brutalised, and Price mounts his cartoon parody movie rescue, the film has to resort to having Russell actually locked inside a cupboard, not so much to keep her out of harm's way, as to lay a tissue-thin excuse over the obvious fact it can't think what else to do with her.

All the way through the film, Russell and Mitchum bat dialogue like sleepy table-tennis masters ready for the shower-room, all the time, this casual, clean, lazy-cat sexual energy

sparking between them. Never more so than in the final scene when, over an ironing board, Mitchum, who's already told her that, when he has no money, he keeps himself busy by pressing his trousers, gives Russell his considered opinion that she 'could be a handy thing to have around the house if a man went broke.' As they go into their closing clinch, the camera averts its gaze, moving in on the iron, left burning a hole in the crotch of Mitchum's trousers, a pulp-minded forerunner of the train-into-tunnel smut metaphor with which Hitchcock would end *North By Northwest* (1959).

Considering the average gorilla-picture hero 'hasn't bathed or shaved or anything', Mitchum does a surprising amount of ironing in this movie. Earlier, Russell discovered him setting up his board in his room, getting ready to *iron his money*. Although he accepted the offer of $50,000 to travel to Morro's Lodge, this really is about as much interest as he ever shows in cash. As he presses the bills, Mitchum informs Russell, reasonably: 'When I have nothing to do and I can't think, I always iron my money.' Mitchum says this with absolute serenity, testing the hot iron with a wet finger, savouring the tranquil insanity. It's an aberrant little scene, the Marx Brothers and Marcel Duchamp hammering faintly far behind it, another senseless flake in a straight-faced blizzard of madness.

The accumulating lunacy and cruelty of the world confronting Mitchum in *His Kind of Woman*, and the downright, down-home existentialism of his response to it, push the film away from Hollywood, in fact, toward Theatre of the Absurd:

"There is but one truly serious philosophical problem: suicide. Judging whether life is or is not worth living amounts to answering the fundamental question of philosophy."[3]

That's Albert Camus famously synopsising the 'to be or not to be' dilemma of being free and finite in a meaningless universe in *The Myth of Sisyphus*. In *His Kind of Woman*, Mitchum ponders the same conundrum. Just returned from another town, where he'd found himself thrown in jail for a crime he didn't commit, this drifter wanders a lonely city night, climbs a rickety flight of steps to the sanctuary of his crummy apartment, only to find three strangers playing cards in the dim light within, waiting there to beat him up, for reasons obscure to him. After they leave him lying on the floor, his phone rings. Answering the salutations on the other end, Mitchum says this:

"I was just getting ready to take my tie off. Wondering if I should hang myself with it."

Then, with complaisant ennui, he accepts an offer he can't make head nor tail of: a lot of money, paid by people he doesn't know, to go away somewhere and do nothing. Nothing in this universe makes any sense to him but, as he wanders the microcosmos of Morro's Lodge, observing the strangeness and danger, waiting for something to happen, something he can only suspect must be bad, he doesn't really attempt to figure it out. Instead, firm in his jaded coolster's sense of himself, a stable and independent state, he accepts it all pleasantly, without surprise, the oddness, the threat and the frequent poundings, beatings he endures like some uncomplaining, masochistic saint.

Lightsome in the mid of all this happy confusion, however, he does eventually, for his own reasons, choose to make a single action, running up his own moral standard. He's spotted a newly wed couple, hanging around the edges of the resort, always looking anguished. He learns that Jim Backus has been fleecing the impoverished young husband nightly at poker and that Backus plans having the little blonde wife repay that colossal debt in kind. Rousing himself to do right, Mitchum sits in on a game and uses his gambler's expertise to enable the husband to win back all his cash – an exact rip-off of the way Bogart's self-centred anti-hero finally made the choice to do good when he took to the roulette wheel to save another young bride from Claude Rains' lecherous intent in *Casablanca* (1942).

Described by another character as 'a lone wolf without friends or relatives, a man who's made it his business all of his life to keep undercover', this Dan Milner character is an yet another unconcerned, individualist drifter functioning on the hazardous border between straight life and the underworld, not antisocial, particularly, but belonging to neither community, and unconcerned by that. Out on his own, surrounded by threat, but moving. Ironically amused. Acting according to his own obscure moral laws, rather than any of the big concepts the rest of society clings to. Relishing absurdity, the way the vodka-fuelled actor behind the character relishes the fact that he's playing a teetotaller tough-guy, constantly drinking milk and ginger ale.

Mitchum's own life presses against the character, in all of this and in other ways. His introduction as just having been released from jail is a very deliberate echo of his own recent real-life spell on the county farm. His conversation jumps with the actor's own beat slang: 'I'm not knocking it, man,' he says about his initial mysterious offer, 'I'm just trying to understand it'; then later, 'I'm hip.' Also, he is given to lapsing into Mitchum's patented hermetic backroads jive: such as when Russell comes to his room in a mood and Mitchum offers this bizarre comment, as though it were an everyday platitude: 'Look, it's a bad night. Along about the cool of the morning, the farmer'll get his cow back.'

In the end, in a decision Camus would have applauded, Mitchum takes Jane Russell over suicide. At one point, as they wander their deserted, ersatz ocean shore together, she gazes out across the night sea, toward a string of islands receding beyond the horizon. She sees there a land of new beginnings and no memory, says she wishes she could flee there tomorrow and start over. Beside her, as if this drifter had killed his time by flipping Sartre in the bus stations, Mitchum recognises Bad Faith instantly. He asks Russell why she would want to go there, what green grass she thinks she'll discover. He explains his thinking once again – the way he did when, in *When Strangers Marry*, he told Kim Hunter how you can't run away from yourself and when, in *Out of the Past*, he told Virginia Huston how every place was the same place. Looking out evenly at the fantasy islands, he says this:

"You're not going to find a thing there except yourself."

It was beginning to look like Mitchum's life's great theme.

Macao

Director: Josef von Sternberg/Nicholas Ray. RKO Radio Pictures, 1952

Synopsis

In Macao, an undercover US policeman is murdered. Days later, aboard a ferry from Hong Kong, ex-GI Nick Cochran (Robert Mitchum) rescues night club singer Julie Benson (Jane Russell) from an over-amorous fellow passenger. Julie steals Nick's wallet. They meet another American, salesman Lawrence Trumble (William Bendix). Going through customs, Nick admits to police lieutenant Sebastian (Thomas Gomez) he's lost his passport. Sebastian reports to crime boss Vincent Halloran (Brad Dexter); Halloran, who killed the US detective, is wanted by American authorities, but untouchable within Macao's three-mile limit. He and Sebastian are expecting another undercover agent to come after him; Sebastian fingers Nick as likeliest candidate. However, Trumble, who clandestinely visits an international police barge outside the three-mile zone, is the real policeman. Julie starts singing in Halloran's casino. Also applying for work there, Nick is told by Halloran to clear out of Macao. The gangster offers to pay him to go but Nick, who's fallen for Julie, turns him down, thinking Halloran wants him off the scene so he can have Julie for himself; Halloran's girlfriend, Marge (Gloria Grahame), reaches the same conclusion. Trumble uses Nick to lure Halloran out, giving him a diamond to sell to the criminal, with the promise of more in Hong Kong. Halloran, though, recognises the stone as one police recovered from his operation and has Nick beaten and imprisoned. However, Marge, anxious Nick should leave and take Julie, lets him escape. Halloran's men chase him through the harbour, where, mistaking Trumble for Nick, they kill the real policeman. The dying Trumble fills Nick in. Thinking Nick's dead, Halloran plans sailing to Hong Kong with Julie to recover the diamonds. Julie and Nick have been conspiring, however, and he stows away on the boat; at the three-mile limit, Nick overpowers Halloran and delivers him to the waiting police. Back aboard Halloran's yacht, he and Julie kiss.

Macao, another tale of mistaken identities, sable-haired night club singers and lands far from home where you don't find anything but yourself, could be built on a rumour. It comes early in *The Lady From Shanghai* (1948), when, learning where Rita Hayworth was born, Orson Welles quietly exclaims in fake Oirish brogue, 'It's the second wickedest city in the world!' 'What's the first,' Hayworth wonders. 'Macao – wouldn't you say so?' 'I would.'

The intention of that unlikely dialogue was to smear murky, short-hand exoticism around Hayworth's icy femme fatale, but a gargantuan shadow lifts off behind the words; the claim tossed out is weird and extraordinary, and difficult to forget. It says there is a place that is the single wickedest place in all the world, a net where all the worst things on Earth are held trapped, and it names that place as Macao. And think what a movie might be made there.

RKO thought so, anyway, and, with the aid of a little postcard-documentary second-unit footage – junks and sampans bobbing a busy bay, thronging rickshaw streets, people occupied in mysterious doorways – set about constructing that imagined Macao on their soundstage. Drifting into its layered darkness, another eternal regular nomad with a stained past, Mitchum found it was, indeed, a city of nets, where bad things happened, but in terms of wickedness, this Macao was only middling. He'd already found far worse back in various San Franciscos and later, in *The Night of the Hunter* and *Cape Fear*, would find far worse again, inside himself.

Macao was released in the middle of 1952 but initial filming was completed in 1950. Again, the hold-up was due to Howard Hughes' fussing – this is the movie for which Hughes issued his legendary four-page memo on how Jane Russell's breasts were to be depicted, and once again, it became a patchwork film. To create this den of exotic intrigue, Hughes turned to Hollywood's old master of imaginary lands, Josef von Sternberg, then on a two-picture studio deal. Sternberg's first movie for Hughes, *Jet Pilot*, a thoroughgoing ridiculous thing in pin-sharp colour, drawn from Hughes' aviation fetish and displaying Janet Leigh at her most beautiful as a debatable Soviet flyer, was also filmed in 1950 – then extensively re-cut, re-filmed and re-messed with, held unreleased until 1957.

Sternberg was the former 'Svengali Joe,' who, in collaboration with Maria Magdalene Dietrich, had conspired to bring to silvery life the creature Marlene, that half-glimpsed, unknowable conflation of the untouchable woman and the woman of the streets, across a series of seven films between 1930 and 1935. Sternberg's adoring camera sculpted Dietrich obsessively, often partially obscuring her with a veil, a fur collar, a bolt of shadow, an otherwise reasonless curtain, then exposing her face all at once with a holy light, like a revelation. Initially a phenomenon, as the phantom landscapes he fabricated to hold Dietrich became more baroquely, hallucinogenically sensual, Sternberg's vision accelerated beyond the depressed tastes of his times. Their two final, most enthrallingly demented films together, *The Scarlet Empress* (1934) and *The Devil Is a Woman* (1935) bombed and their partnership came to an end. Dietrich went on to other directors, in films that attempted echoes of Sternberg; the film-maker himself, once Paramount's favourite, fell from grace. For the rest of his career, he drifted for hire, stripped of his once complete control.

The *Jet Pilot* farrago had been a disastrous but instructive experience for Sternberg, one that intensified his already profoundly haughty snobbery. When Hughes handed him this pulpy *Macao* confection he more or less turned his nose up. A self-made autocrat, Sternberg had been notorious for antagonising and alienating casts and crews even on his happiest, hand-picked projects of the 30s. On *Macao*, his disdain curdled. Both Mitchum and Russell would later speak of how unhappy the set was, how Sternberg adopted a divide and rule strategy, attempted playing the actors off against one another. Mitchum's favourite story revolved around the time the cinematographer, Harry J Wild, got so fed up he lashed out and kicked 'the apple box' the short director used to stand on, sending Sternberg flying. Russell's favourite story concerned how Sternberg refused to allow any food on set and so Mitchum took to sloppily making and eating the biggest, greasiest lunches he could concoct, picnic style, right on the little altar-like lectern that Sternberg used to hold his script. At that, the director is supposed to have warned the actor that, if he wasn't careful, he'd be taken off the picture.

Pointed banter in pointy hats with Jane Russell and William Bendix in the wickedest place in the world.

'If anybody's getting taken off,' Mitchum responded, perhaps between mouthfuls, 'it'll be you.'

And so it was. As well as winding up his co-workers, Sternberg, making no secret of his loathing for the story, had kept his own interest up by ignoring all the boy/girl/gangster/cop stuff, to concentrate instead on bringing *Macao* to life as a memory of the special interior symbolist worlds he used to spin for Dietrich, from a riot of moonlit- and sunlit-textured shadows, smoke and nets and veils, old Chinese men looking anciently enigmatic, lizards on walls, Sikh cops directing traffic, Russian doormen, black cats in brick alleys of the night. This was probably why he was hired in the first place but RKO hated all this atmosphere, and, wanting to get back to straight-ahead narrative, tried taking it all out, but the picture left made no sense. In Mitchum's succinct description, 'There was no way they could glue it together –

I kept meeting myself.'[1] Another director was called in to fix it up.

The seventh, out of eight, of his movies to be photographed by Harry Wild, *Macao* had already become a site of reunion for Mitchum. He was happy to be acting again with Jane Russell, and looks on approvingly at the work done by William Bendix, his gorilla nemesis from *The Big Steal*: in the going-through-customs section, Mitchum, white fedora pushed back in proleptic resemblance to his *Cape Fear* look, steps back to react with deadpan delight to Bendix's skit with a suitcase full of stockings and cigars. The film also saw him once more with the fantastic Gloria Grahame, playing the girlfriend of the gangster of the piece, and tossing out the best line in the movie as Mitchum enters the casino to sell his stolen jewel: 'You're up early for a loser.'

At one time, Grahame, classically trained, possessed of quick, feline intelligence and a kinky sense of humour, shared an apartment with Jane

Greer. Like Greer, her career was affected by Howard Hughes' refusal to let her out of her contract: at the time Hughes sent her unhappily to *Macao*, Columbia had wanted Grahame for the coveted lead in the comedy *Born Yesterday* (1951), the part eventually going to Judy Holliday, who picked up an Oscar for her ditzy blonde turn.

Grahame and Mitchum went way back. Around the time *Macao* was released, in fact, Mitchum's brother, John, was divorcing her sister, Joy. Mitchum had first acted with Grahame on stage as early as 1940, in a play called *A Maid in the Ozarks*, and she had also been memorably strange and seedy and sweet as a dancehall girl in *Crossfire*, although their paths never crossed in that film. Later they would work together more closely, him as an unthinkingly ambitious youngish doctor, her as an alcoholic party girl, exchanging looks over cigarettes in the bizarre Dr Kildarian soaper, *Not as a Stranger* (1955), in which his fellow unlikely medical students included Lee Marvin and Frank Sinatra.

But it was Mitchum's reunion with the drafted-in director, Nicholas Ray – Grahame's estranged husband – that proved most significant. When he was called to mend *Macao*, Ray and Grahame were in the process of divorcing; they had recently made *In a Lonely Place*, a film that looks like a sad, abstract tracing of the dissolution of their marriage. Grahame didn't feature in any of the new footage Ray was shooting – most of her scenes in the film are Sternberg's.[2] However, according to legend, having already seen an early cut, she told Ray that if he edited her completely out of the picture, he wouldn't have to pay any alimony.

Through Grahame and the lunch tables of the RKO commissary, Ray and Mitchum had known one another for a while. They had hoped to work together on Ray's first movie, *They Live by Night* (1948), with Mitchum as a villainous one-eyed Indian bank robber who menaces the central doomed doe-eyed young lovers on the run. RKO had, however, balked at the idea of their rising star playing a baddie, especially an Indian baddie, and vetoed the notion. At the time of the *Macao* re-shoots, however, the actor and the director had recently worked together, as Ray had been called in to do exactly the same sort of patch-up job on Mitchum's previous movie, the semi-noirish *The Racket* (1951). A remake of the silent gangster flick Howard Hughes had produced successfully in 1928, *The Racket* was among the first projects trumpeted when he bought RKO. Mitchum plays a middle-rung, decent, but placidly stressed cop, employing faintly underhand tactics in fighting a middle-rung old-school gangster (Robert Ryan, seething in a barber's chair) who's on his way out due to his refusal to change with the times. Sam Fuller, the blessed maverick pulp-tabloid movie-maker, had written a baroque, punching update of the film for Hughes, but his draft was unfortunately scrapped.

As made, the film presents cop and hood as reflections of one another, hinting the real rackets go on far above their heads, in the hands of the politicians running their unnamed city. In some respects, the movie suggests a preliminary, reined-in sketch for the savage cop neuroses Fritz Lang would unleash in *The Big Heat* (1953). The credited director, John Cromwell, had made a dark-sheened, but fairly stagy piece out of it. Working uncredited, Ray came in to direct the best sequence in the movie, a chase from basement to rooftop through a darkened multistorey car park, Mitchum pursuing hoods who have just tried to blow up his home. Even though playing a pillar of society, with doting suburban wife, Mitchum's restive aloneness chafed against the role, texturing the film, but the script, leaning toward a blanket celebration of police tactics – something the ex-billy-clubbed vagrant, ex-chaingang escapee, ex-fitted-up-dope-fiend jailbird might well have regarded with amusement – allowed this little outlet.

Exemplified by movies like *In a Lonely Place* – about an embittered, fracturing Hollywood screenwriter destroying his one chance at happiness; *On Dangerous Ground* (1951) – about a dysfunctional, brutalised rogue-cop on the wintry edge of breakdown, and his most famous movie, *Rebel Without a Cause*, Ray's preferred beat was a cinema of loneliness, devoted to misfits skirting society. His films mounted an ongoing exploration of a peculiarly male, but never macho, sense of isolation, the curse of independence. Having worked for the Government during the Depression as a researcher, collecting field recordings of songs and stories from the mountains and backwoods, antihero ballads and weird local legends, Ray also shared Mitchum's firsthand experience of travelling the length and breadth of a folksy, nonconformist America. Of all the directors Mitchum collaborated with, he was the most attuned to his particular sensibility; after working together inadvertently on this enjoyably disposable movie, the two would pool resources to make one of the best films of either's career, the weary lonesome cowboy story, *The Lusty Men* (1952).

Ray's arrival brought about one more reunion for Mitchum – he found himself returning to writing. New scriptwriters were working on the film but pieces still didn't fit, so to make the picture work, the director and the returning actors had to come up with new scenes on the spot. As Mitchum put it: 'They turned it over to Nick. Nick, Jane and I looked at each other, and finally Jane handed me a pencil and a piece of paper.'[3]

For three weeks, Mitchum wrote in the mornings, ensconced in Victor Mature's empty dressing room. In the afternoons they filmed what he had written. The scenes were throwaway, but entertainingly so, and neatly crafted, smoothing jagged edges between episodes and hustling story along, without being seen to hurry. Above all, they had their own, laconic, easy humour.

Among them is the early sequence aboard the ferry, a deft, deceptively compact piece of exposition and character sketching, which moves at a languid, deadpan clip, the steamer's whistle hoot-hooting occasionally to underline the joke. As in *His Kind of Woman*, Russell's entry is memorable: in a little cabin aboard the ship, a sweatily deranged looking rat-faced little man does a ridiculous, jerky cartoon mambo, spinning and twitching and shimmying on his own; across the room, the camera pans up from a rhythmic pair of black high-heels to reveal Russell standing beside the blasting record player, assessing his routine, flashes of cross-eyed surprise disturbing the sullenly amused set of her face, all the while her hip rocking absently to the music, like some idling soft machine.

Later – once Russell has hit the passing Mitchum on the head with a shoe, and he's punched the sweaty little jiver unconscious; and Russell has stolen Mitchum's wallet while he was stealing a kiss from her as a reward – she encounters William Bendix on the top deck. Guessing her size with a practised eye, he pops open a suitcase to give her a free pair of nylons

which she instantly begins to change into. On the deck below, Mitchum leans on the rail, gazing toward the approaching port, when one of Russell's discarded old stockings floats down past him. He reaches out to harvest this unexpected manna from the air, runs it appraisingly through his fingers, then wanders up the stairs in time to see her, bending over in her bamboo coolie hat to finish snapping the clasps on her second stocking:

'Enjoy the view?' she says to Howard Hughes as much as Mitchum.

'Well, it's not the Taj Mahal or the Hanging Gardens of Babylon,' Mitchum allows, face chasing some slight teasing delight, 'but, eh, it's not bad.'

Russell: 'Anyone ever tell you what big blue eyes you have, grandma?'

She leaves, and Mitchum and Bendix introduce themselves and chat and watch her undulate away. As he speaks, Mitchum folds her stocking and slips it into his jacket pocket, saving it for later – and in an extremely efficient bit of wrapping up, this is how he realises his wallet and identification papers are missing, leading straight into the next scene at customs, and the whole muddied identity idea that drives the rest of the film.

Jitterbugging lechers, music, shoes hitting heads, kisses, pickpocketing, stockings floating from heaven like flip gossamer promises, pointed banter in pointy hats – Mitchum the writer, goofing off but getting a job done, positively crams these early minutes with blithe business, the dialogue hopping with phrases recognisably his: 'fold up your tent,' he instructs the little crazy dancer who's been getting hot under the collar for Russell.

Something of Mitchum's behind the camera handwriting might be spotted in these amused sticking-plaster scenes, but his usual signature is otherwise all through the film: the character he plays, Nick Cochran, is archetypal, another radically unlikely hero, outcast and adrift in the big world. Five years before the movie caught up with him on that ferry from Hong Kong, he fled New York City forever, thinking he had murdered a man. Since then he's been floating, putting the various skills he learned during the war to whatever uses seem most likely to keep him alive. Looking for work in the gangster's casino, he tells him how he used to work for a gambling house in Singapore, then:

"…after Singapore, I nursemaided a shipment of machineguns to Iraq, then I went to Cairo, got rid of a handful of stones for a couple of refugees who wanted visas. That dough, I blew on slow horses. Worked my way back to China on a freighter…"

Gun-running to Iraq, taking jewels from refugees in return for black market visas? This isn't the sort of thing included in the usual good guy resumé. In *Casablanca*, the rogue antihero played by Bogart had fought the good, fascist-killing fight for the Republicans in the Spanish Civil War; Mitchum's self-serving history here has more in common with the anxious black-market business conducted by Peter Lorre's *Casablanca* character. His Mitchum-ness, however, ensures he gets away with it.

Wandering the hemisphere as if it were an interconnecting network of back alleys, picking up whatever backdoor jobs present themselves, the character is the usual rootless cocktail: ability mixed with moral ambivalence mixed with an overriding delinquent laziness – all that money gambled away – and a complete, somnolently cocksure independence, simultaneously shot through with melancholy: while touring the moonlit bay in a sampan with Russell in a moment of peace, Mitchum lets slip a confession that both explains why he looks so contentedly accustomed to being exiled in the world, and gives away how it feels:

"I've been lonely in Times Square on New Year's Eve."

Alongside the recurring traits, however, one other, unprecedented, Mitchum could also be seen in *Macao*, a figure described in the fragmented scraps of the film shot with Sternberg's sensualist's eye that remain scattered throughout the body of Ray's re-mixed collage. As he had with Dietrich, Sternberg lavishes the women in the film with an almost holy light: here's Russell, sheathed tightly against the smoke of an indifferent Casino in a silvery metallic dress, throwing off light as she stakes a rueful claim on 'One for My Baby'; here's Gloria Grahame, arms encased in shoulder-length black gloves encrusted with dragonish filigree, a private, loaded half-smile playing her face as she strangely shakes a cup of dice in her own arcane little dance, a delectable black ribbon joking her hair as she nods to herself.

Passing through the shadows of the movie in his glowing white linen suit, glimpsed through beaded curtains, a sweat sheen catching the light, shirt open at the neck, sometimes shirtless, thick hair mussing, Sternberg eulogises Mitchum's casual physicality with that same desirous gaze. The best scene in the movie is pure Sternberg, almost to the point of parody, when Mitchum escapes the house in which he's being held and hurries through the night to the docks, pursued by two knife-wielding assassins in black silk. It begins in an eroticised prison room – probably Gloria Grahame's boudoir – caged by soft bars of shadow. The door opens mysteriously, of its own, and, as if startled, the camera retreats back from it, finally to discover Mitchum, alert on a bed, framed behind a fine-meshed black veil of mosquito netting. A calm, dreamlike scurry of a chase begins, Mitchum fleeing across rooftops, down onto a flagpole that snaps beneath his weight, dropping onto a canvas awning that rips, then quickly through streets where tin cans drop from roofs, on into the cloistered back street passages toward the harbour.

Finally, arriving at the wharves, Mitchum discovers a shrouded, spidery cathedral of black fishing nets, rising maze like from an unstable floor of loose planks that float unsteadily, ankle-breakingly on black water. As he progresses silently through this half-formed, deeply textured sequence, clambering and running with unpolished grace, an indolent house cat slowly shedding domesticity to rediscover innate alleyway agility, the movie changes. Practically silent, it becomes purely about the movement of this figure against this dim confusion of net, concrete, brick, wood and water. Forgetting all the backstage chaos, the disruption and animosity, the joking and the pulpy plotting and the patching-up, *Macao* momentarily remembers what else a movie can do. For a few minutes it becomes a heightened, abstract poem, conceived purely in honour of Mitchum's careless athleticism, a poem about Mitchum in noir, simply the way he looks and the way he moves through the invented dark and painstaking moonlight, chased by murder in a place that, briefly, looks like the wickedest in the world.

Noir Movies
Angel Face

Director: Otto Preminger, RKO Radio Pictures, 1952

Synopsis

In Los Angeles, ambulance driver Frank Jessup (Robert Mitchum) and his partner Bill (Kenneth Tobey) respond to an emergency call from a Beverly Hills house. Arriving, they find the wealthy Mrs Tremayne (Barbara O'Neil) almost asphyxiated from gas poisoning. She survives. Drawn by the sounds of piano-playing, Frank encounters Mrs Treymane's step-daughter, Diane (Jean Simmons). When he tells her her step-mother will live, Diane becomes hysterical. After work, Frank phones his girlfriend, Mary (Mona Freeman) – however, Diane has followed him. Frank breaks his date with Mary and takes Diane dancing. He tells her of his ambition to open a garage specialising in sports cars. The following day, Diane tells Mary that Frank had been with her; Mary dumps Frank. Diane persuades Frank to give up his job and become the family chauffeur. He accepts and has a frustrated affair with Diane, who's anxious her parents don't find out. Finally, suspecting Diane of trying to kill her step-mother over jealous feelings about her father (Herbert Marshall), Frank quits. That afternoon, however, Diane rigs the family car to send her step-mother crashing to death over a cliff; but her father is killed, too. Traumatised, Diane is put into the psychiatric ward of the prison hospital pending trial, jointly accused of murder with Frank. Diane's lawyer concocts a publicity stunt that sees them married in prison in an attempt to elicit the jury's sympathies – it works, and they are acquitted. Following the case, Frank attempts to reconcile with Mary, but she plans marrying Bill. Back at the Treymane house, Frank rejects Diane's protestations of love and calls a cab, planning to go alone to Mexico. Diane offers to drive him to the bus station. As they are about to leave, she reverses her car at speed over the cliff top, killing them both.

If you want to find punk attitude inscribed across a few frames of film, forget Malcolm McDowell kicking the tramp's head in *A Clockwork Orange* (1971), or Brando in leather in *The Wild One* (1953) when asked what he's rebelling against, asking in return 'Waddaya got?' In *Angel Face*, a completely demented movie but fabricated with such hazy, dreamy elegance you almost don't notice how nuts it is, Mitchum's negligent poetry makes all that look like stuff spelled out in building blocks by busy kids.

Around midway, following the double auto-smash-murder of the wealthy couple he's been working for, Mitchum walks into a police station for questioning, wearing a chauffeur's cap. That's all it is, a man walking across a room while a few other men sit around, but these seconds of film show independent, causeless, bored anarchy in reluctant motion: something about the heedless way he walks, the tilt of that ridiculous cap, the look on his face about having to wear the thing *and* go to the bother of coming in here to answer questions – simultaneously disdainful and indifferent – generates the same field projected in that courtroom photograph three years previously.

In Preminger's film, playing Frank Jessup, the malcontent low-class ambulance driver who dreams only delinquent dreams of tinkering with girls and hot-rods and maybe spinning those dangerous little cars along fast blank racetracks, Mitchum essayed the most extreme manifestation of his RKO loser-antihero protagonist. Here is a man who exudes an utterly monumental sense of detachment, dereliction and disenchantment, exhibits an unhealthy willingness to drift whichever way takes least effort and seems likeliest to lead to a warm bed.

Angel Face was put together quickly and, once again, moulded in the image of Howard Hughes' secret agenda, a mania this time concerning Jean Simmons, owner of the titular kisser. Simmons was 21; Hughes first noticed her a few years earlier, wrapped in a Technicolor sarong in *The Blue Lagoon* (1948). Obsessed, he subsequently bought her contract. For her first RKO movie, *Androcles and the Lion* (1952) he drafted detailed instructions as to how thick her mouth was to look. Following the usual patterns, his fixation developed to the point where Simmons and her then-husband, Stewart

Getting tired of Jean
Simmons, a lost,
lonely lunatic.

Granger, half-seriously devised a murder plan involving throwing the millionaire off a balcony. With her RKO contract almost up, the aggravated actress finally resorted to taking a pair of scissors and, knowing how Hughes had a fetish for lush brunettes, hacking off most of her own hair, figuring that not only would it bug Hughes, but that it would also preclude her from appearing in another movie for him.

Hughes, however, still maintained control over Simmons for four weeks and determined he would see her once more with a headful of long, glossy black locks. She was called in and fitted for a wig and *Angel Face*, a movie made as an act of control and revenge, a movie made about sex and hair.

Otto Preminger, then at Twentieth Century Fox, was loaned to Hughes as a man who could get a good job done quickly. Hughes summoned Preminger to a mystery midnight meeting in a car parked on a Hollywood boulevard. Preminger mentioned that he didn't like the script. Hughes said he could do what he wanted with it, adding: 'Look, you come into the studio tomorrow morning. You just walk in like Hitler, and you take over.'[1]

With Simmons' contractual clock ticking, the film, adapted from a long-mouldering script called *Murder Story*, itself based on a real-life teen patricide, had to be completed in 18 days, and so Preminger adopted a bulldozing, autocratic approach to the shoot, similar to that Josef von Sternberg had failed to maintain on *Macao*.

The most notorious story from the disgruntled set regards the early scene where, to calm Simmons, hysterical over news that the step-mother she's just tried gassing to death will live, Mitchum slaps her. It's notable because there's the usual blatantly sadomasochistic tilt going on – on receiving her slap, Simmons regards Mitchum for long seconds, and then, all sorts of eager, kinky connotations erupting, forcefully slaps him back, prompting his lazy admission that he's 'been slapped by dames before' – but also because, famously, some of that vibration spilled behind the camera, to where Preminger, head filled with Hughes' whispered instructions, was sitting.

The slap was filmed in close-up and Mitchum really had to hit Simmons; Preminger, however, kept calling for take after take. With Simmons'

face getting redder and redder Mitchum became increasingly anxious, disturbed that he was hurting the petite actress. Finally – according to Stewart Granger – as Preminger called 'Again!' Mitchum turned and cracked the director across the face, asking: 'Would you like another, Otto?'[2]

Despite or because of the animosity permeating the set, as with *Macao*, the co-stars bonded. This, in fact, wasn't their first movie together. Before *Angel Face*, Mitchum and Simmons, sporting a rather cropped do, worked together in *She Couldn't Say No* (aka *Beautiful But Dangerous*, 1952), cheerfully directed by prolific veteran Lloyd Bacon, a one-time regular collaborator of Charlie Chaplin's. Featuring a plot about the harm wrought by a flighty heiress who decides anonymously to spread money around the oddball inhabitants of a bucolic Norman Rockwell town – they'd funded a life-saving operation for her as a child – the movie had been Hughes' attempt to revive the screwball comedy, but the script lacked anything like the necessary speed and pungency. In compensation, Mitchum relaxed into the rural small town setting and set his own backwoods pace as town doctor, romancing Simmons and a local blonde who makes coleslaw, contentedly fishing the quiet river and mixing ice-cream sodas.[3]

In the same way that *Out of the Past* and *The Big Steal* form a set, Bacon's film stands as a reflection of *Angel Face*, illuminating Hughes' fantasy vision of Simmons: in both she plays the young, upper-class, sophisticated but naïve daughter of a phenomenally wealthy man, in both she needs taken in hand and introduced to the rougher edges of the world and in both there is talk of her being put away in an insane asylum.

In *Angel Face*, Simmons is a lost, lonely, lovely lunatic, a pampered little onyx-eyed Electra assassin, hating her step-mother and wanting only to be as close as possible to her ineffectual father (a fine, spineless, ingratiating performance by Herbert Marshall, a veteran English actor who had lost a leg in the First World War, by that stage of his career into playing a series of weak husbands). She buys him special presents which she hides in his bedroom; he uses his wealthy wife's money to buy his daughter snazzy cocktail outfits, seemingly never considering that his wife might appreciate a similar gesture.

In the movie Simmons dimly recalls losing her real mother in an air-raid during the evening infernos of the London Blitz, nights probably spent clinging close to dad, lost in the story-book worlds he must have spun to get her off to sleep. Now he's run out of stories; a once-famous novelist, he's dried up, as impotent a writer as he is a husband, spending his days alone in his study, as his wife chides, 'sharpening his pencil'. His daughter, though seems to have inherited his fiction gene, or perhaps is still lost in the fantasy landscapes he created for her as a kid. One night, after she's persuaded Mitchum away from his ambulance driving and ensconced him in the room over the garage as the twisted family's pet chauffeur, she comes to his room. It's 2.40am, and she spins a dark, wide-eyed, shivery spook tale about her step-mother gliding into her room while she slept, to murder her.

While she talks, Mitchum listens silently, waiting for her to finish, fishing in his dressing-gown pocket for cigarettes, faint traces of mild irritation battering his blinking eyes. When she comes to the end of her story, something unexpected happens. Until now, it has looked as though Mitchum is a patsy, ready to believe whatever she says, blow along with whatever she cooks up. Here, though, it becomes clear he's recognised her craziness all along but seems to have figured, what the hell, she's cute with it and able to fund the auto-shop he's been dreaming about. However, it's nearly three in the morning, he needs his eight hours and he can't be bothered. He's 12 years older than she is and her childishness is beginning to annoy him – particularly the way she gets all coy in clinches and backs off without putting out, wanting him on-tap in his chauffeur's cap to creep around under her parents' noses, meeting for chaste, romantic-paperback trysts in obscure spots near the crashing sea. So, startling her from her little wicked step mother reverie, he says: 'If I was a cop, and not a very bright cop at that, I'd say your story is a phoney as a three-dollar bill.'

Stung, Simmons asks: 'How can you say that to me?'

And Mitchum, with the frustrated sarcasm of a tired man fed-up with unconsummated girly games, hits her with: 'Oh, you mean 'After all we've been to each other'?'

A surprising frankness about sex is one of the major elements of *Angel Face*'s busy background nuttiness. Photographed by Harry Stradling like a bad dream, at once hazy and clear, in the main the movie forgoes the sharp shadowlands of the noir night to unfold in daylight amid the layered, bright affluence of the wealthy family's Beverly Hills home. Preminger's cool objectivity and sense of taste and pace give this cold-fevered pulp a respectable sheen, but, there are strange, off-kilter things: the way the monumental doors of the ambulance depot hang in the thick Los Angeles evening like the closing gates of heaven behind Mitchum; the way that sick house is perched right on the edge of a crumbling precipice.

The film gets crazier as it goes, tossing around as if trying to wake itself. When Simmons has rigged the family jalopy so it will send her step-mom and, accidentally, her father, hurtling to death over that cliff, the crash comes like a sudden, ridiculous, rip in the movie, brutal, fast and furious. Later, when she's been put in the psych ward of the woman's prison, Simmons' fellow inmates are a weird crew: toothless, witchy old wrinkled-apple women with straggling, dry grey manes, lapsing into strange, folksy hymn-singing when Mitchum and Simmons go through their sad, cynical fabricated pre-trial wedding in there.

It's that open, casual sexiness that's really strange though, particularly for a movie filmed in 1952, when the production code had congealed into its most solid state. While Mitchum seems frustrated by the black-haired teen killer, it's extraordinarily clear that he and Mary (Mona Freeman), the blonde nice, homey girl he ditches for her, have long been sleeping together: giving Simmons a bored description of Freeman, Mitchum mentions how she wears pyjamas in bed; Freeman comments on how Mitchum knows it's impossible to hear the telephone from her shower; when Mitchum goes to attempt a reconciliation with her in her apartment, Freeman's semi-naked in her slip and they talk comfortably in the bedroom as she dresses, with him finally zipping her up as though it's a routine operation.

More explicitly, there comes this exchange when Mitchum, who is oblivious to the fact that Freeman knows he broke their date the previous night to go off with Simmons, fluently lies to her about where he'd been, and she snaps back at him with the bitterness of a woman used to going out with a man who gets slapped:

MITCHUM: "I'd have been useless company last night. 10 minutes after I left Harry's, I was in the sack."

FREEMAN: "I can believe that. Well, you can head for that same sack tonight."

And, more or less, he does. Throughout the movie Mitchum goes through a cycle of dallying with Simmons to see if it gets him anywhere, then, when it doesn't and he's bored, trying to drift back with Freeman, mildly surprised when she turns down his offers of a steak or a movie. Utterly, serenely, unable to comprehend how either girl could think that any of this stuff matters, his lack of commitment is awesome; furthermore, friendless and seemingly not looking for friends, it applies to every aspect of his life.

He gives up his ambulance-driving at the drop of a hat to start chauffeuring – like the ambulance men glimpsed in *Where Danger Lives*, he's not involved in the job for humanitarian reasons – then gives up chauffeuring just as easily. Cars and driving, that's all he knows and all he cares about. He's happy to gaze at Jean Simmons, but it's her little zippy roadster – a snappy buggy the witch-girl refers to as her 'broomstick' – that really casts a spell on him and gets him dreaming in hopped-up lingo about his greasy future surrounded by engine parts, polished chrome and smooth bodywork painted in bright pop colours:

"I've got an idea for a power plant that'll make this mill look sick."

Except, it's not the future he's looking to find. He seeks a return to the past, to 10 years previously, when he was a young man roaring wildly around race tracks, careless in perhaps different ways. His hot-rodding days were interrupted by being called on to do another kind of driving, steering a tank through the Second World War, and that's either changed him, or confirmed something he always suspected. It's no coincidence the movie discovers him driving an ambulance, licensed to go screaming through city streets at

reckless speeds at night, seeking injury and death. Even if driving is all he can do, he could have found a job driving a bus or a delivery truck or a taxi; buried in the performance, the garage dreaming, is the suggestion he's looking to rediscover some part of himself that's since gone numb; that or searching for obliteration in speed and metal. He's trying to pretend the war never happened and still living it, still sees the things he saw through the little slit window of the tank he drove through Europe, the things he did with its guns and its crushing wheels and its flamethrower. Maybe that's a shared signal he picks up from Simmons, like him marked by the conflict, carrying her visions of the charred graveyard of the Blitz. In any case, this is something that has fed his breathtaking disregard.

It is inconceivable that the man Mitchum presents in this movie could possibly care less about anything: friends, love, work, cash, attempted murder, actual murder, cops, prison, marriage or a lonely young woman's insanity. It's what motors the casually extraordinary moment, when, the morning after her night-time visit, Simmons comes back to Mitchum's room again to find him packing, and he makes it clear to her that he knows, has known all along, how sick she is, knows that she has murder games on her mind – and makes it clear that he couldn't care less, so long as he's not around to get caught in the fall out. For all he cares, she can just get on and kill the old lady. This former hospital worker certainly has no intention of doing anything, alerting anyone either about the plan or Simmons' illness:

"I'm not getting involved – how stupid do you think I am? You hate that woman and someday you're going to hate her enough to kill her, it's been in the back of your mind all along."

In fact, only twice, at the very death of the movie does Mitchum express any real concern: first, when he nearly spills some champagne in a car because Simmons is a bad driver and rough on the gears; then, a second later, when he's rocketing backwards to a plummeting death of twisted metal and mangled flesh amid baking rocks and stubborn Beverly Hillside grass.

Just after Simmons has hurled them back over their cliff top to crashing hell, the taxi Mitchum had called to take him to the airport trundles into the driveway of the house and forlornly, funnily, honks its horn at the empty house. Receiving no answer, the driver gets out, honks again, pushing his cap back as the dust blows softly past his feet. The ending recalls Mitchum's earlier comment to Mona Freeman when – after she's dumped him for his reliable, bow-tie-wearing square driving partner, Kenneth Tobey, after the double murder, after his trial and false marriage to the little psycho – he laments, yeah, if only their call out to Simmons' refined hell-house had come in five minutes later, he'd have missed it and everything would've been OK.

As Freeman points out, though, Tobey was on that call, too and nothing happened to him. He wasn't lured into mischief by the siren sounds of Simmons' weird piano playing. Mitchum had it programmed into him, he was looking for it. So, maybe if that final taxi came five minutes earlier, he would've made it down to Mexico as planned, but it's clear that that would've just been postponing the inevitable. Down there he'd have sought out some other dark-eyed deviant oddball, someone looking like Jane Greer, maybe, and worked out another way to get himself killed. New starts and second chances are things he knows deep down he doesn't really believe in. As it is, going out fast in the brilliant sunshine with a cold bottle of champagne, a pretty girl, and, above all, a good-looking car with its engine roaring and its tyres screeching – you suspect it's about all he ever hoped for.

Once again, dead in a car, thoughts of Mexico draining from his mind. The movie Mitchum made for RKO after *Angel Face* could be seen as picking up the hopeful threads left torn and dangling where that film ended, the way *The Big Steal* seemed to have grown out of the final moments of *Out of the Past*. In it he's made it to Mexico, where he discovers gangster's girl Linda Darnell, another black-haired woman in trouble, but with more curves. The picture, cleanly directed by Rudolph Maté, was even called *Second Chance* (1953).

Filmed in sharply-coloured 3D, Maté's movie was a crackly, straightforward pulp confection. It eventually moves into a studio-bound, back-projected world, but the early sections, shot around the bleaching, busy little streets of Cuernavaca and Taxco, are drenched with a cluttered sense of place and heat. Once again, Mitchum is a man trying to outrun his past; he plays a troubled (but not too troubled) boxer, who, like John Wayne the year before in *The Quiet Man*, has killed a man in the ring in New York and is haunted by it. Now he's down in Mexico fighting all comers in crowded afternoon bullrings, trying to shake off his fug and get to the stage where he can throw his right hook again. Maté films one good, simple, undesigned boxing match, offering glimpses of what Mitchum might have looked like 17 years earlier as bum-fighter navigating the smoky rings of Nevada.

Again, he drifts into trouble after sex, ditching a willing willowy blonde in the bar after his fight to wander hazily off after the promise of Darnell on another man's recommendation. As it happens, she's being pursued by her former lover's psychotic hit man, Jack Palance, who himself harbours a deranged erotic obsession with her. In his grey suit, with his hair shining blackly, Palance's reptilian, Chet Bakerish ugly beauty, partly the result of plastic surgery undergone to correct injuries sustained when a bomber he was flying crashed during the war, is at its most pronounced. Palance spattered an astonishing fit-to-bust energy across every movie he was in during this period and is memorably unhinged here, jerking around the screen looking for bad things to do with a straight angular vigour the film can barely handle, maniacally trying to kick through the constraints of his role.

The movie ends with a dumbly thrilling fist fight between Mitchum and Palance – an ex-prizefighter himself – on the observation platform of a cable car stalled and swinging between two high mountains, the overhead wires beginning to fray. Palance goes hurtling to his death, Mitchum prevails, trundling down to solid ground and a happy future with Darnell, who turns out to be a decent girl after all. After all the murk and ambiguity and violence and absurdity of his career exploring the varied noir worlds of RKO, this was a straight, happy ending in brightly coloured sunshine.

Not a bang, but a contented popcorn sigh, it was the last film he made for the studio.

Noir Movies
Cape Fear

Director: J Lee Thompson, Universal Pictures, 1962

Synopsis

In Savannah, Georgia, lawyer Sam Bowden (Gregory Peck) receives an unexpected visitor from his past, Max Cady (Robert Mitchum), a rapist he testified against eight years previously. Bowden realises Cady is stalking him and his family around town and asks his friend Chief Dutton (Martin Balsam) to keep an eye on the newcomer, but Cady is careful to remain inside the bounds of the law. The Bowden's dog is mysteriously killed. Meanwhile, Cady's lawyer demands a meeting with Bowden and Dutton to protest the continued police harassment of his client. Bowden hires a private detective (Telly Savalas) to follow Cady, which inspires him to attack a girl, assaulting her so viciously she refuses to talk. Cady begins insinuating to Bowden he plans exacting his revenge by doing the same to the lawyer's wife Peggy (Polly Bergen) and young daughter, Nancy (Lori Martin). Nancy is terrorised by Cady the next day at school. Bowden tries to buy Cady off; realising he will not be swayed, however, he hires three thugs to drive him out of town. Cady hospitalises the men, one of whom confesses to police that Bowden had paid them. Facing losing his job and a possible jail sentence, Bowden hatches a desperate plan: he sends his wife and daughter alone to their houseboat far along the Cape Fear river, hoping to use them as bait to draw Cady out. Bowden then makes a circuitous journey to join his family, and, with another armed man, awaits Cady's attack. Finally, as expected, Cady makes his move; in the savage fight, the other man is killed and both Peggy and Nancy are nearly assaulted; finally, though, Bowden bests Cady and delivers him to the authorities.

By the time he appeared in *Cape Fear*, cutting an insolent channel through the bright heat of a wide Savannah main street to bring pain and flagrant, obscene evil up the dignified steps of a colonnaded courthouse, pausing to check the asses of two huddling typists leaving for lunch, Robert Mitchum hadn't messed with noir outright for nine years, not since his contract with RKO had puttered out.

In his time as a freelance actor and occasional half-hearted producer – he set up office on Sunset Boulevard, but spent most of his time there writing night club material for his sister and poetry for himself – he'd ventured only twice into outlying, rural areas of noir's jagged gloom: once, as the doomed moonshiner in *Thunder Road*, playing the familiar dissident loser-antihero; and once, as the killer preacher stalking Charles Laughton's *The Night of the Hunter*, playing the strangest, wickedest thing alive. In both those movies, however, he found not noir's cold-fevered heart, but things almost like it, bent in different shapes. Close, but no cigar.

In J Lee Thompson's film, however, he had his mouth around that rank cigar, led with it, a tumescent thing wounding the air before him. In later years, historians would decide the high noir cycle had ended in 1958, in the dirty canals of *Touch of Evil*, but no one had ever thought to tell Mitchum about that. Back again in the genre that had played him so often for a patsy, freed from contractual obligations to always come through as the reluctant good guy, he had scores to settle. He was back into the black to show it how bad bad could get.

This Max Cady character was something new in Mitchum's lexicon; now into the 1960s, he let loose with stuff he could never have vented before. Cady was a relentless reflection of the Preacher who would so blithely kill women and kids in *The Night of the Hunter*, but Laughton's Preacher had come through the looking glass, fed on ogre stew, fairytale dust and children's nightmares, and Mitchum, pitch-perfect, had conceived and played him in a way as abstract as the picture book Depression landscapes Laughton created; played him, that is, as a kind of *idea* of evil.

Cady wasn't drawn from any picture book. He'd been places and done things. He knew what dirty bar room floors looked like, and savoured the thoughts that swam into focus while staring at them. He knew darkened car parks and the shadowed sites under piers at night and what could happen there. He'd seen the walls and ceilings and carpets and bedspreads of cheap

Doing bad things in bad places, with Barrie Chase.

rooms. He'd washed in jailhouse water and counted slow nights through bars. Cady stinks sharply of the world and Cady makes you wonder.

Cape Fear was shot in Savannah, Georgia the town where, 29 years earlier, the 15-year-old Mitchum, making one of his cross-country hops, had been arrested for vagrancy and tossed on a chaingang. In the film, the police chief, chumming up with Gregory Peck's harassed lawyer, tries to have Cady run out of their gentrified borough for vagrancy, too, only to discover he has thousands of dollars in his bank account. In life, the young Mitchum hadn't been so lucky; he'd arranged with his mother for a little money to be forwarded to the post office for him, but was picked up before he

collected it, and soon found himself shuffling the hot, overgrown roadsides at gunpoint, rooting out weeds and sour grass until, slipping his shackles one night, he made a bolt into the bewildering murky maze of the swamplands.

Cady makes you wonder, though, about the road Mitchum took as a skinny 14 year old, out alone into the big, dim, depressed US, where the fractured tramp legions drifted the highways and railroads, men looking for work, or a warm body, or something usable, setting up tin-can camps in the night, sitting in the dark boxcar corners, nursing thoughts and fear and fatigue and looking for ways to brief oblivion. Men who had lost hope and family and knew they couldn't sink any further, no matter what they found themselves doing. At night, in the emptied cattle cars, in the track-side hobo jungles, in the whispering, bone-weary bunkhouse of the chain-gang camp – who did that kid find waiting for him? Cady offers clues. When he laughs, he is the only one who knows what the joke is, his voice is stained with more than tobacco.

With the hard light of the locale lending sharp edges to the picture, Mitchum made Max Cady the most real bad man the American movie screen had presented until that point. To this day, he remains disturbing, precisely because his conception has nothing to do with cinema or the stage or 'acting'. You could easily meet this man in the street, on a bus, in a bar, a wrong-turn alley; he's the guy wandered in from parts of town you don't want to know about, looking for amusement, whose eyes you try not to meet, the guy leering at other guys' wives to see what they – the other guy, the wife – will do. Ready to go.

Unspeakable, but entirely credible, he was unregenerate, but he was clever, and he was sane, and he was intractable, entering the film with a clear head to pursue one vile, vindictive mission, from which he would not be diverted: to rape, with extreme brutality, the wife and little child of Gregory Peck, the lawyer whose testimony at another rape trial had put him in a cell for eight years. And to let Peck know that this is what he's going to do before he does it.

One of the most soiled scenes comes when Mitchum turns up, sucking a can of beer, dressed in a stripy Bluto T-shirt, dripped stain at the belly, to haunt Peck's family at a sunny, busy little weekend dockside, full of middle-class families getting ready to go boating. Dragging his gamey smell into that happy afternoon, mocking the atmosphere with hat pushed back, he leans over the rail of the dock with lascivious grace, to watch Peck's daughter, Lori Martin, working obliviously on their bobbing launch below. Martin was 15 when she appeared in the film, but could easily be two or three years younger. As Peck approaches and confronts him, Mitchum gestures toward this small girl: 'Say, she's getting to be, uh…' he pauses to take a brief swig, and while he does, his mind, a greasy machine, computes how to complete the sentence. In a fraction of a second, the can still at his lips, he's composed the words and snorts a satisfied laugh to himself: '…getting to be almost as juicy as your wife, ain't she?'

Cady goes about his single-minded assignment with awesome determination. We are told how he sold his family farm to raise the money to come after Peck: there's the sense of his having jettisoned his history, making himself over in some destructive rite, reshaped himself to fit the task of retribution, his new life's work. He speaks of how, in jail, he 'burned for eight years' refining his nightly thoughts of revenge, elaborate scenarios now, evolved from simple, slow, bare-handed murder fantasies into a nuclear-family-sized variant on The Chinese Death of a Thousand Cuts: 'First they cut off a little toe? Then a piece of finger? Piece of your ear? Your nose?'

Cady discovered his model for torture in the voracious reading he did in jail, between the law books he devoured with deviant application, loading himself up with ordinances and civil rights and loopholes, so he'd be sure not to step on the cracks while he set out to break the back of Peck's family. His towering relentlessness itself touches abstraction; he could easily have become metaphor, death-angel in white-trash chic, the avenging force descended on this bright little town to shred the veneer and threaten the complacent dog/patio/cocktail situation Peck and his peers inhabit: we see the lawyer and his police friend meeting to discuss what to do about this outsider, cosy men from some straight 1950s *Night of the Living Dads* scenario, dressed in back-slapping slacks, sipping beers from the cooler in the backyard garage, hung with poppa toys, DIY equipment and fishing rods, little ladies out of sight indoors.

But Cady, of course, deprives Peck and the policeman of their main weapon – the law – and uses it as a shield. Depicting the forces of authority as crumbling and helpless against a loathsome one-man tide of evil, *Cape Fear* prefigures the right-wing calls to arms and vigilante fantasy movies spawned in the wake of Don Siegel's – itself sharp and ambiguous – *Dirty Harry* (1971). When, in 1991, after all those death-wishing vigilante pictures, Martin Scorsese remade *Cape Fear*, he amplified and explored the themes of the family unit and conventional values under attack, and of the notional hero having to go outside the deficient law to protect himself. Scorsese added echoes, inversions and layers of complexity to Thompson's template, creating a movie that was less a remake than a comment on the original.

Most obviously, he re-used the unforgettable score Bernard Herrmann composed for the 1962 film, music that by turns sounds strident, descending alarums around Mitchum's sauntering rampage, or pauses in eerie, tensely lyrical lulls. Herrmann's score emphasised a sub-Hitchcockian vibration in Thompson's film, and Scorsese teased the Hitchcock out, then sent it crashing around in nervy, over-caffeinated patterns. This second *Cape Fear* also brought back Mitchum and Peck, appearing as monumental grey phantoms amid the noise and colour, in roles that reversed the moral polarities of their original characters: Mitchum as the helpful, but faintly unconcerned police-chief, Peck the slimy lawyer defending the new Cady, Robert De Niro, against him.

The threatened family in Scorsese's update was imagined not as the tight, wholesome brood of the original, but as already distrustful, fracturing from within. The lawyer resorting to attempted murder in the remake, played by Nick Nolte, had himself already taken the law into his own hands before; where in Thompson's film, Peck merely testified as a witness against Mitchum, in Scorsese's, De Niro comes after Nolte because, when acting as his defence years before, the lawyer had deliberately suppressed evidence which would have mitigated his sentence.[1]

Scorsese's complex meta-movie was about interrogating these themes, and, within this schema, his vengeance-dealing Cady was reduced to a figure of pure abstraction: Robert De Niro, eye-rolling, cackling, gibbering in tongues, swaggering in his sailor's cap, looked like a nightmare dreamed by a fevered Popeye cartoon. De Niro's Cady, assembled with text-book precision, was an outright movie monster, a fantastical beast; Scorsese made this explicit, placing him among the abandoned stage set of a school production of *Little Red Riding Hood*, declaring: 'I'm the big bad wolf.'

Mitchum's Cady was not about to start turning any Grand Guignol horror movie tricks and was no psychologically profiled bundle of psychotic neuroses. He was drawn from life, conceived at gutter level, where the trash collects easily and play-acting looks foolish. His Cady didn't strain a muscle – he wasn't metaphor or an instrument of fate. He was a man, as unpredictable as a man. Representing only himself, acting according to his own choices. The 1991 Mitchum walked into Scorsese's movie as if to point up how absurd it was. He enters as a shock flash from the original, muttering in close-up about an English Setter he once had, on his way to supervise the new Cady's strip search. Looking on, placidly unimpressed, as De Niro strips down, Mitchum's reflection floats in the one-way mirror over the younger Cady's image; De Niro's body is toned, in six-pack shape, the product of exercise, something the original Cady would have scorned. His body had been beef-slab tough, broiled into shape by the life he chose.

De Niro's Cady is covered in maniacal jailhouse tattoos, messages of mixed up biblical revenge, protesting too much. Gazing on, Mitchum mutters the second-best line in the movie: 'I don't know whether to look at him or read him.' (The best line in Scorese's film is Mitchum's, too. He has suggested to the splintering Nick Nolte the best way to deal with De Niro is to lure him somewhere quiet, then blow his head off. Nolte is outraged by the suggestion, explodes haughtily and stomps off. Mitchum, watching him go, sends the following sailing serenely after him: 'Well, pardon me *all over* the place.')

Scorsese's movie was an intertextual fun fair rollercoaster freighted with ideas. Thompson had neither the talent nor the ambition of the younger director, but his movie makes Scorsese's appear bloated. The themes Scorsese worked over were there, of course, in the original – Peck delivers a fine portrait of suffering upright nobility pushed to breaking point – but Thompson left them lying on the surface. Clean-boned, crisp and fast, his picture was concerned with nasty, driving, straight ahead shock. As such, the original *Cape Fear* was all about its bad guy, leaving a less cluttered backdrop for Mitchum to work against, and, more than any other of his movies, it became entirely about his performance.

The entire film steps back to watch what Mitchum is doing, the way the cops in that interview room step back, cowed by his physique, to watch his strip search. It's one long bar room solo, exploring base human evil. You realise that, at some level, he connects with this character. Some part of him identifies, understands. Often, from behind a look of amused contempt, he appears quite delighted with himself, and, at some level, his sympathy begins to rub off on us, insidiously assaulting the audience, creating a profound unease.

Mitchum's Cady was grown from dirt he'd observed on the highways he'd travelled, but was rooted, too, in blown-up splinters of his own image. He had Mitchum's rambling roadhouse hipster thing going on – 'Hey, daddy,' he calls to the old courthouse cleaner at the start of Thompson's picture – like a hypertrophically swollen version of the 'Robert Mitchum' square America eagerly imagined to occupy its deviant reveries around the time of his drug bust. Cady was Mitchum as cop-hater – 'start reaching for those,' he spits at a deputy whose hand wanders toward his billy club while asking him to leave a waterfront bar, 'you better call for the riot squad, man' – and as drug fiend: during his strip search, down to his white shorts, Panama hat still on his head, as he hands his clothes to the policemen, he taunts them: 'you better check that shirt, I gotta coupla jolts of horse stashed under the collar.' Degenerate, without morals, following unknown pleasures, consorting with loose women, doing bad things in bad places.

Very bad things. He picks up Barrie Chase, who's been slumming around waterfront dives, and drives her to a rooming house. On the way, as she excitedly runs him down – 'you're just an animal, coarse, lustful, barbaric… you're rock bottom' – he notices he's being followed by Telly Savalas, the private eye Peck's hired. As Chase babbles smugly on, you see Mitchum thinking ahead. There follows a bedroom scene recalling the murder room in *The Night of the Hunter*: Mitchum prowls strangely, his back almost arched, gauging his fist, regarding the girl laid out on the mattress. She looks suddenly fearful and then, off screen, he destroys her, purely as a taster for Peck. We never learn what he does; she's discovered later, rendered speechless, moving like a wounded animal. It's violence of a design beyond the film's imagination, but whatever it is, Mitchum is capable of it. All the cops can say is: 'Something kinda weird's happened to her.'

Later, Mitchum sits Peck down in bar. Realising that, unbelievably, Peck still hasn't quite got the message, hasn't fully grasped what he plans for his family, Mitchum tells him a story by means of example. A hideous monologue that ranks among his best work, the tale is all suggestion, but, pushed along by the unencumbered pleasure he takes in the telling, sounds pornographically explicit. Vague, shifting pictures are conjured around the words. The story concerns Mitchum's wife, who divorced him while he was inside, taking their kid with her:

"She married a plumber. They wound up with a litter of kids; my own kid doesn't even know me. So, when I got out, I went to visit her. The plumber was off plumbin' someplace and the kids were all in school. She picked up a poker and tried to hit me over the head with it. And I took it away from her and calmed her down and she crawled in the corner. And I took her to a little spot about 50 miles down the road… That night, I made her call up the plumber and tell him she was taking a little vacation from him and the kids. Then I made her sit down and write me a love note. Asking me to invite her on a second honeymoon. She dated it and signed it. Made her write a lotta dirty words. Then I… occupied her time for three days. Beginning to get the picture, counsellor?

Finally, coming after the family now, as they hide up along the dark, choking Cape Fear river, Mitchum leaves suggestion aside. His films often feature passages that are solely about the way he moves through an environment, confident this can absolutely convey the emotion of a scene: it happened in the chase through *Macao*; when he walked across the deserted arena of *The Lusty Men*; when he went foraging silent and alone into the Japanese camp in *Heaven Knows, Mr Allison*. It happens twice in *Cape Fear*: at the beginning, when he walks that main street as though shouldering his way through civility, hat shining like a shark-fin; and again here, when he comes carefully through the night for violence.

Stripping off for the water that sends light reflecting across him, cocking his head to listen to the trees, the chirping cicadas, the frogs, Mitchum becomes a lizard thing, poised on rocks, prowling through reeds, clambering deftly on all fours, all the time coming forward. Lori Martin sits alone in a building beside the river, playing table tennis with herself, and, out there, Mitchum pushes back branches to see her: a dire close-up, wet hair plastered, half in the light, as he sees her, he slowly dips his head down into the shadows, bathing himself in dark.

First, though, after smiling while drowning a man, he goes for Peck's wife, Polly Bergen, in a sadistically vicious confrontation on the houseboat. Mitchum proclaimed his disdain for The Method often enough, but Bergen testified that she didn't know who he was anymore, or what he was going to do next. That he had disappeared into Cady, and that, as he started punching, slapping her in mounting frenzy, she was beginning to get frightened. 'It just suddenly got carried away… he was totally berserk…'[2] Part of his assault is to offer her a chance to sacrifice herself to save her daughter – at least for the time being. As she begs incoherently, he busts an egg in his fist, sending its contents spraying over her, like the shell of her life breaking.

As Peck stumbles blindly around after him, Mitchum goes back to get Lori Martin, who, hiding behind her ping-pong table, lifts a fire poker pathetically against him, just like Mitchum's wife did in that story. As he drags her out, there comes a horrible, bluntly hellish image, her little girl face clamped against his brute wet-meat carcass of a body.

Peck, of course, finally gets Mitchum, saves his wife and child from him, but he's far too late to save the movie. Holding Mitchum at gunpoint, Peck refuses to kill him, because that would be crossing the line, becoming like him, letting him win; but Mitchum has long already won – he owns the film, and he brought stuff to it no one was expecting, horrible things, and, more than that, the suggestion that horrible things hold their own bounty.

As the family – and the audience – leave *Cape Fear*, it's hard to say whether they're supposed to look as though they have survived to sail boldly into new solidarity or whether they are simply irrevocably shattered, flinching from the revealed world. The question is overshadowed, anyway, by Mitchum's last words, spoken down the barrel of Peck's gun:

> "Go ahead. Go ahead. I just don't give a damn."

The lines have been said in countless movies but rarely have had so much of a matter-of-fact abyss about them. The entire weight of Mitchum's performance leans behind the statement, squashing it convincingly, dreadfully flat. The living end.

The Friends of Eddie Coyle

Director: Peter Yates, Paramount Pictures, 1973

Synopsis

Eddie Coyle (Robert Mitchum) is a middle-aged father of three and small-time career criminal in Boston. He buys guns from young operator Jackie Brown (Steven Keats) for the mobster Scalise (Alex Rocco), who specialises in robbing suburban banks. A three-time loser, Eddie is awaiting sentencing for a previous scam – he was caught smuggling in an operation organised by his friend, Dillon (Peter Boyle), who runs a bar in town – and is facing a long jail term. Worried about what will become of his family if he goes inside, Eddie looks to cut a deal with treasury agent Dave Foley (Richard Jordan): he'll provide information if Foley will help him with the judge. Foley says he'll see what he can do and Eddie tells him about a machine-gun deal Jackie's planning. Acting on the tip, Foley arrests Jackie but then tells Eddie it's not enough to keep him out of jail. Foley asks about Scalise and Eddie realises the agent wants him as a permanent informant. Eddie bitterly refuses but a few days later contacts Foley to say he will inform on Scalise. Foley, though, tells him he's too late; acting on other information, he's already arrested Scalise. Knowing about Eddie's upcoming trial, the mob assume he was the informer and issue a contract, hiring Dillon to perform the hit. Oblivious, Eddie accepts Dillon's invitation to join him and his nephew at a hockey game. During the match, Dillon gets Eddie so drunk he later passes out. While his nephew drives, Dillon executes the sleeping man, dumping the body in a bowling alley car park. Days later, Dillon meets with Foley. It becomes clear it was Dillon who informed on Scalise. Foley agrees not to investigate Eddie's murder too closely.

In 1971, thinking of Howard Hawks' *The Big Sleep*, the critic Manny Farber wrote: 'One of the fine moments of 1940s film is no longer than a blink: Bogart, as he crosses a street from one bookstore to another, looks up at a sign.'

Farber cited that fragment as an example of something he believed had since been largely lost as movies had become increasingly over-conscious and overblown, what he described in a 1966 essay *The Decline of the Actor*, as: 'those tiny, mysterious interactions between the actor and the scene that make up the memorable moments in any good film. These have nothing to do with plot, 'superb performance' or even the character being portrayed. They are moments of peripheral distraction…'[1]

Looking back at *The Big Sleep*, however, you discover Farber's memory is off: Bogart's looking-up-at-a-sign pause isn't instinctive; in fact, he doesn't look up at a sign at all. He pauses to look at the sky, responding, on cue, to the thunder Hawks has put in to signal the imminent rain storm that lets Bogart play a foxy waiting scene in a sheltering bookstore with a pretty clerk who twists a pencil between her fingers.

Even if Farber's memory is imperfect, his thesis of the fugitive moment, throwaway splinters that lodge and reverberate, is sound. One of the fine moments in 1970's film comes in *The Friends of Eddie Coyle* and is no longer than a blink: Robert Mitchum, after he dumps his heavy garbage can on a cold, bright morning sidewalk, watches his children run past him to their shiny yellow school bus, and touches his hands momentarily, absently, to the knees of his trousers, wiping off the dirt.

From his tired entry to the film, wandering out of a thronging night into a half-empty diner, to drink coffee, eat apple pie and buy guns among fatigued nurses and strange old ladies in hats, through the scene when, having dumped his garbage and seen his kids go to school, he goes back inside to where it's warm, a tiny kitchen with bread in a plastic bag, where he happily slaps his wife's behind, washes his hands and makes toast, to the simple, genuine pleasure animating his face toward the end of the movie, when he watches an ice hockey game and the film looks for a while like a documentary that's only about a weary, oblivious guy happily drinking beer and watching ice hockey, Mitchum's performance as fated three-time loser Eddie Coyle is a frazzled symphony of focused distraction, moments that feel real, spontaneous

and are interesting to see, that simultaneously have nothing to do with plot, yet capture the entire point of the movie.

Peter Yates' properly shabby adaptation of George V Higgins' downbeat debut novel is less than perfect – the decision to spray it with the wac-ca-chow sub-funk music endemic to cop shows and crime movies of the era betrays uncertainty over what sort of a picture it's supposed to be – but it's a film that only grows with time. Certainly, placed alongside the noisy confusion and superheated conventionality of an entertaining but deafeningly over-praised contemporary like *The French Connection* (1971), Yates' film is criminally neglected.

In terms of Mitchum's career, it's an important movie not only because of his

performance as the doomed Eddie Coyle – one of his best, pitched at a low ebb that fits the abandoned, mundane beauty of the film – but because here, a decade on from the spasm of *Cape Fear*, and 20 years since his RKO reign as uncaring king patsy ended, noir claimed him again, took him back to a world that suited him and kept him there to stage an amber-tinged black renaissance through this, *The Yakuza* and *Farewell, My Lovely*.

His last-but-one film, *Going Home* (1971), set amid a similarly downbeat, dead-end world, a place of cheerless suburban streets, palpably dying mill towns near the sea, had showed the black impulse stirring. In an excellent, burned-out performance in that movie he played Harry Graham, a simple, rough ex-con, trying to look

Killing time in the bar run by chummy executioner Peter Boyle.

undaunted but bowed down under a sad load of guilt, just released from a long prison stretch for killing his wife, his son's mother, trying to build a small, new life. After some overly worked out grimness – the confused, raging son, played by Jan-Michael Vincent, turns up, rapes the father's new girlfriend, the father beats the son near to death – the son finally asks Mitchum why he killed his wife, and Mitchum, with a flat emptiness that makes the movie, bluntly confesses 'Because I was drunk.'

Since the high noir of the 40s and 50s – with vigorous exceptions like *Cape Fear* and *Point Blank* (1967) – noir had been tamed somewhat, commodified, forced into constrictive TV threads like *Dragnet* and *The Untouchables*. Its most obvious traits and tics inventoried, if not its essence, noir had become something to be called up, played with or played against. By the early 1970s, though, conditions were right, bleak enough for the mood to rise unhindered again. Noir was originally born from anxieties engendered by world war and its revival in this period – in movies like *Chinatown, Night Moves, The Conversation* and *Taxi Driver* – can be seen as a reaction to the rupture and upheaval of the American 60s, a new paranoia born of assassination, the unrest of civil rights and anti-war demonstrations, a violent generation gap, the freezing Cold War and the revelation of high-level, invasive political corruption.

The Friends of Eddie Coyle a film entirely about betrayal, conspiracy, time running out, the ending of things, autumn fading into winter, appeared in the middle of 1973 and fitted the wearied, cynical mood of the times. America's beaten troops were returning from Vietnam and Watergate was in full flow. The movie was released just as the news about the attempted wire-tapping of the Democratic offices in the Watergate complex by President Nixon's men was being given a new spin, with the disclosure that Nixon himself had secretly recorded every conversation that took place in his Oval Office.

While a film like Francis Ford Coppola's *The Conversation* was explicitly about the fear of electronic surveillance, unseen observation was felt more insidiously in *Eddie Coyle*. The paranoia in Coppola's film was intense, jagged, insistent – in *Eddie Coyle* it was wearier,

accepted as part of the atmosphere, like water in taps. Everyone was watching everyone else and reporting back to someone else again. Surveillance wasn't the film's main theme but it played a part in its creation: George V Higgins' fine novel had been praised, above all, for the way the story was carried by the authentic dialogue of its characters. At once colourful and toneless, these conversations – many incorporated intact in the movie – had the awkward, dumb repetitions, dead ends and side tracks, pauses, silences and non-rhythms of real speech. Over the years, Higgins had been a truck driver, a crime reporter, a lawyer and, latterly, assistant attorney general of Massachusetts. He had long developed a talent for eavesdropping in bars, restaurants and courts of law, and, as a federal prosecutor, had certainly had access to wire tap evidence collected by police and federal agents. The banal poetry of the men in his story could have been lifted verbatim from tapes of bugged real-life criminals (coincidentally, in 1975, Higgins wrote a non-fiction book on Watergate, *The Friends of Richard Nixon*).

Shot in and around Boston, the film of *Eddie Coyle* described a burned-out USA, a spent nation. Mitchum's Eddie, whose dreams have long since shrunk and who is now confusedly weighing up where his past has left him, is content, like the Harry Graham of *Going Home*, to keep his head down and just do enough to survive. Although a few scenes take place at night, Mitchum's world is mostly one of empty mornings and abandoned afternoons; everyone else seems to be away, at work, living a better life. There's a tension between the flat, commonplace ugliness of the washed-out urban–suburban settings the movie is mostly trapped in and the half-glimpsed splendour of the surrounding season: crisp autumn and the leaves that haven't yet fallen like the brown carpet in Mitchum's backyard riot in burns of purple, red, orange, yellow and green.

The friction between beauty and drabness lends the movie a beguiling atmosphere of melancholy dereliction. The almost constant dreariness of the scenery combines with the golden light to conjure a workaday surrealism, heightened by the sight of bank robbers moving against this backdrop in grotesque disguises: transparent moulded masks; rubbery old-men masks; blank ski-masks with slit eyes and squiggly sewn-on mouths. The landscape of the film is extraordinary, *Eddie Coyle* presents a daylit eulogy to unremembered areas at unremembered times of day. Not just the neglected diners, vacant bar rooms and functionally dismal peripheral bank branches but forsaken bare roadways running alongside forgotten lakes on the outskirts of town, left-over spaces behind those little bungalow banks, a badly designed concrete plaza in drizzling rain, slag-heap mineworks and deserted waterworks are all captured.

Mitchum and the vain, self-serving treasury agent subtly played by Richard Jordan first meet in the most thoroughly beautiful spot in the film: away from the city's grey wash, in a stretching empty piece of parkland where the trees are a cacophony of colour and, far-off, an unseen chainsaw buzzes beneath the sound of the breeze dryly stirring all the leaves. Nodding to Jordan's zippy roadster in the car park near the forsaken kids' play-area, Mitchum recognises seized merchandise and the two have a conversation that seems like an elegiac in joke, recalling Mitchum's *Thunder Road* days:

MITCHUM: "Nice machine you got there. Anybody I know's?"

JORDAN: "I don't think so. Fellow over in the western part of the state was using it to transport moon. Poor bastard. Paid cash for it and got hooked on his first run."

MITCHUM: "Well, you get away with it sometimes..."

The primary location of the movie, in fact, is the car park. There can't have a been a feature that spends so much time haunting these places: car parks of banks, bars, multistorey car parks, car parks of cut-rate shopping centres, the car park of a small suburban railway station where the big trains never stop. These blank, transitory arenas, places of elision for straight society, are where Mitchum plies his trade, conducts his meetings, lives.

While certainly not a member of that straight life passing busily around him, neither is Mitchum fully part of the underworld. Nor does he want to be – he'll buy and sell handguns but the idea of using one himself seems never to enter his mind and he physically recoils from the sight of a machine gun. He's known as a 'stand-up guy,' because he never squealed when he was caught smuggling Peter Boyle's booze; partly because of Boyle's reputation as a killer, partly because he never wanted to think of himself as a squealer, still half-believing codes that hold him trapped and are destroying him. But 'a stand-up guy' is by definition a guy who got caught, a loser. The crooks are civil to him but don't really seem to know him or take him seriously. They use him, the way Jordan's treasury agent uses him. It's Jordan, in fact, who supplies the best description of how Mitchum drifts back and forth across the borderline through the film: 'He's like a stray dog.'[2]

In physical terms, the wary, downcast way Mitchum moves as Eddie is an inversion of Max Cady's brazen stride. Mitchum retreats into his bulk, like a man who long ago learned not to trust his size and muscle to save him, who, in fact, hopes no one will notice he's a big guy and take it the wrong way. He has reason. His nickname is 'Fingers,' earned years ago when he sold a man a gun and the gun was traced and the man ended up in jail. Mitchum had to make amends to the man's friends, as he explains in his Boston accent, a flat sound chased by whining:

"Shut my hand in a drawer. Then one of them stomped the drawer shut. Hurt like a bastard. You got no idea how it hurt. There you are and they tell you very matter of fact that you made somebody mad, you made a big mistake and now there's somebody doing time for it and it isn't anything personal, you understand, but it just has to be done. Now get your hand out there... I know what's going to happen, like I say, and they put your fingers in a drawer and then one of them kicks it shut. Ever hear bones breaking? Just like a man snapping a shingle. Hurts like a bastard."

The impression is Mitchum started out in criminal life because it beat working and got stuck there, never climbing any higher. And now, at 56, he's facing up to it being too late. His life's about gone.

Wary and downcast:
Mitchum as Eddie.

He let it go. *Eddie Coyle* was Mitchum's first genuine, calm probing into ageing, how it can creep up, how time runs out and how that, as he always seemed to be aware, is just how it is. Although themes of age had started appearing in his films – *El Dorado* had been all about it, looking for last chances with a wry smile – his noir triptych of the early 1970s was specifically about lost youth, turning the bend and facing the home straight. The portraits in these films are all the more effective because it was Robert Mitchum

painting them, in noir, an icon rousing himself along with the genre that first appeared when he appeared, that he grew up in.

Eddie, this small-time crook who never made the big time, surrounded only by autumn, could once have been exactly the sort of guy the young Mitchum pushed around back in the 1940s; he could have been one of Kirk Douglas' low-rung henchmen from *Out of the Past*, left drifting after his boss was killed by that crazy woman. Like the Mitchum of that film, *The Locket, Angel Face* and

Thunder Road, he was doomed to die before the film finished spooling through the projector. The movie treats Mitchum cruelly: facing losing everything, the little genuine warmth of his cluttered home, he makes a decision that goes against everything in him – to rat out his friends – only to find he's reached that painful place of compromise too late. Meanwhile, all around him, others sell him out without thinking twice.

The one mean kindness shown him is courtesy of Peter Boyle, the man who set him up, the man who kills him to cover his own trail. Boyle's chummy execution of Mitchum is a drawn out ritual, distressing to watch for the victim's blissful ignorance. As if fattening him for slaughter, Boyle treats him to a good meal, some wine, then an ice hockey game with beers, the chance to see the famed, brutal Boston Bruins of the early 1970s, and their star player, Bobby Orr in rushing action. Mitchum watches with glee and admiration as a fight breaks out on court, sloshing beer over his trousers, happy and grateful for a night away from his worries, in an atmosphere full of crowding life, what looks like friendship by his side. Of course, once the game is over and he's lulled to sleep by beer and the rocking motion of the car home, Boyle puts him down like a stray dog and dumps him, his coffin a car ditched in a fitting graveyard: another deserted car park, wet tarmac stained with the pink and flashing blue neon of a bowling alley sign.

Maybe it was some flicker of guilty compassion deep in Boyle, or maybe it's just the last demonstration of how utterly oblivious Mitchum is, how he's manipulated and toyed with even though he's sure that he's the one being foxy, the one who knows what's going on – but he leaves in a dumb kind of peace, floating into oblivion on a cushion of alcohol, still thinking about the game, dreaming of youth, and bright tomorrows:

"Can you imagine being that kid? What is he, 24 or something? He's the best hockey player in the world. Christ, 'Number Four – Bobby Orr.' What a future he's got…"

Noir Movies
The Yakuza

Director: Sidney Pollack, Warner Brothers, 1975 (aka *Brotherhood of the Yakuza*)

Synopsis

San Franciscan businessman George Tanner (Brian Keith) asks his friend Harry Kilmer (Robert Mitchum), a retired private eye, for help: a yakuza mob — Japanese gangsters — have kidnapped Tanner's daughter, holding her in Tokyo to force him to help their gun-running operation. Accompanied by Tanner's nephew, Dusty (Richard Jordan), Kilmer journeys to Japan to meet Eiko (Kishi Keiko), the woman he loved during the Second World War but who mysteriously refused to marry him, bringing their relationship to a close. He asks to see her brother, Tanaka Ken (Takakura Ken), a renowned former yakuza. Tanaka is bitter toward Kilmer but indebted to him for looking after Eiko and agrees to help. Rescuing the girl, the two kill a number of the kidnapper's men and the yakuza faction issue a contract on Tanaka. Kilmer, meanwhile, discovers Tanner's daughter was really kidnapped because Tanner had reneged on a deal with the yakuza; now the businessman is working happily again with his gangsterous partners and has agreed to have Kilmer killed. An attack by men working for Tanner leaves Dusty and Eiko's daughter dead. In revenge, Kilmer goes after Tanner, killing his friend. He then helps Tanaka take on the ganglord who wants him dead; before setting off, however, Tanaka's brother, a respected yakuza counsellor, reveals to Kilmer that Tanaka is not Eiko's brother but her husband, whom she had thought dead when she first met Harry. In the bloody final battle, Tanaka kills scores of his foe's men, including his estranged nephew, his brother's son. Afterward, Tanaka meets his brother and follows the yakuza tradition of cutting off his little finger in penance. Kilmer sets out for home but turns around and goes again to see Tanaka. While taking tea, Kilmer cuts off his own finger as a sign of regret for the pain he has brought into Tanaka's life.

In *The Yakuza*, the past for Mitchum really is another country – Japan, where his character, Harry Kilmer, served with the occupying forces after the Second World War. As much as the film is about cultures watching each other, about karaoke singers in Tokyo singing *My Darling Clementine*, about loyalty, moral codes and twisting nets of obligation, and about the pure pulp thrills of gangsters and straight violence, it is predominantly about a man going reluctantly back to the landscape of yesterday, where they do things differently. Beneath the movie's static calms and storms of chopped-up brutality runs a weary current of sadness.

Shot in Tokyo and directed with oiled efficiency by Sidney Pollack, the script was composed by two of the most loving noir connoisseurs of the New Hollywood, Paul Schrader and Robert Towne. Schrader scripted initial drafts in collaboration with his brother, Leonard, recently returned from a four-year spell in Japan, where he had gone to teach English to avoid his army call-up. Loitering in bars, Leonard began recognising the Japanese gangster class, observed them up close, and when he returned to the States had the idea of writing *The Yakuza* as a novel; his brother enthusiastically hijacked the notion and turned it in the direction of film.

A film critic, Paul Schrader was desperate to write a movie, and had already started work on what would become his neo-noir masterpiece *Taxi Driver*. In 1972, *Film Comment* magazine published his analytical article *Notes on Film Noir*, among the most important English-language pieces written on the subject. Schrader had studied and cracked the codes of noir, knew how to reassemble the constituent pieces. In the same way, for this movie, he isolated the generic prerequisites of the yakuza flicks that were the dominant, disreputable mainstay of Japanese cinema across the 1960s. If a musical needed songs and love, a yakuza picture required abrupt violence, cynicism, conflict between a man's loyalty to others and his own personal honour, a cutting-off-the-finger scene, an apocalyptic finale.

By and large, such a movie also needed the presence of Takakura Ken, who was as emblematic of the genre as Mitchum was of the noir mood, and who, like Mitchum, knew

how to wear a raincoat. A Japanese institution, Takakura, a master of the kendo swordplay displayed in the stately orgy of violence toward the end of Pollack's movie, had made countless yakuza films. The greatest star of the Toei studio, which specialised in factory-like production of these wide-screen gangster outings, he averaged between 10 and 15 movies a year during the early- to mid-1960s, making more than 20 features for his vengeful-jailed-gangster *Abashiri* series alone.

Schrader's script blended Japanese systems with American noir strains but perhaps the blend proved too formulaic; Towne was called in to provide a rewrite. With the extent of his input into epochal movies including *Bonnie and Clyde* (1967) and *The Godfather* (1972) the subject of speculation, Towne's script-doctoring was revered in Hollywood. He had also recently written *Chinatown* (1974), his own, masterly invocation of high-noir, describing a parched, urgent memory of the Los Angeles of the late 1930s. Directed by Roman Polanski, *Chinatown* hummed to the tune of Chandler but worked sly inversions and comments into its amber melody; the private dick played by Jack Nicholson was not Chandler's lonely man of knightly honour but a rattier dude on the make, too cocky to realise what a fool he is – like the Jeff Bailey Mitchum essayed for *Out of the Past*. But, like Bailey, something still struggled and shone through his tarnished armour. *Chinatown* was at once revision and homage; despite its air of hard despair, it exhaled nostalgia.

For Nicholson's character, LA's Chinatown was a state of mind, a site of uncertainty and

Into the past: In Tokyo with Kishi Keiko.

disruption; once a cop, he used to work that neighbourhood, until something, something very bad happened there. Although *The Yakuza* is a pulpier work, and the neutrally rendered landscape of the city never becomes a character in the movie as LA did in Polanski's, Tokyo represents something similar for Mitchum; something he never understood happened to him there, and the time has come for him to return and confront it. Like Nicholson in *Chinatown*, like Marlowe in all those Chandler stories, like James Stewart in *Vertigo*, he's a detective, hired under false pretences; not simply an iconic symbol, like *Chinatown's* period hats and cars, however, Mitchum's timeworn presence in *The Yakuza* provided a physical bridge to the old noir world, showed it was still pressing behind the skin of the present. He gives the movie its black and white skeleton.

Takakura's character is at one point described as 'a relic, left over from another time,' a reference to the ritualistic systems of morality and battle he follows, codes as old as the samurai way of bushido. But the movie is at pains to present Takakura and Mitchum as burdened lone-wolf doubles and the description is tailored to fit both. Where, in his previous film, Eddie Coyle had been a man without a future, Mitchum's Kilmer is a man practically without a present, held in stasis, snagged on the unresolved friendships, enmities, loves and wounds of three decades before. Of all the men Mitchum had played, Kilmer most resembles a future, solitary version of Keeley, the cynical sergeant returned from war to a dark, neurotic city in *Crossfire*.

Thirty years may have passed but for Kilmer the war might just as well have ended yesterday and, for all the violence of the mean streets surrounding him wherever he goes, might as well be still going on. His life since leaving the forces – police work, private detection, no family, the easy wariness with which he handles weaponry – serves to illustrate the problem that Samuels, the murdered man in *Crossfire*, posited all those years before: 'We don't know what we're supposed to do – we're too used to fighting.'

The disruptive violence of the movie, stylised by sudden flurries of staccato editing, catches attention, but it's Mitchum's tow of stoic loneliness that haunts the film. He moves like a man who has pushed his way through unending decades of war; unlike Eddie Coyle, Kilmer is alert enough to see through the traps life and other men set waiting for him – but he's fatigued by all the years of having to.

Trying both to explain Japanese gangsterdom to an audience who had never heard of yakuza before and also to delineate a complex skein of relationships, the script occasionally trips over itself in exposition. Far more eloquent are the shots simply holding on Mitchum's face as he drifts the changed, once-familiar streets of Tokyo, beat by it all, on his way to meet again with the woman he loved and lost without knowing why.

Mitchum's bittersweet scenes with Kishi Keiko are hushed, actor and actress exchanging silent solos, harmonising their different kinds of quiet to build moments far more expressive of hope, regret, warming memories and lost time, awkward distance and the yearning to be close than any writing could hope to encapsulate. These scenes are some of the most tender in Mitchum's career, almost as delicate as his empathetic work with Deborah Kerr in *Heaven Knows, Mr Allison* (1957) and *The Sundowners* (1960).

As Kishi and the tightly reined Takakura demonstrate, the tradition of restraint in Japanese movie acting could extend into its populist mainstream and there's a *frisson* from seeing Mitchum's complementary but particularly American stillness – the minimalist detailing, the constant, unstressed suggestion of inner life – operating alongside theirs.

There's a direct correlation between the distinct-but-complementary nature of Mitchum's acting in this setting and the character he's playing; again, he's caught in his own orbit, a lonely misfit observation satellite floating between worlds. He's described as a 'strange stranger' – an outsider uniquely attuned to Japanese mores. During the war, this affinity set him apart from his American counterparts, but he could never fully join Japanese society. Dumbfounded by his lover's refusal to marry him, he drifted back to the States to live a limbo life, triply isolated by his war experience (mention is made of his ordeal during the raging Tokyo firestorm which claimed countless lives), his romantic wounds and his intrinsic, solitary difference. He's first seen in the movie alone in

his towelling gown – a sartorial echo of the life he might have had in Japan – on the wooden balcony of his beachfront house at the very end of the world, sadly examining the potted plants he tries to maintain against the salty air, one turning sickly brown, about ready to die.

By the end of the film, it looks as though the good guys have triumphed, kind of, but Mitchum has found out his best, his oldest friend had betrayed and then tried to kill him and, in turn, has had to kill him. He's resolved his differences with Takakura somewhat but in the process has given up his chances with the only woman he ever loved; he's watched a girl he once regarded as a daughter and a young friend he used to babysit die on a floor together. He leaves the film alone flying west, carrying God knows what souvenirs in a small blue Pan-Am bag, his bandaged, mutilated hand another badge of difference. As it climbs up and away from the airport runway, the plane carrying him out of the film back to that empty house by the sea is destined neither for blue skies nor sunset but heads into lowering, mountainous banks of endless grey clouds. He looks doomed to a life of patient loneliness, without hope, but intact, which is where the movies next found him.

Conflicting loyalties and abrupt violence: Takakura Ken (centre) settles scores.

Noir Movies
Farewell, My Lovely

Director: Dick Richards, Avco Embassy, 1975

Synopsis:

Private Eye Philip Marlowe (Robert Mitchum) accepts a case from gargantuan ex-con Moose Malloy (Jack O'Halloran), who's trying to find Velma, the dance-hall girl he went out with years ago. Following a lead from Tommy Ray (Walter McGinn), a trumpeter who played in Velma's club, Marlowe meets Jesse Florian (Sylvia Miles), whose husband owned the joint. From her information, he tracks Velma to an insane asylum. Meanwhile, Marlowe is hired by Lindsay Marriott (John O'Leary) to help buy back a necklace stolen from his "friend". In the meantime, Malloy informs Marlowe the asylum inmate isn't Velma. Marlowe accompanies Marriott; at the designated spot, he's knocked unconscious and Marriott is killed. Investigating, Marlowe eventually locates the stolen necklace's owner, Mrs Grayle (Charlotte Rampling), young wife of an elderly judge. At his office, Marlowe is beaten and taken to lesbian madam Frances Amthor (Kate Murtagh); she wants to know where Malloy is and has Marlowe drugged. Awakening from hallucinations, he discovers Tommy Ray's murdered body. He escapes and tries to get information from Amthor, but she's killed in an argument with one of her henchmen. Marlowe next encounters Mrs Grayle's friend, gambler Laird Brunette (Anthony Zerbe), who offers him $2,000 to bring him Malloy. Learning that Florian is in contact with Velma, Marlowe arranges to have Velma phone Malloy. Following his phonecall Malloy goes to meet Velma, but it's a trap and a shoot-out ensues. The cops are called and, investigating the set-up, Marlowe and police lieutenant Nulty (John Ireland) find Florian murdered. That night, Marlowe and Malloy board Brunette's floating casino; confronting the gambler, they discover Mrs Grayle with him. It transpires she and the missing Velma are one and the same – the whole affair has been her attempt to hide her former life as a hooker. Mrs Grayle kills Malloy, and Marlowe kills her. He decides to give Brunette's $2,000 to Tommy Ray's widow and child.

There's a moment in *Farewell, My Lovely* that looks like time rippling. Well, there are a few, because time rippling is mostly what this picture is about – but one moment in particular, unforced and accidental, when it's as if a tiny crack opens in the movie, allowing a rustle from decades before to push through. It comes around half an hour in, at night, down amid the dusty darkness of a forsaken place Raymond Chandler called Purissima Canyon, running off a coastal highway near LA. Robert Mitchum, as Philip Marlowe, has come here accompanying John O'Leary, as fragrant ratty ladies' man Lindsay Marriott, to help buy back a stolen necklace of Fei Tsui jade from criminal parties unknown, supposedly hiding in the pale surrounding brush.

This being a Chandler adaptation, the surface plot – all that Fei Tsui jade/stolen necklace/unknown criminal parties stuff – doesn't matter. What matters is the darkness and the loneliness and the possibility of danger, the sense of the city sitting corrupt and cooling back along the gloomy highway like a milk spill of light over the desert, the sense of dim, unconcerned stars high above and the idle crashing sound of the sea, the heedless lap and fade of waves nearby as, leaving O'Leary hiding in a fat, glinting car to be murdered, Mitchum saunters warily down through all of this to the white painted barrier that floats in the night at the end of the dirt road.

Vaguely searching the pressing murk beyond, a gun in his hand, Mitchum paces the length of the barrier, and it happens just as he approaches, then turns and looks away from the camera. The film has been pushing for this moment all along, calculating on the accumulation of night, certain equations of light and architecture, but suddenly, genuinely, there's something about the way Mitchum turns, half in apprehension, half in bored exasperation, the way the back of his neck appears above a raincoat collar, the angle of his hat. For a few frames, with the worn evidence his face openly carries – the evidence of thirty years of suspicions confirmed – obscured, the movie mainlines a real, pure old noir jolt. You could be watching *Out of the Past* again, its monochromes blushing, colourised by a subtle genius.

The sight of the 1975 Mitchum as Marlowe, sashaying a weary, 58-year-old tread through a painstakingly recreated 1940s – and the sound of him, breathing out chorus after chorus of voice-over narration – does a lot of this film's work for it. Chandler's novel had been filmed before. Rewritten by eventual *Out of the Past* scripter Frank Fenton, it first appeared in disguise, as part of RKO's debonairly low-cost *Falcon* series, *The Falcon Takes Over* (1942), the faux-Marlowe role filled by George Sanders, whose imperturbable, amused urbane disdain and elegant insolence resembled a polished, Anglophilic reflection of Mitchum's

misfit Yankee ennui. Then, in 1944, Edward Dmytryk turned in a version good enough to be called the greatest straight Chandler adaptation (*The Big Sleep* being the greatest messed-up Chandler movie), a film that, defining noir's cosmopolitan expressionism, looked like the sordid nightsweats of a nation at war and, playing Marlowe, gave fantastic, hard-lined new life to former icky crooner Dick Powell.

The 1975 *Farewell, My Lovely* however, bypassed these, taking its lead from two other, recent movies: Robert Altman's modernist hijacking of Chandler's *The Long Goodbye* (1973), and Roman Polanski's and Robert

The old urban armour out of mothballs as Charlotte Rampling stirs up glowing memories of femmes gone by.

Towne's corrupted pastel Chandleresque reverie *Chinatown*. While the revision of *Chinatown* had an air of regret, Altman's contemporary remodelling of *The Long Goodbye*, scripted by Leigh Brackett, who co-scripted Howard Hawks' *The Big Sleep* with William Faulkner, was gleeful, near savage in its cynicism. Set against the dippy landscape of early 1970s LA, Altman's Marlowe, Elliot Gould, was a shabby mess, out of time, wandering an indifferent world where his rigid code no longer functioned, where, instead of allowing him to navigate a sure, unmean passage through the mean streets, his moral compass left him high and dry.

In Chandler's original, Marlowe sets out to prove a friend innocent of murder, and, more or less, does; in Altman's update, the friend is guilty all the way, uses Marlowe, and, in a retaliation Chandler's Marlowe would not have countenanced, the stung Gould finally tracks the guy down and kills him, dancing into the final credits to the soured sound of 'Hooray For Hollywood.'

Directed by former photographer Dick Richards, *Farewell My Lovely* shied away from Altman's radical repositioning, and harboured a nostalgia, a desire to eulogise, far straighter than *Chinatown*'s; simply put, it wanted to be a 1940s film, but could not ignore the fact that mounting an unadulterated, unaware old school private eye picture had been rendered all but inconceivable.

Mitchum's sheer presence, though, a unique combination of undiminished, still-potent strength and the undisguised onset of age, bulldozed a path through this dilemma, by allowing Richard's movie to be the 1940s and the 1970s at once. Like the hats and fire hydrants and curving fenders littering the bleaching streets around him, like Marlowe himself, Mitchum is an authentic piece of the mythic 1940s, can get his mouth easily around the smooth, hardboiled shapes of Chandler's words and the fine facsimiles scriptwriter David Zelag Goodman has added ("I was having some Chinese food when a dark shadow fell over my chop suey..."). The pristine hat and the raincoat he belts against the night look exactly, to the last stitch and fold, like his rumpled *Out of the Past* armour, as if they had been vacuum packed in an RKO vault, awaiting his return. The film places him again on a beach at night, with a spider-woman in his

arms; once again he's in a world prowled by gorillas, waiting to shoot him up or pound him to death. However, he is patently not the 1940s Mitchum. The fatigued evidence of his face, the heroic maintenance of his body – upright but looking as though sagging dissolution will set in as soon as he rests – are reminders of how far removed the film is from the period it describes.

Around him, following his cue, the entire movie sets out to simultaneously evoke, pay homage and offer bittersweet comment. More so than *Chinatown*, which, for all its anguished retro strategies, felt urgently present tense, it becomes a memory movie, bedimmed by shadows of old films and a vanished city. *Farewell, My Lovely* presents a Los Angeles in quotation marks. This is clear from the first: beneath the titles comes a close-up of palm fronds in a limp breeze – later, glimpsed in the background of bars and nightclubs, it becomes evident these are fake leaves of fake trees. Then comes a montage of found, treated footage: moving lights of city streets busy at night, a neon line drawing of a woman's face on a theatre marquee, thronging sidewalks, headlight glares from chubby silhouette cars, all oblivious stock images, slowed down and coloured roughly, as though put through an ancient tinting process, to push them further away.

All the while, the main musical theme gives a sad trumpet the chance to explain itself, anticipating the sad trumpeter whose peripheral death will affect Mitchum more than any other in the movie. The final image of the sequence is a high, overhead shot, looking down into the vanished, happy motion of a long-gone street. Choking on a rising haze of lights, the boulevard appears as a burning canyon in an engulfing night, consuming itself in an amber inferno.

This overture then gives way to the complementary sight of Mitchum as Marlowe; the camera crawls up the brickwork of a dingy hotel to reveal him alone behind a greasy window, looking out into that abyss, bathed in a red glow from nearby neon, a cigarette dangling his lips, one hand holding the grimy net curtain back, the other nursing whiskey. Mitchum as Marlowe, alone, looking out at the world, a broke down icon carved in celluloid. Chandler once explained, in a 1951 letter, how Marlowe was 38 and would always be 38 – even though he was

writing five years after the 46-year-old Bogart made *The Big Sleep*. Mitchum is a full two decades older than Chandler's detective ever was, touching 60, but carries himself exactly the way you imagine Marlowe might had he made it to that age. He has Marlowe's unimpressed amusement down pat, but appears battered by a life of seeing the soiled laundry of so many other people, looks worked over by the years of sadness and violence, the traps, the perversion and the betrayal.

Again, Mitchum's unforced Mitchumness adds to the scene, allows the film to do more than it might: the preternatural cynicism present in that face is far more profound and unaffected than anything Robert Altman conjured – Altman is mocking of old movie tropes; Mitchum's wearily derisive Blackfoot skepticism is aimed at the cosmos. Still, it's a poignant cynicism; this face is shot through with a tired, but tenacious kind of bruised romance, a sheltered belief in the possibility of poetry. It's this that makes his eyes light up when he sees a happy kid with a toy baseball, that makes his eyes turn down when a faded party girl drunkenly tries on routines from her long-gone girlhood; and it's this that initially leads him into taking a hopeless job for a lovelorn big ox too dim to see that love can make a hard life harder.

Like the titles, the world of the movie proper is painstakingly fashioned solely to frame this resonant incarnation. The faces and shapes of the

A sepia-tinged world of hats and gorillas.

Trying to make a tiny difference: grilled by John Ireland and Harry Dean Stanton.

cast around him have the peculiar singularity and vitality of a lost age: as Nulty, the downtrodden policeman who finally remembers why he became a cop in the first place, there's John Ireland, a familiar face in the crackling 1940s noirs of Anthony Mann, but by that stage into a slump of exploitation movies (prior to Richard's film, Ireland completed horror cheapies *The House of Seven Corpses* – with Faith Domergue and the grisly, self-explanatory *The Mad Butcher*). As the purring, duplicitous killer femme, Charlotte Rampling stirs up glowing memories of Lauren Bacall, crossing her legs in a red dress to make explicit all the insinuations in Bacall's Look and, like her, possessed of a beauty that could be glacial or mischievous, and

the intelligence to work against it. Then there's old Jim Thompson as the frail, silvery Judge Grayle; Sylvia Miles, tremendous as the soused, blousy Jesse Florian, muttering how she used to have pep; Kate Murtagh, like a vicious, blubbery, deceptively mobile kid sister of Sidney Greenstreet as the mean lesbian Madame Frances Amthor; Harry Dean Stanton, a combination of William Burroughs and a half-opened jackknife in his flimsy suit as the corrupt, racist, petty-thieving cop trying to out-sneer Mitchum all the way; and ex-boxers Jimmy Archer and Jack O'Halloran as, respectively, Georgie the news-stand guy and the towering, dimly sentimental, annihilating lummox Moose Malloy.

The film is designed by Dean Tavoularis, who arranged the oilpaint New York glooms of the first two *Godfather* movies, and photographed by *Chinatown* cinematographer John Alonzo. As in the latter, LA itself becomes a character: Tavoularis scoured the city to find stubborn remnants of Chandler's town, discovering locations like Sylvia Miles' beat-up Echo Park residence, exactly as Chandler imagined it: "a dried-out brown house with a dried-out brown lawn in front of it." Tavoularis and Alonzo combine to suggest that the rot discovered in *Chinatown*'s 1937 has really set in. Walls of rooms – the seedy hotel Mitchum is holed-up in at the start of the movie, the barren office,where goes to sit out the nights, gazing out his window in the dark – are often sickly yellow, the paintwork looking clammy, about to start running with sweat.

Yellows and sad browns saturate Alonzo's photography, all at once suggesting the look of sepia photographs, the oxidised pages of discarded old paperbacks, jaundice, and a world stained by billowing nicotine clouds; playing private eyes brings out the chainsmoker in Mitchum, at one point lighting one cigarette from the smouldering end of one he's just finished, discarding it in his overflowing desktop ashtray, butts piled in a pale Golgotha of tobacco and ash.

Goodman's script, while maintaining intense fidelity to Chandler, closes down the book and works in slight changes, to amplify the feeling of a world running down. It seems Mitchum's Marlowe has fallen into the seamy kind of divorce work Chandler's detective took pride in avoiding, and, finally, in the film, unlike the novel, it is the detective himself who fires the gun that kills the manipulative green-eyed killer femme. This runs like a betrayal of the original Marlowe's code of chivalry, but then the original Marlowe had never been shot in the crotch by an almond-eyed Jane Greer. Some mistakes you learn from.

Mitchum's first words are Goodman's, spoken in a voice-over that is another *Out of the Past* echo, played like a melody carried on the rhythm of his physical performance. This Philip Marlowe was about the softest Mitchum ever played: it's there when he talks to the little kid with the baseball, when he throws gently delighted combination punches beside the news-stand with Jimmy Archer, when he watches with exquisite sadness tinged with disgust – at her, at himself – as Sylvia Miles tries to climb inside the bottle he's brought to pry information out of her. If *Out of the Past* was Mitchum as Miles Davis blowing 'So What,' *Farewell, My Lovely* is Mitchum as Coltrane breathing 'It's Easy To Remember'·

"This past spring was the first that I'd felt tired and realised I was growing old. Maybe it was the rotten weather we'd had in LA. Maybe it was the rotten cases I'd had – mostly chasing a few missing husbands, and then chasing their wives once I'd found them, in order to get paid. Or maybe it was just the plain fact that I am tired, and growing old."

The film is set one year after the novel, in 1941, when America teetered on the brink of WWII, and that feeling of something about to change, of something coming to an end, shimmers faintly throughout. One of the script's finest additions is a running parallel between the progress of Marlowe, who keeps a baseball amid the spare rubble of his desktop, and the unbroken, record-busting clean batting streak of New York Yankees legend Joe DiMaggio. It allows Mitchum a musing about DiMaggio that brings up the ghost of the Eddie Coyle, who wondered at the youth of an ice-hockey hero:

"Would he hit safely in every game forever? And why not? He was only 26, and playing baseball in the sunshine."

Of course, DiMaggio's run is finally ended, another reminder to the tired gumshoe that his tenuous luck is going to give out, too, one of these days, and he really has no idea where that's going to leave him, why he keeps moving, doing his melancholy little jobs, trying to make a tiny difference when he knows it won't make any difference at all.

"I'm tired… everything I touch turns to shit. I've got a hat, a coat and a gun. That's it."

But, of course, he will keep moving, shouldering his sadness and tiredness and his bruised hopes and beliefs, clutching deadpan bitter humour to him like a shield and treading a decent path through the tattered, swarming, dusky red meanness of the city night. Entering affairs that never work out, and usually worse than that. Taking the jobs that come before him. Wondering mildly at the stuff people get into, the stuff they do to each other, themselves.

Mitchum gets all of this into the way he turns and walks out of the film, walking away from the camera, tossing his baseball up in the dimming air, a symbol that, just because one run has come to an end, that's no reason for not trying for another with the time left (or perhaps it's another symbol, in that it recalls a line from another of *Out of the Past* director Jacques Tourneur's most famous movies, *The Leopard Man*, in which man's condition in the universe is compared to a ball kept spinning in the air by the water from a fountain). He's last seen as a shadow, disappearing behind the frosted glass door of the beat-up Crescent Hotel where a trumpeter's widow and kid live, off to do a small act of great goodness, before returning alone again to his patient office. Watching him go is like reading one of the last things Raymond Chandler ever wrote, a letter in which he defined his eternal view of Marlowe. In this movie, Mitchum merges with the words:

"I see him always in a lonely street, in lonely rooms, puzzled but never quite defeated."[1]

That makes for a nice fade to black, and would be a good way for Mitchum to walk finally out of film noir. In a lot of ways, *Farewell My Lovely* was his farewell to noir, but the dark stuff hadn't quite finished with him yet. Three years later, he was back as Philip Marlowe again, in Michael Winner's bizarre *The Big Sleep*, a movie that imagined Marlowe transposed, operating in the England of the late 1970s, but, unlike the updated *The Long Goodbye*, failed to do this for any good reason. Otherwise the movie stuck rigidly, doggedly explicit, to Chandler and saw Mitchum sharing screen space in a hothouse with a visibly wilting James Stewart, then saw him wrestling Joan Collins.

Mitchum's pace, resignation and monumental weariness are the only things that make the film watchable, and his voiceover is a pleasure to hear, but the reports that he only made the movie because he got to keep the 12 Savile Row suits he wears in it are easy to credit. More satisfactorily, for the movies, he was back moving briefly through *Cape Fear* again, for Martin Scorsese's 1991 remake, adding a necessary skepticism.

The real site of the slight noirish reprise in Mitchum's late career, however, was in television. The first movie he made for TV, *One Shoe Makes It Murder* (1982) saw him as a retired, beat-down, shabbily Marlowe-esque detective, hired to find the missing wife of Nevada gambler Mel Ferrer. He manages to find her corpse and, hooking up with hooker Angie Dickinson tours a faintly deadbeat world trying to solve the murder.

The following year, Mitchum dusted off his reprehensible, cold-to-the-bone Max Cady persona to give an extraordinary performance, full of the old evil-has-its-own-rewards stuff, in *A Killer In the Family*. He played a white-trashy murderer serving life, who persuades his wide-eyed sons, James Spader, Eric Stoltz and Lance Kerwin, to spring him and a jail-buddy. With the boys in tow, the two men rampage across Colorado territory. As they go, they kill a carload of people – a family – in a scene that remains difficult to watch. Mitchum busts the film apart.

In 1986, he was back behind bars, wearing jailhouse denims and glasses while patiently scrutinising a book in his cell at the start of *Thompson's Last Run*. For this he partly reiterated Eddie Coyle: safe-cracker John Thompson is a habitual criminal, an old three-time loser resigned to ending his days inside. Thompson has more horse-sense than Eddie ever had though, and Mitchum made this gentle, rueful, last-chance chase movie – he's reluctantly busted out by his long-lost niece, and pursued by an aging cop who, Jimmy Cagney-Pat O'Brien style, was his childhood friend – into an extended blue-note study, thinking his way through the character from the inside. Filmed around rundown rural areas of Dallas, the movie gave him the chance to drink whiskey, drive backroads, fish in a lake, dance to country music, and sit reading to five tiny kids from a picture book.

Finally, in 1989, he played the title in *Jake Spanner, Private Eye*. A light-hearted spoof intended only to gently kid the old noir traces, this movie mostly misfires, but Mitchum goes through it like a dancing bear doing a soft-shoe, and it contains a few fine things. One of the finest is the first sight of the 72-year-old actor, sitting looking supremely, exquisitely bored on a sunny park bench, clutching a crazy-golf putter and wearing a Hawaiian shirt. Just prior to this, carried along on his weary voice-over, explaining how he'd been to too many places, and even if he hadn't always prevailed, he'd survived, the film has run through a sequence of clips from *Out of the Past* , showing the young Mitchum losing Virginia Huston, kissing Jane Greer in moonlit Mexico and roughhousing with Steve Brodie.

Cutting from that young man whispering how, if has to die, he's gonna die last, to the idling old fella soaking up sun on the bench forty-two years later, looking faintly surprised that, around him, people are bothering to kid themselves that they're having fun, the movie asks: what would a man from that lost old precarious black-and-white planet do if he'd made it out, what would Philip Marlowe make of this changed Los Angeles if he'd managed to survive and drag himself all the way into 1989?

The plot has this jaded old gumshoe haul himself reluctantly out of retirement, agreeing to help rescue the kidnapped granddaughter of aging mobster Ernest Borgnine. Plot twists ensue, Mitchum tours Echo Park again, and the film ends with him and Borgnine wandering off to spend a suitcase full of cash together somewhere warm and far away.

Beneath the final credits, under the sound of Mitchum singing, comes a happily ridiculous epilogue. We see him lounging in a basket chair, attended by an adoring group of young Hawaiian girls. He's wearing another, even gaudier Hawaiian shirt, has a Bluto sailor's cap stuck on his head, and a truly mammoth cigar hanging from his mouth. He started the movie thinking back to Jeff Bailey; here, as he holds a cold drink aloft and raises his eyebrows at one of the women, there are all sorts of questions alive in his eyes. He looks for all the world like Max Cady, reformed in heaven. Good enough.

Chapter Six
War Movies

The Second World War was Mitchum's era. The actor was drafted into the US Army in the middle of 1945, just as the conflict in Europe was coming to an end. Although spending seven months on active duty as an infantryman, he remained in Stateside camps – helping out as an assistant to the medical officer inspecting his fellow troops for haemorrhoids, if the version of his army career he gave to interviewers was to be believed – never seeing any action. He was eventually discharged on a hardship ticket, to return to work and support his extended family, for whom he was sole breadwinner. He would, however, continue fighting the conflict off and on around the globe in pictures for over 40 years, finally, at the age of 71, in his most mammoth acting undertaking, for some of the largest audiences the world has seen.

Having already spent a year at Lockheed helping build the quick, rickety planes the Allies were sending up against the Nazis over Europe, he first entered movies just as the US was entertaining new doubts about the war it had reluctantly, angrily finally entered after the bombing of Pearl Harbor and the crippling of its Pacific Fleet at the end of 1941. Still reeling from that blow, encountering unexpectedly proficient enemies and suffering unanticipated setbacks across the theatre of conflict, the cocksure US was beginning to realise this wasn't going to be a case of simply stepping in and quickly smacking down the bad guys. Consequently, the vast majority of the movies Hollywood produced during this period that were actually about the war – as opposed to being designed to take audiences' minds off of the war – were fundamentally propagandistic in intent, morale-boosters less concerned, on the whole, with interrogating the reasons behind or the true nature of the conflict, than with flag-waving and

playing up the idea of noble Yankee boy heroes and their allies selflessly off fighting inhuman, dehumanised villainy. Never mind that the newsreels playing before those films, just after the Loony Toons, were showing varied glimpses of apocalypse, ghost cities on fire.

A good-looking, but regular-looking and beat-up-looking Joe in his mid-20s, Mitchum was initially drafted as a sideline dog face into a number of these variously soapy or comic book heroic war pictures. When he wasn't in cowboy gear, he was in uniform, playing a soldier 10 times between 1943 and 1945.

It went this way: first, in *The Human Comedy* (1943), a folksy small town-at-home-in-wartime movie, with li'l Mickey Rooney scooting around the hamlet delivering telegrams to mothers telling them their sons were dead, Mitchum briefly played a not-dead-yet soldier, trying to pick up Donna Reed; in *Doughboys in Ireland* (1943), he was a commando cooling his heels and attending parties while in training in Ireland; he was fleetingly glimpsed in the background as a sailor aboard the destroyer Randolph Scott was attempting to steer safely through cold waters and Axis attacks in the vigorous, laconic, Howard Hawks-produced *Corvette K-255* (1943); then a Sergeant, overseeing a pair of squabbling buddies through their pre-combat basic training in the zero-budgeted *Aerial Gunner* (1943); then under Randolph Scott again, in the ultra-patriotic *Gung-Ho!* (1943).

In that film, both he and Scott were members of the ferocious Marine unit known as Carlson's Raiders. Mitchum, looking young and dumb-punkish, sporting a buzz cut, undergoes specialist training, then is off fighting dim, dirty jungle warfare on a Pacific Island, trying to recapture territory from the Japanese. The character he plays is among the most vivid of his

early bit parts, a roughneck former prize-fighter known as 'Pigiron,' he's been a street fighter since childhood and has a bad reputation for brawling. After signing up for the mission to capture the Island, he takes a Japanese bullet in the throat, but keeps going.

Next came the cheap and shaky *Minesweeper* (1943) with Mitchum a sailor in training again; he was then a wounded soldier tended by cute, heroic nurses like Margaret Sullavan in a makeshift Army hospital in the Battle of Bataan in *Cry Havoc* (1943); in the last reel of *Johnny Doesn't Live Here Anymore* (1944), he turned up on leave in New York, hoping to find someplace

quiet to go with his young wife; he followed Spencer Tracy as a flier on Doolittle's Raid, that against-all-odds affair when American bombers attacked Tokyo as a morale-boosting gesture after Pearl Harbor, in Mervyn LeRoy's low-key, earnest *Thirty Seconds Over Tokyo* (1944); and, in *Mr Winkle Goes to War* (1944), a faceless Corporal ordering mild-mannered, middle-aged Edward G Robinson, recently drafted, through the induction process. 'Faceless,' by the way, is meant literally: Mitchum is simply a booming voice and massive uniformed body in this picture, his head cut off by the top of the screen while little Robinson looks meekly up at him.

Battered on the beach: refighting D-Day for *The Longest Day* (1962).

By and large in these films, Mitchum is hardly around long enough to do more than register, create a fleeting, odd texture against the grain of the surrounding film and disappear. In life, he spent the weekend before registering for his enlistment in jail, after some muddy, boozed-up misdemeanour, protesting he'd been billy clubbed by a gang of cops – he carries into these pictures the face of an anti-authority guy, who has decided to lay off goofing-off for a while and help out.

The propaganda messages most of the war films of this period dealt in would have held little appeal for his fundamentally cynical, sceptical intelligence and, in general terms, the collective heroism of the army group-movie was by its nature anathema to the solitary outsider aesthetic Mitchum responded to and cultivated as a leading player. Consequently, although he worked often and long in war movies, the films he made in the genre are among the least representative of his career.

As a young man with a young family during that time, however, he did have an insight into the individual reluctance, apprehension, resignation and fear that any other drafted soldier would experience – the sorts of emotion the 1943–44 war pictures preferred to be kept under wraps. When he finally received his own invitation to join Uncle Sam's forces in April

of 1945, he didn't saunter cheerfully, boldly off to fight:

"When they took me away, I still had the porch rail under my fingernails."[1]

Mitchum's sympathies lay more with the realities of individual men caught up in war than with any of the grand, broad-brushed statements endemic to the genre. In the 1966–67 period, without any fanfare, he participated in 152 missions as an observer in the Vietnam war zone, surprising American troops on the front lines by suddenly appearing from a helicopter. He spent his time there talking and drinking with the soldiers, then spent the weeks after his return contacting the families of the soldiers he had met, delivering messages to parents and wives, and talking about the waste.

Only with a couple of war movies would he have the chance really to express and to explore such ambiguous feelings, emotions that were outside the remit of the regular army flick. One such opportunity came just before his induction, when returning to the celluloid front lines he put all of those feelings and that intelligence into play for one magnificent, sober, muddy and miserable masterpiece of war.

The Story of GI Joe

Director: William A Wellman, United Artists, 1945

Synopsis

In 1944, war correspondent Ernie Pyle (Burgess Meredith) joins with Company C of the 18th US Infantry in a North African desert to accompany them as they march and fight their way into Italy. The men — including Sergeant Warnicki (Freddie Steele), who carries a phonograph record of his baby's voice around with him, searching for a record player, and Private Donardo (Wally Cassell), a dedicated lothario — are under the command of Lieutenant Bill Walker (Mitchum). Pyle stays with the company through a number of battles, then leaves to report from another area of conflict. Later, he rejoins Company C, to find that Walker has been made Captain and that several familiar faces are now absent. The unit becomes hemmed-in, unable to move below a mountain-top monastery that's being used by German forces. On Christmas Eve, Pyle shares a bottle with Walker as the captain writes letters to the families of the men who have been killed. A few days later the order comes through to attack the monastery; the push is a success but Walker is killed in the battle. Pyle and the men of Company C leave Walker's body and join the forces marching north.

The story begins with desert dust, lines of waiting trucks filled with waiting soldiers and a dirt road stretching into the north. A young Lieutenant, gruff and hard-headed but with a peculiarly sad set to his eyes, is speaking to the disappointed troops slouched together under his command, telling them to get rid of the big-eyed little puppy they seem to have found somewhere out here in the empty middle of nowhere. Soon the dust will turn to an endless vista of churned-up, rutted black mud, the soldiers' faces will begin to change and disappear and be replaced but the dog will stick around for a while and the waiting will never end.

That puppy sends out a misleading signal. As James Agee – the poet, critic and author who would end his career adapting *The Night of the Hunter* for Charles Laughton – commented in his glowing review of William Wellman's film, *The Story of GI Joe* was released into 'a world which is generally assumed to dread honesty.'[1] A young soldier boy gently cradling a little scruffy pooch would seem to be an image made to humour that world, suggesting that the most clichéd, maudlin kind of movie is about to unfold.

Indeed, Wellman's film features character types which by 1945 had already become stock stereotypes of the army genre but, as the film unfolds you see through the cliché to the simple truth behind: these kinds of characters exist. Here, forced together in the mass of the unit, Company C of the 18th US Infantry, they are clinging to their broad-brushed character traits like drowning men to planks of wood, although they betray themselves in surprising ways. Their various peculiarities, sometimes so relentlessly adhered to that they border on being symptoms of neurosis – as in the case of Wally Cassell, the Brooklyn–Italian wolf of the troop, whose ladies man obsession has grown to resemble a terrible secret addiction as he clandestinely sniffs a perfume bottle at night – are the only remnants left of life at home, the only thing to differentiate them, apart from their dog tags. Watching the film you accept that if a certain kid out there found a puppy someplace, he really would want to try and look after it.

Often in these army pictures, one or two colourful types – a joker, a poet, a psycho, a neurotic, a hero – would stick out from the anonymous herd, as the film focused on the actions of individuals within the group. Wellman's film, though, is about the collective, but it's a khaki cluster made up of individuals. Eventually, Mitchum as the Lieutenant (who, during one of the periods when the film has lost sight of him, gets promoted to Captain for unexplored actions) emerges as the most recognisable, and finally the most haunting face among the soldiers, but the way the film turns so often to him is in keeping with the way the men he commands turn to him.

Burgess Meredith takes notes as Mitchum takes orders.

Even then, none of the men, Mitchum included, ever comes very close to us, although they sometimes come just close enough to offer a few hints about the kinds of guys they are, or were, back where they came from. The film is based on the famously intimate sketches of foot soldiers' lives that the journalist Ernie Pyle filed from the front as he trekked with American troops into Europe from Africa, and Wellman keeps that perspective; superior officers and the enemy are completely absent from the film, only their influence, coming down in arcane ways, is felt. Characters drift in and out of the film's gaze the way the changing rows of tired faces must have streamed past Pyle. Those moments when Wellman allows them to swim into brief focus are very delicately balanced, enough to put notes of common tragedy resonating through the movie.

Whether or not the world was wanting anything like honesty, Wellman was ready to begin addressing the realities of the war. *GI Joe* was filmed in April of 1945 as Berlin was falling to advancing Soviet troops and the Allies were making the unimaginable discoveries of Belsen and Dachau. When the movie was released, in September 1945, the month the war ended, it was only weeks since atomic bombs had dropped on

Hiroshima and Nagasaki. Not counting the civilian deaths in concentration camps and firebombed cities across the planet, estimates put military fatalities alone at around the 20 million mark. Ernie Pyle was himself killed as the movie was being made, cut down by machine-gun fire while reporting on the fighting around Okinawa.

Wellman's movie has this ghastly reality running through it. Sam Fuller, the ferociously iconoclastic director who had formerly served as a soldier with the 1st Infantry Division, fighting along this same path out of North Africa toward the concentration camps of Czechoslovakia, praised *GI Joe* for 'its feeling of death and mass murder.'[2]

Shot by the great Russell Metty, who would later photograph *The Stranger* and *Touch of Evil* for Orson Welles, and *Spartacus* (1960) for Stanley Kubrick, the movie looks as though it has been filmed on a weary, dirty desperate graveyard planet, a cold place, alternately assaulted by lashing, filthy rain and light hot enough to daze eyes, parch mouths and dry out stiffened, heavy clothes just in time for the next freezing downpour. Soon after the convoy of trucks moves off out of that opening scene, the first young body has already been left lying in the dirt by the side of the road – Wellman shows the silent faces of the GIs regarding the corpse of this kid they hadn't yet gotten to know in an intensely humanist series of dumb close-ups – and a new silence has entered the film.

Nights are filled with choppily edited battle darkness: flares and strobing explosions, dim confusions of figures falling and fighting. The men, flinching, huddled against a small blasted wall as mortars explode close by, turn hollow-eyed and mechanical as they progress through this terrain, begin sleepwalking, stiff-legged in their exhaustion.

One of the most admirable aspects of the film, particularly for its period, is the willingness to depict enlisted men who are uncertain, fearful, bored waiting and suspicious of their orders, never quite knowing where they're going or why. Guys who want to be lazy, bitch about how their superiors manage to get turkey at Christmas, while they seem to get passed by. Who lie about late at night in their desert truck camp and are genuinely tempted by the insinuating radio purr of 'Axis Sally,' giggling lazily in their ears and

broadcasting morale-crippling blasts of homesick Artie Shaw from Berlin.

The film drifts in and out of time. There are ellipses, lost periods. You see the toll the experience is taking on the soldiers in the lines of their faces beneath the beards they grow and shave off and grow again, the trudge of their walking, they way they talk and keep quiet. Some of them are crying, and some of them just aren't there any more, disappeared faces, their absence unmentioned by their comrades. Then new, younger, fresher recruits arrive to take their place, trying hard not to look as terrified as they do.

And when the new kids arrive, it's up to Mitchum to look after them, straightening up so as to appear reassuringly intimidating, but coming apart inside from watching all these boys turning into killers.

Wellman cast Mitchum after he'd noticed him in one of the happily clip-clopping B-Westerns the actor had made for RKO, but he picked up on something those films had no time for. Even so, the director was unprepared for what he got; he often repeated how he wished he had filmed Mitchum's test against proper scenery:

> "Really, for I saw something so wonderful, so compelling that I was mad at myself for not having built the set before, so that I could have made the test the actual scene that came out in the movie"[3]

Wellman uses Mitchum in the film as a man of action – there's a superb silent battle in a bombed-out church, when, as if relieved to have something to do after all the trekking and waiting, Mitchum and his Sergeant go about taking out their hidden enemies like two men contented at work – but also as a man of extreme, observant stillness and silence. Working with supreme restraint, Mitchum gives a performance of an interior nature that's quite audacious, hinted at only previously in the lull moments of *When Strangers Marry*.

He often looks confused, but distantly, as though he's by now long used to being confused by what's expected of him and sickeningly used to the ceaseless, phantasmagoric parade of dirt and bodies and violence and gore. As the film develops, he becomes a kind of half-glimpsed regular soldier saint, one who doesn't want to be a saint, and doesn't want to be a soldier.

His silence is eloquent. He stands in silence to watch a man pray. He stands in silence as his Sergeant reels off the names of the men killed on the latest reconnaissance mission, pauses for a long half-second, then says, 'OK Sergeant, you better go get some chow.' Then he burns with a vicious, steely silent anger when he catches one of his men goofing off (the playboy Wally Cassell, sneaking back into camp from a liaison in a nearby village), before hissing at him to start digging latrines as a punishment: 'nice deep ones.'

As finally filmed, the scene that Mitchum made as a test for Wellman is the most quietly astonishing in the movie, cracking open the inner-life of the character, revealing his sad intelligence and jaded humour. Ernie Pyle, played with low-key grace by Burgess Meredith, has come through the muddy night to Mitchum's quarters, a hovel constructed in the corner of a blasted building, a rough, strung-up blanket serving as a door. It's sometime near Christmas and Mitchum is hunched with a pencil over a pile of papers – toying abstractedly with the pencil as though he's used to late nights writing – trying to compose letters to the mothers of the men killed that day.

Meredith has a bottle of grappa – as Mitchum puts it, 'Italian moonshine' – with him, and Mitchum swigs into it, the liquor working quickly on him because he's already befuddled by fatigue. The journalist is trying to get a handle on this tall figure he's seen striding through the carnage, part of the group, but apart from it, shouldering a different burden. He learns that Mitchum would like to head west one day, when he gets home, that he was once married, but it didn't last long. Mitchum turns his head down to the next in his pile of death letters, groggy:

"Name?... Jesus..."

Slurring to Meredith, his pencil poking at his lip, he begins composing aloud, a very sad, slow and sarcastic sing song about the waste of it:

"Dear Mrs Smith,

Your son died bravely today on the...

Then he breaks off, blowing out a laugh. Exhausted, disgusted and boozy, he goes on a burned-out fragment of a slurry speech about all the 'names and addresses and the hills to be taken,' about all the energy of all the men working all around the world for war, about what could be achieved 'if only we could create something good out of all this energy.' He finishes up idly thinking about getting some rest, letting slip his cultural preferences back home:

"It reminds me of WC Fields' sure cure for insomnia – get plenty of sleep."

This street-level soldier saint finally ends up sleeping the big one. At the end of the film, after a furious battle to take a monastery that the soldiers knew they should have taken weeks before (incorporating genuine, ground-tilting combat footage John Huston had filmed for his documentary on the bloody *Battle of San Pietro*), the men are regrouping at the bottom of a hill. Other soldiers are marching up the hill, but a silhouetted line of donkeys are making their way down, laden with corpses. Flung over the back of one they finally notice Mitchum, killed in some unseen incident up the hill.

His corpse is left lying among all the others, shaded by trees along a little Italian roadside. As the soldiers file off past him on the road to the next hill to be taken, the soldier he had lambasted a few nights before, Wally Cassell, pauses to hold his hand and touch his face, the stillness and silence pouring off of him now, even more articulate than before.

Mitchum received his only Oscar nomination – for Best Supporting Actor – for *GI Joe*, but he didn't bother to attend the ceremony. In the event, the statuette went to James Dunn, for playing a drunken singing waiter in *A Tree Grows in Brooklyn* (1945).

After the notices he received for *GI Joe*, Mitchum was a hot property. The day he returned from his army service he was put to work by RKO. The first thing they had him do was... return from the army. The movie was Edward Dmytryk's *Till the End of Time* (1946), one of the first in a wave of films concerned with the experiences of the boys coming back from the front.

After his *San Pietro* report, John Huston had made another, extraordinary, film, *Let There*

Be Light (1946), a clear-eyed but tender documentary on the subject of painfully traumatised war veterans undergoing therapy and gradually being helped to re-adjust to life; the film was withheld from the public for many decades by a shocked War Department, more or less because, simply by focusing on the faces of these shattered men, Huston's film gave the lie to every piece of wartime propaganda produced, and would have gone some way to ripping apart any future attempts at recruiting by Uncle Sam.

Nevertheless, as the noir movies were beginning to reflect, the figure of the returned soldier was an intriguing new character, and the difficulties and the adjustments of the demobilisation process were not only an unfolding social phenomenon, but fertile ground for melodrama. A few months after *Till the End of Time*, *The Best Years of Our Lives*, telling a very similar story, would appear to Oscar-winning effect.

Dmytryk's movie concentrates mostly on the flat-faced spectacle of Guy Madison trying to be bitter and surly and upset his mommy as he returns to leafy small town streets. Madison's uptight turn doesn't come off and the film soon bogs down in maple syrup – but Mitchum cuts a memorable figure. Injured during fighting, he now carries a silver plate somewhere beneath his long mess of hair, which is bad news because, a lanky cowboy lad, he used to make his living as a top rodeo rider. There's a fine scene when, months after mustering out of the forces, he shows up in the dark garage of Madison's parent's suburban house, really bitter, unshaven and bumming money, but still meanly appreciating the blackly funny side of things, knowing he's the butt of the joke. Later there comes a fantastic fistfight in a bar when he finds out some guys in the place are racists and, dressed in denim, losing his white hat, long hair

drooping, sets enthusiastically to beating the tar out of one of them.

The next time he was a soldier it was for Dmytryk again, having difficulties coming home again, and cynically amused again, as he found the itching, inky city of *Crossfire* awaiting him. He lost his uniform for a few years but, when he wasn't making Westerns, the movies he appeared in – all those noirs and a weird Christmas romance called *Holiday Affair* (1949) – all placed him explicitly as a veteran, still trying to figure out what he was supposed to do now.

By then, the Korean war was beginning to infiltrate Hollywood and, promoted to Colonel, he appeared in one of the first films based around the conflict, *One Minute to Zero* (1952). This was a mostly routine RKO churn out, blending rickety sets with newsreel footage, stirring together an action–romance formula – fighting in a foreign land, the Colonel falls for a nurse while, between battles, his GIs teach local kids how to chew bubblegum – but it contained one extraordinarily hard moment when Mitchum's character takes the grim decision to start shelling a convoy of civilian refugees who are fleeing the conflict because he suspects enemy troops are hiding among them.

During the 1950s, after a hiatus, Hollywood had started turning back to the Second World War again. A new wave of war movies began to appear: sometimes the films were intended as slightly prejudicial history lessons; sometimes they attempted to pick over events with a little more detail, cynicism and savagery than would have been previously allowed; and, often, they used the war as a dangerous backdrop for pure escapist entertainment, adventure stories and romance. Mitchum's next spell in uniform fitted into the latter category but, directed by the man who had been Hollywood's most active documentarian of the years of conflict, the fantasy was infused with a strange, roughened, reflective grain.

Heaven Knows, Mr Allison

Director: John Huston, Twentieth Century Fox, 1957

Synopsis

1944, somewhere in the South Pacific, US Marine Corporal Allison (Mitchum) drifts in the ocean alone in a tiny dinghy. He is washed up on a lush, green atoll. Warily exploring a deserted village, he encounters a solitary nun, Sister Angela (Deborah Kerr). Sister Angela is alone, left behind when the mission settlement was hastily evacuated. As they forage for food, a friendship grows between the marine and the nun. Japanese reconnaissance planes strafe the island and they shelter in a hillside cave. When the planes return the island is firebombed, preparing the way for Japanese troops who arrive and set up camp. Allison and Sister Angela hide in the cave, but food grows scarce. Fearing for the nun's health, Allison sneaks into the Japanese camp to steal supplies while Angela frets alone. When the Japanese unexpectedly leave, the relationship between Allison and Angela is tested by the attraction he feels for the nun, who has not yet taken her final vows. He proposes to her and is stung by her rejection. That night, he discovers a bottle of sake Japanese soldiers left behind. Drunk and bitter, he scares the nun and she flees into a rainstorm, collapsing by a swamp. Allison finds her unconscious and fever stricken. When the Japanese return, he raids their camp for blankets for Angela. A soldier discovers him and he kills the man. The next day, Angela's fever has broken, but the Japanese are hunting for the soldier's killer. American ships appear and bombard the island in preparation for a marine landing. Allison sabotages the Japanese guns, ensuring a safe landing for the Americans and is wounded in the process. On the hill, Allison and Angela savour their last few seconds alone and swear eternal friendship as marines appear to take them back to the world.

Built entirely on the very real, unique chemistry flowing between Mitchum and Deborah Kerr, *Heaven Knows, Mr Allison* develops as a funny, sad, meditative humanist fable, one that touches on a simple, optimistic mysticism, but is still sprightly and entertaining, sprinkled with old-fashioned adventure and the sound of explosions.

All through John Huston's movie, Mitchum, playing an uneducated, low-ranking marine, engages in some of the most delicate acting of his career. He has to, because a step wrong by anyone involved would wreck the film. The pitfalls inherent in the situation explored are gapingly obvious. The film has a plot that could easily become a sickening star-crossed lovers' story, and sounds like the opening of a bad, bawdy joke: '*A nun and a soldier are stuck on a desert island...*'

Certainly, the then highly influential censoring body of the Catholic Church, The Legion of Decency, were all over the movie while it was being made, sending a representative, Jack Vizzard, to the Tobago location to oversee the production. This situation at first rankled Huston and his crew but they soon began drawing entertainment from the man's presence, pretending to shoot improvised salacious scenes whenever he appeared:

"Mitchum came over to Deborah and put one hand down the front of her dress and the other up her skirt. She kneed him and Jack said 'You can't do that!' And Huston said 'I don't see why not...'"[1]

By then Mitchum and Huston had bonded, brought together by boxing, among other things. Huston was hoping to turn a crew member into a prize fighter, and asked him to spar with Mitchum. Mitchum knocked the man out, which perversely persuaded Huston to go ahead with the plan, setting the man up with a few disastrous fights in London. Before the film, the director had been uncertain of using Mitchum, put off by stories of the actor's capacity for being 'difficult.' In fact Huston had originally conceived, *Mr Allison* as a Marlon Brando movie – Brando turned the picture down, to Huston's disappointment. By the end of the shoot, though, Mitchum and Huston had formed a friendship that would last the rest of their lives, and the director had formed his own opinion of the actor:

"...one of the finest actors I've ever had anything to do with. His air of casualness, or, rather, his lack of pomposity is put down as a lack of seriousness, but when I say he's a fine actor, I mean an actor the calibre of Olivier, Burton and Brando... he is in fact capable of playing *King Lear...*"[2]

In his approach to film-making as above all an excuse for adventure, Huston cut an almost Hemingwayesque figure. A story-teller first and foremost, working exclusively from literary sources, it's often said he had no deep commitment to his pictures, beyond his relish for the peril of getting them made, testing himself and his cast against the story and the extreme locations he preferred. However, his careful reworking of the *Mr Allison* story, and the close relationship the film bears with Huston's movie of five years previously, *The African Queen* (1952), points toward his personal concern with the themes the film explored.

Mr Allison was based on the novel by Charles Shaw which had indeed ended with the nun and the soldier falling in love. Before Huston's involvement, William Wyler had planned to film the story, and, hoping to circumvent The Legion of Decency, had a script prepared with a get-out built in: in the Wyler script it was finally revealed that the woman had never been a nun at all, had simply adopted a disguise, hoping the habit would keep her safe from the Japanese invaders.

Huston recognised this ending as a gimmick, one that was entirely unfaithful to the story that had proceeded it. However, the scandalised protestations of The League aside, he was also entirely sceptical about the conventional trash conclusion of Shaw's novel. He determined that Sister Angela should remain true to her vocation and devote herself to God, whose presence becomes almost a third character in the movie. The war – seen rumbling and flashing strangely beyond the horizon as Mitchum and Kerr gaze towards two distant destroyers slugging it out in the night – functions as a fourth. In this, the film works as a deeper meditation on the more wholeheartedly comic *The African Queen*, another two-handed tale of an earthy roughneck and a pious woman marooned alone together in a world at war.

Whereas in the earlier movie Humphrey Bogart's cheerfully unwashed, irreverent engine rat and Katharine Hepburn's bible-reading schoolmarm found love as they journeyed down the Congo into the heart of sweetness during the First World War, in this remarkable film Mitchum and Kerr establish a more complex, even spiritual kinship.

Kerr, back in the wimple 11 years after playing another nun navigating choppy carnal waters in the hallucinogenic *Black Narcissus* (1946), was initially troubled by Mitchum's roustabout reputation. On this film she became another lifelong friend and would go on to be his most frequent female co-star (they would make another three movies together). Their playing together is exquisite here, an eggshell-treading call and response of unsure looks and gestures, half-understood and unspoken words, buried meanings, a strange, beguiling, increasingly confident little symphony performed by two people who have never played music before.

What they ultimately find in each other is not romantic, sexual love, but the strength to walk their own separate paths; they leave the movie not with a kiss, but with an eternal bond, as Kerr explains in her final words to Mitchum before the representatives of the bloody world come to take them back again:

"No matter how many miles apart we are, or whether I ever get to see your face again, you will be my dear companion always, always."

Where great stretches of the river in *The African Queen* were recreated in a studio, *Mr Allison*, filmed entirely on location, maintains an intense relationship with the physical world. The film presents the natural landscape simply, but reverently, and in that balance there functions an immense lyricism. The opening is a seven-minute silent sequence, one of those pieces of film that are all about Mitchum moving through a landscape; another comes later, in the wordless 14 minutes when Mitchum raids the Japanese camp for food, then, almost discovered, has to lie in utter stillness while strange rodents crawl over him and close by – something unimaginable 10 years previously – Japanese soldiers bitch, are sleepy, read books, play games, dance to the radio and steal drinks just like regular men.

There's a moment elsewhere in this quiet, dreamy film that serves as a fleeting masterclass in Mitchum's approach to screen acting. The little South Pacific island they are stranded on has just been blanket-bombed by a squadron of Japanese planes. Formerly a plentiful garden paradise, the place is now just scorched earth and burned and burning palm trees surrounded by empty miles of glinting ocean: the fruit they had been living on is destroyed; the buildings they had been living in have been reduced to smouldering, collapsing blackened frames; the raft they have spent days constructing, hoping to sail to civilisation, has been blasted into ash.

Just as he's weighing up the devastation and accepting that things couldn't really get much worse, Mitchum turns and notices something off screen – what he has noticed, we realise with the next cut, is that things are about to get a whole lot worse indeed. A Japanese destroyer is appearing around the headland, bound for the island, carrying troops who will very soon set up camp.

So, that's the scene: a single marine, with a nun to protect, armed only with a knife, suddenly faced with the sight of a few hundred heavily armed representatives of the enemy bearing down on him. The obvious way to play this, the way any two dozen other actors would have played it, would involve some permutation of fearful eyes popping cartoon-wide, furrowed brows, a raising hairline, anguished grimacing, pointing, vivid, gnashing despair, alarm.

Instead, confronted with this fresh hell, Mitchum elects to play it this way: regarding the beat-up island as he talks with Kerr, he turns slightly away, then pauses in his turn, glancing off screen. As she continues speaking, an almost imperceptible change comes across his face. Taking place near the edge of the screen, all his movements kept small and natural, this event is so minimal, almost subliminal, that it's easily missed: there comes a grim little *that-figures-just-my-luck* almost smile, a blown-out bantam sigh, an infinitesimal slump of the shoulders. The

look that he gives could be that of someone who, after a run-of-the-mill bad day, has just remembered he forgot to pick up a newspaper with the baseball scores on his way home. And it works.

Although Mitchum plays with some of his greatest restraint in this film – and that delicacy is doubly fitting because he's playing a big barrack-room lug who's consciously, constantly watching himself, trying to mind his manners and impress a very gentle lady – it is also one of his most physically demanding roles. Huston has him clamber trees, cling to rocks battered by waves and get dragged along the ocean bed by a giant turtle he's trying to catch.

The film begins with the discovery of the soldier lying alone and semi-conscious in his dinghy in the middle of that glinting, empty sapphire sea – a Moses basket that has been floating for days or weeks or months – then charts his first triumphant, then quickly wary landing on the shore. As he dives and crawls through the trees and undergrowth, swims the pools of fresh water, his boots around his neck, then explores the deserted village in an alert, confused cat prowl, the camera lingers over the textures around him: lush foliage, grass, bamboo. The soundtrack is hushed by the constant sound of waves, wind through leaves, bird noises and the cries of strange animals.

In sequences like this, Huston's movie looks forward to Terrence Malick's *The Thin Red Line*, another South Pacific film that is almost more a mesmerising environment than a movie, a vision of a paradise about to be lost. Huston's film, too, tells its own strange Eden tale – as is made explicit when Mitchum tries to serenade Kerr under the moon with a brief, faltering rendition of *Don't Sit Under the Apple Tree*.

As in *GI Joe*, this film gave Mitchum the chance to play not an iconic soldier hero, but a downbeat individual. Allison, a man floating alone in an ocean, has always been alone: an abandoned orphan, he escaped the care home when he was 14 and hit the road, getting in trouble until he found the strange, harsh surrogate family of the marine corps. Mitchum's other loners were secure enough in themselves to wander independently through the world – Allison, although he falls reflexively into the certainties of his training when under physical threat, is otherwise far less secure, stays a marine

speaking peculiar marine language because he as yet has no idea as to how to function and communicate in the world outside war. The war has given him a respite from having to face reality – but it is his brief time with Angela, so certain in who she is, that saves him. At first he sees in her the chance to build another little family shelter for himself and turn his back on the war, and he turns mean and bitter on her when she remains faithful to her God. Ultimately measuring himself against her, though, he comes to realise that he is someone, after all.

Huston had seen a lot of what went on during war, what men did to each other and what the conflict did to them. This poetic lull-time film floats like a dog face dream: with its warm, beautiful island far away, its pristine beautiful woman and its tale of decent heroism, it could be a fantasy lingered in by a man lying in a cold muddy field, waiting for the next assault. Or the last vision of a dying soldier in a dinghy floating alone in an endless, sapphire sea.

The remainder of Mitchum's career in the celluloid forces allowed him little opportunity for such shading, but there was still duty to be done. In *Heaven Knows, Mr Allison*, Mitchum's character had been cast adrift before the film began when the captain of a submarine had

suddenly submerged the boat under fire – 'which is according to his book, but a little tough on us gyrines' – leaving Mitchum and his fellows being blasted like drowning rats. Back in service later that year, he was at sea again, and troubled by another submarine captain, playing an incredibly tense game of cat-and-mouse in *The Enemy Below*. The film was directed by former Philip Marlowe Dick Powell, and Mitchum played the world-weary new captain of a US destroyer, involved in a perilous, chess-like battle in the South Atlantic with German U-Boat commander Curt Jurgens. He followed this by taking to the air, again under Powell's direction, playing 'The Iceman' in the somewhat less successful Korean War flier's flick, *The Hunters* (1958), a film that gave Mitchum little to do on the ground, but featured aerial sequences Howard Hughes would have loved.

Then the Second World War called long and loud once more. He was a GI again, enjoying himself as Bilko-esque scamster Archie Hall in *The Last Time I Saw Archie* (1962); the real Archie Hall didn't enjoy it, though, and sued the film-makers for invasion of privacy.

By now, the heroes of the original war pictures were much older, and consequently the movies were busy promoting them. Factually based pictures about famous figures taking part in famous events were the order of the day, inflated to star-studded epic status. Of these star chariots, the first was the greatest, Darryl F Zanuck's meticulous re-staging of the D-Day landings, *The Longest Day* (1962). Lining up for action were John Wayne, Henry Fonda, Robert Ryan, a wounded Richard Burton and, for some reason, Fabian and Paul Anka. The finest stretches, though, came on the battered, inclement grey Normandy beach where General Mitchum, fresh from scraping the slime from the opposite end of the scale in *Cape Fear*, was still ready for action, getting down and dirty with his men, trying to lead his beleaguered troops up the dunes and to get his cigar to light. He slouches and runs through the fusillades as though he's been doing it all his life, booming out fantastic lines: 'There are only two kinds of people on this beach – those that are dead, and those that are gonna die!' Then, after the three hours of the film are up, he swings into a passing jeep, finally unwraps a new cigar and heads off for the next objective: 'Okay, run me up the hill, son.'

Fourteen years later, they tried to call him up again, and he reluctantly provided the only life itching amid the bloated battle of *Midway* (1976). He really was itching: the producer, Walter Mirisch, had first offered Mitchum the chance to play either of the lead roles, but he turned them down and Henry Fonda and Charlton Heston stepped in. Mirisch next offered Mitchum the third lead, but he turned that down, too, and Glenn Ford got the part. Finally, the absurdist in him playing up, Mitchum agreed to play the part of Admiral 'Bull' Halsey, who missed the battle because he was confined to a Pearl Harbor Naval hospital with a skin disease.

He sits up in bed dressed in blue pyjamas, scratching himself constantly, neck and hands smeared in white paste as Henry Fonda comes and asks for his advice. Mitchum's advice is : 'When you're in command, command.' A little later, Glenn Ford comes to ask his advice, too, and Mitchum, still in the pyjamas and paste, scratches some more before suggesting to Ford he should: 'go find Yamamoto and chew his ass.' Meanwhile, out across the Pacific, a handful of Japanese commanders, among them Toshiro

Mifune, handed a picture of Mitchum around a table in a war room and nodded. It was one day's work and when it was done he had his cheque sent to a charity.

He was handed a brief demotion to play a Colonel being kidnapped by a German Richard Burton in *Breakthrough* (1978), an uncertain semi-sequel to Sam Peckinpah's furiously despondent anti-war flick *Cross of Iron* (1977). Burton, a disenchanted sergeant of the Third Reich, wants Mitchum to know about a breakaway plan by his superiors to assassinate Hitler. Mitchum doesn't look too interested but he goes and tells Rod Steiger anyway.

In 1983, Mitchum was 65, and hadn't been bothered by a uniform for five years. He must have figured he'd done his duty and had finally managed to slip off AWOL without anyone noticing. Then, the last of the *Longest Day* leaders left standing, he was conscripted into something that looked like the rampaging bastard son of Zanuck's movie, something called *The Winds of War*. Thirteen months later, after having turned up for work in locations all across the globe, Mitchum found out he'd somehow managed to become the keystone in the biggest television event up until that time.

In this somewhat sprawling adaptation of Herman Wouk's epic novel about the years leading up to America's entry into the Second World War, produced and directed by Dan Curtis, Mitchum played Commander, later Admiral Pug Henry. He's sent by President Roosevelt to trot around Europe, keep an eye on the development of the conflict across the water where Hitler, Stalin and Churchill are hard at it, and send word back home, all the while trying to keep a soapy tangle of sub-plots from choking the screen. In all, the series ran to 16 hours and Mitchum was onscreen for most of it, solid, hardly moving, taking it all in as a strange, endless parade of cardboard characters crashed and folded around him and the world went all to hell and gone. He was like a rock for the audience to cling to, or navigate by.

Shortly after the *Winds* died down, a TV movie *Reunion at Fairborough* (1985) threw him forward in time again, to the present day. He was an ex-Army flier going back to the English country base he was stationed at during the war, reuniting with the English rose he had

The conflict never ends: *The Winds of War* (1983).

loved while he was there, 40 years ago. The woman, delightfully, turned out to be Deborah Kerr, and the old soldier finally got to kiss her. Otherwise, it was mostly low key stuff; still, just to keep things from getting too square, Mitchum started this amiable, gentle movie with a scene that found him sitting alone in a hotel room with a can of beer and his old service revolver, getting ready to blow his brains out. He ends the film in trouble with the cops, with Kerr offering to put the kettle on.

The Winds of War had ended with Mitchum preparing to go to war. In 1988, at the age of 71, there seemed little chance of that, but the next thing he knew, there he was in command of a Navy cruiser, sailing off out of Pearl Harbor into the sequel, *War and Remembrance*, again based on a book by Herman Wouk, and again put together by Dan

Curtis. For this, he was first sunk in the Pacific, then sent off into Europe again.

This time, the filming took 21 months and the end result unfolded across 30 hours. Mitchum, acting on reserve, walked through it all doing just as much as he felt was needed, looking idly out for a good line. In both this massive undertaking and its prequel, the stoic sag of his face bespoke a man who had seen it all before and was sad and weary of a world – or a TV show – that was forcing him to view it once again. Mitchum's stillness and his monumental reluctance were pushed to the outer limits, becoming a radical new philosophy of TV acting. By the end of it, he looked as though he'd gone through a war and was beginning to accept that he'd probably have to fight yet another, because there was no one else left.

Chapter Seven
Weird Movies

The noirs, the wars and the westerns were Mitchum's usual beat. Not every movie he made outside those areas was necessarily weird but a lot of them were. In general, there are two types of weird Mitchum movie: movies that were already weird and that he happened to be in and movies made weird solely by his being in them.

A good example of the latter would be *Holiday Affair*, a Christmas movie. The idea of Mitchum being in a Christmas movie is just odd, somehow, as is the idea of him playing an Australian shepherd, the rutting patriarch of a sweating Southern small town soap opera, or a mild, impotent Irish school teacher. The idea of him, aged 38, playing a medical student along with Frank Sinatra, is just bizarre, but it happened, in *Not As A Stranger* (1955).

More occasionally the two stands would smash together and you would get what was an already weird movie made even weirder by dint of Mitchum's presence. A good example of that would be *Matilda*, a film he made in 1978 together with his fellow former Philip Marlowe, Elliott Gould. *Matilda* was a kid's movie about Gould, a theatrical booking agent in New York who's on his uppers – like Woody Allen's *Broadway Danny Rose* (1984) – and is representing the titular dame, a boxing kangaroo, around Vaudeville. In it, Mitchum plays a campaigning sportswriter who throws in with the kangaroo. Quite often in the ring, the kangaroo looks like a man in a kangaroo suit.

What is notable, though, is how often across these aberrant movies, the characters he played still fitted the profile of the solitary Mitchum persona he had articulated so often in noir films and Westerns. Some of his most notorious portrayals of misfit difference came in the oddest movies of his career, *Holiday Affair*, *The Night of the Hunter*, *Home From the Hill*, *The*

Sundowners, and *Ryan's Daughter*. The film that comes closest to Mitchum's personal statement of intent *Thunder Road*, is itself about the strangest of the lot.

A groovy, bitter, nasty satyr: *Secret Ceremony* (1968).

Weird Movies
Holiday Affair

Director: Don Hartman, RKO Radio Pictures, 1949

Synopsis

Christmas in New York. Connie Ennis (Janet Leigh) is a war widow with a six-year old son, Timmy (Gordon Gebert). Still faithful to her late husband, she's been seeing Carl (Wendell Corey) but avoids his marriage proposals. Connie works as a comparison shopper checking prices in a rival store, buying an electric train from Steve Mason (Mitchum), a toy department salesman. When Connie takes it back, Steve refunds her money, even though he knows what she's up to. This gets him sacked. Encountering Connie as he leaves, they wander Central Park. Steve helps Connie with her work until they're separated in the crowds. Connie returns home, where Carl and Timmy are trimming the tree. Steve turns up. When Carl leaves, Steve tells Connie no man can compete with her husband's ghost. As he leaves, he surprises her with a kiss. The next day she asks Carl to marry her. On Christmas morning, a train set arrives for Timmy from Steve. Connie tries to return his money and finds him in Central Park. After she leaves, Steve is arrested for suspicious behaviour. Carl and Connie are called to the police station to verify his story. Steve accompanies them to Connie's apartment for dinner with her parents and announces that Connie should marry him, not Carl. Connie throws him out. The next day, Timmy takes his train back for a refund, wanting to give the money back to Steve. As they go to deliver the cash, Carl tells Connie he knows she's in love with Steve. She goes to him but he tells her he's not going to compete with her dead husband. On New Year's Eve, Steve boards a train for California – as the train leaves, he discovers Connie has come aboard after him and they kiss.

An all but forgotten Christmas movie, *Holiday Affair* unfolds in the same airless fake RKO city that played home to all the studio's urban noir stories. The cinematographer on the picture, Milton Krasner, had arrived from assignments in some of the most hopeless neighbourhoods in the noir zone: photographing the fate-drenched locations of *The Woman in the Window* (1944) and *Scarlet Stree*t (1945) for Fritz Lang, discovering corpses in unlit rooms in Robert Siodmak's *The Dark Mirror* (1946) and exploring the dirt shadows of the broken down bowery of Robert Wise's *The Set-Up* (1949).

The difference this time, however, is that the lights are on. It's daytime, there are crowds of people bustling happily around the place and the streets are sprinkled in shining snow that falls soft and constant, white flurries looking like soap flakes and sugar. The city is called New York but it's a cheap cardboard Christmas card Manhattan, covered in glitter and glue.

However, despite its chintzy surface of hokey seasonal cheer, despite the toy shops and love stories, the busy throngs of people carrying armloads of packages, and despite the ickshy-cuteshy presence of Gordon Gebert, a six-year old kid with ruffled hair and missing teeth, *Holiday Affair* goes seriously against the grain of the prevailing idea of a Christmas film. Although it's very lightly handled and finally ends with a kiss on a train on New Year's Eve that's as sweet and warming as mulled wine, it's a clear-eyed, anti-sentiment, strangely modern little movie.

The story, unfolding over the space of the week between Christmas Eve and New Year's Eve, is all about Janet Leigh's frightened, blinkered and sweetly bitter young war widow – who would rather marry a man she doesn't love than disturb the memory of her late husband – being given a shake and bluntly told to open her eyes, stop pretending and above all, rejoin the living. Mitchum plays the flip stranger who has blown into her life and, while everyone else tiptoes around, has started doing the shaking.

The film, directed by Don Hartman, who came from Danny Kaye pictures and the Hope and Crosby *Road* flicks – is a comedy, but in the unshowily anarchistic figure Mitchum cuts, it celebrates a rejection of conformity. Mitchum follows a line of thinking that regards such normal ideals as safety and security as shackles, and takes a bluntly hard-headed, but blithe and calmly philosophical approach to death.

When he turns up, covered in the studio snow, at Leigh's little apartment to find his rival in love,

a super-square Wendell Corey trimming the tree while Leigh goes to fix drinks, he picks up one of the photographs of her dead soldier husband that litter the place, and Corey tells him admiringly how Leigh speaks to her little kid about the dead guy all the time:

COREY: "It's wonderful how she keeps him sort of… alive."
MITCHUM: "Is it? After all – he's not alive."

Death! In a Christmas movie! Of course, a little darkness to be overcome was a vital element in any worthwhile Yuletide flick. The greatest of thcm all, Frank Capra's glowing *It's a Wonderful Life* (1946), had despondency and despair in spades, so much so that Gloria Grahame had turned up to flooze around the shadows and James Stewart, preparing to commit suicide, discovered the anguished core he'd later mine with Anthony Mann and Alfred Hitchcock.

Created for a world coming out of war, however, Capra's peerless, timeless, seasonal fantasy about the badlands of what-might-have-been ultimately delivered a message about staying in your station. *Holiday Affair* was made three years later for a world still haunted by the war – one the most strange, disturbingly everyday lines comes when Mitchum and Corey, waiting for Leigh to come back with their drinks, make uncomfortable small talk about how the snow seems different these days, and agree that it's probably something to do with the atomic bomb – but the message it delivers is exactly the opposite to Capra's. While all the other adults are drumming into little Geber the values of keeping your aspirations low, Mitchum tells him: 'If you aim higher than your mark, you'll stand more chance of hitting it.'

Mitchum's advice sounds like a particularly American piece of thinking, designed to gee-up an audience that's about ready to throw off the grey mourning rags of the 1940s and stride confidently in the brightly coloured 1950s for a spree of rampantly optimistic consumerism. But it's not that, either. Mitchum's character rejects that, too. He's anti-materialism, anti-capitalism, anti-get-up-and-go-ism.

In *Holiday Affair*, Mitchum doesn't fit in anywhere, nor does he want to. A veteran himself, it could be that his indifferent, philosophical nature was forged by the horrors he saw overseas, or it could be that he's just naturally inclined toward a personal brand of pragmatic Zen existentialism:

"You gotta take everything that's coming to you, all the surprises good and bad… every surprise isn't a telegram from the War Department, you know."

Either way, in this movie he essays a true proto-beat attitude. He goofs off at work on simple joys like making a toy train whistle for little kids or wearing a rubber monkey mask and saying to pretty girl: *'Well, Hello!'*

Once he's been fired, as they wander through a postcard dream of Central Park in the snow, eating hot dogs, he tells Leigh how he once followed the work-hard-and-get-on ethic but soon tired of all the rat-eyed cut-throat stuff going on around him and dropped out, jumped on a boat to South America and bummed around.

Now, like Kerouac working on the railways and in the forests to fund his writing, he takes whatever jobs he can get for as long as he can stand them – he's not interested in working, doesn't care when he gets fired, but he's trying to save a little money so he can go to California and spend his life building boats. In the meantime, he has no home, drifts around from cheap room to cheap room, spends his nights hunched over a drawing board, designing sail ships. He prefers to eat his lunch and breakfast – coffee, with donuts for dunking – alone in the park, chatting with the seals in the zoo, because none of them wants to be president of a bank. He goes clambering behind rocks with crumbs to feed a little squirrel, because it needs feeding.

Above all, he hates hypocrisy, doesn't see why he shouldn't speak his mind – and so he does, with a bluntness that's still surprising. After having known her for only a few hours, he tells Janet Leigh that he'd better split because he might fall in love with her and it wouldn't work because she's hung up on a dead man. Again, in a late scene where he shares a cozy, happy Christmas dinner with Leigh, Corey, Leigh's parents and the kid, and, after Corey's speech about how he's loved Leigh for such a long time and is so glad he's about to marry her and join her family, Mitchum, a stranger in the house, gets up and calmly announces that that's all well and good, but really, Leigh should marry him.

Earlier, just after Leigh has demanded that he leave her little apartment because he's given her a hard time about how she clings to her sainted husband, before he goes he grabs her by the shoulders and roughly, lingeringly plants the realest screen kiss 1949 audiences had seen square on her mouth (Howard Hughes had been after Leigh in this period, trying every trick he had to wow her, cars and planes, the whole bit, but she hadn't been impressed, and kept bringing her parents along on

dates – you suspect the kiss might have been one of his designs).

The way Mitchum sees it, if a man loves a woman – any woman, even someone else's – then she's fair game; he's says as much, right to the face of Leigh's do-good, nice-guy, fiancé with her parents looking on. This stuff was hardly part of the 1950s family plan. *Holiday Affair* was Mitchum's second movie after the marijuana imbroglio and the film uses him as a genuinely disruptive, benignly dangerous element. As soon as he turns up, Corey, Leigh and little Geber – the nuclear family – have all started arguing. Later, the cops take one look, can't figure him out and throw him in a cell on suspected assault and vagrancy. The police sergeant (Henry Morgan, who would years later turn up in the M*A*S*H TV show) spells out his apprehensions, the suspicions of the materialist world:

> "The guy's without a job – broke. Without a bed to sleep in. And he buys a kid an electric train? Gives Christmas presents to tramps? Gets Christmas presents from a little girl with a balloon on her head? Eats in the park with the seals, is mother and father of an orphaned squirrel – you don't think this guy's a suspicious character?"

Forty years later, Mitchum made his only other Christmas movie, turning up in the Dickens revamp *Scrooged* (1988). He played Preston Rhinelander, ageing, deranged, but widely feared president of a TV network. He was still hanging out with animals, asking his executive Bill Murray: 'Do you have any idea how many cats there are in America.'

He then goes on to suggest that they should start by targeting the potential pet audience in their output:

> "I'm not saying build a whole show around animals. I'm merely suggesting we occasionally throw in a little 'pet appeal'. Some birds, a squirrel… Remember Kojak with the lollipops? What about a cop that dangles string, that's his gimmick? Lots of quick, random action…

He ended the movie on Christmas Eve, drinking beer in a room full of cats.

The Night of the Hunter

Director: Charles Laughton, United Artists, 1955

Synopsis

In 1930s Ohio, Preacher Harry Powell (Mitchum) drives away from the corpse of the 12th widow he's killed and robbed, talking to God as he goes, and is arrested for driving a stolen vehicle. Meanwhile, in Cresap's Landing, little John (Billy Chapin) and Pearl (Sally Jane Bruce) see their father Ben Harper (Peter Graves) arrive home, chased by police. Harper has murdered a man and stolen $10,000. Before the police arrive, he hides the cash. Harper shares his prison cell with Preacher, who tries to find out where the money is. Harper says nothing and is hanged. Preacher travels to Cresap's Landing, where he woos and marries Ben's widow, Willa (Shelley Winters). On their wedding night, Preacher rejects Willa's sexual advances and tells her to reject the sins of the flesh as ungodly. A war of wills develops between Preacher and little John as he tries to break the children and make them reveal where the money is hidden. John tells Willa what her new husband is up to but she doesn't believe him until she arrives home early and overhears Preacher threatening Pearl. That night, Preacher kills Willa, dumping her body in the river. Telling the locals she has run off with another man, he sets about breaking the children. He finally discovers that the money is stuffed inside Pearl's rag doll but the terrified children manage to escape him and flee down river in a tiny boat. Hunted by Preacher they travel through the Depression landscape and are finally taken in by a kindly widow, Rachel Cooper (Lillian Gish), who runs an unofficial orphanage. Preacher arrives and lays siege to the house. Rachel finally shoots and wounds him. Police take the Preacher away to be hanged for Willa's murder. John and Pearl settle in the safety of Rachel's home.

Filled with monsters and poetry, moonlight, dust and rabbits, *The Night of the Hunter* is a children's movie that has lost its parents, curled up into a ball and fallen asleep alone in the corner, only to have bad, half-formed but vivid nightmares.

The movie hangs like a dream forming on the edge of sleep as, trying to stay awake, a bedtime kid drifts in and out of consciousness: over the credits, set against a starry black sky, a lullaby is heard, then comes a vision, the disembodied head of a kindly nearby story teller, Lillian Gish, merging with the dream, floating oddly among those same stars and planets, then fading from sight as the dream takes over, only for her to appear later as a face within the fantasy, like one of the Kansas farmhands who turn up in Judy Garland's Oz.

Charles Laughton's only film as a director represents a unique moment in Hollywood, an achievement that only blossoms with time. The reputation of this film has grown exponentially down the decades, to the point where, having been buried soon after release, it is today probably Mitchum's most famous, best-loved performance, the figure he cuts as the psychotic Preacher with LOVE and HATE writ in jailhouse blue tattoos across the knuckles of his hands, his most recognisable incarnation.

It's not that critical opinion has been revised; when the movie first appeared it received a raft of positive, thoughtful, slightly confused reviews. It was the confusion that won over – Mitchum was making the hospital soap *Not as a Stranger* (1955) with Frank Sinatra for the same studio the same year, and United Artists, who only agreed to back Laughton's movie because of Mitchum's involvement swung their weight behind that more familiar kind of movie, uncertain how to handle Laughton's film, uncertain even what it was they were handling. Audiences stayed away and the dismal financial failure of this deeply personal project hit Laughton so hard that he never directed again. The film, though, wouldn't leave the minds of the people who did see it and so it grew, out of the light.

Laughton adapted his film with James Agee from Davis Grubb's best-selling novel, a tumbling, dense but clean masterpiece of Southern Gothic, drenched in the impressions, characters and Bible-haunted folklore of the Ohio river valleys where Grubb grew up. Like

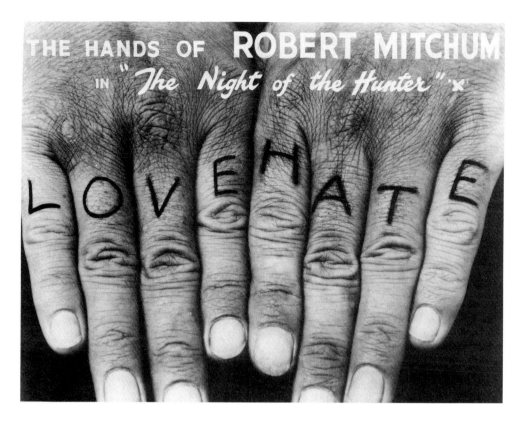

THE HANDS OF ROBERT MITCHUM
IN "The Night of the Hunter" 'x'

LOVE HATE

Mitchum, Agee had travelled the country during the Depression period Grubb's novel recreated, working with the photographer Walker Evans to chronicle the existence of dust bowl share croppers, a project that grew into the book *Let Us Now Praise Famous Men*. The film is infused with the sense of their personal involvement – Mitchum even directed the children in several scenes after Laughton lost patience with them.

From his first reading of Grubb's book, Laughton immediately saw the kind of film that he would make. Not a movie specifically about the Depression, although that wave of uncertainty moves under the film, not a thriller, not a melodrama but 'really, a nightmarish sort of Mother Goose tale.'[1]

The picture tells a horrified fairy-tale, an intensely American one, with its Huck Finn catalogue – steamboat whistles, fishing poles baited with wriggling worms, yummy-smelling fresh-made fudge and chequered table cloths at bright riverside picnics – laid out in dappled bucolic light. From the corners of the frame, though, the sharp old shadows of Grimm European expressionism creep in. The fishing rod's hook doesn't bring up catfish; it gets snagged in the deep parts of the water on the windshield of a car in which a drowned woman sits like a mermaid with her throat slit, 'her hair wavin' lazy and soft around her like meadow grass under flood waters.'[2]

Filmed with a masterly control of light by cinematographer Stanley Cortez – who had shot Orson Welles' *The Magnificent Ambersons* – the look is a unique blend of the jaggedy Germanic style, the daylit classical language of the DW Griffith movies Lillian Gish was synonymous with, and the radically stripped down aesthetic Laughton had brought to the stage productions he and his producing partner, Paul Gregory, had worked on in the early 1950s.

Throughout the movie, scenes take place in bare sets that have little to do with reality, but are just detailed enough to give a suggestion of place: strip joint, courtroom, prison cell, bedroom. This is child's-eye expressionism: shadow houses on a horizon loom like enormous felt shapes and the horizon itself is either table-top flat, or rumpled and bumped like a mess of bed blankets.

Similarly, the strange, conscious symbolism fits this picture book mode: as in the very haunting sequence as the children drift safely in their little boat out of Preacher's reach – a strange, broken, giant crucifix of light playing on the black surface on the mother river, their flight sympathetically observed by a cast of big-eyed rabbits, spiders, owls, turtles, sheep and foxes – it doesn't get in the way of the movie, it becomes the whole texture of the film.

More than the Preacher's hunt, more than the parcel of stolen cash, more than the battle between good (Lillian Gish, the pure face from the Eden age of cinema) and evil (Mitchum, the modern, fallen reprobate), *The Night of the Hunter* is a film about being a child and built around children's conceptions of evil: unspeakable things may happen to them but they can deal with them and can relate to them only with the tools they have, and only in the language they know. Thus, the film unfolds, as François Truffaut had it in his review,

"like a horrifying news item retold by small children."[3]

Laughton, who knew Mitchum from Hollywood parties had pitched the movie to him this way:

LAUGHTON: "Mitchum, I'm directing this film and there's a character in it who's a diabolical shit."

MITCHUM: "Present."

Often, if a movie was too overblown, too clumsy, too unconvincing, Mitchum would simply ignore the film around him, accept the gusts of art as regular weather, and instead burrow into the truth of his character – you can see him doing it in strange films like *Ryan's Daughter* and Joseph Losey's artily grubby psychological rag-bag *Secret Ceremony* (1968). It's a measure of Mitchum's respect for

A horrified American fairy tale.

Laughton that he here gives a performance that is keyed exactly to the pitch of the director's conception. Allowed for the first time really to explore and give vent to the creatures that fermented in the more perversely creative corners of his imagination, he creates a Preacher who's part fairytale, part cartoon villain, part horror show ogre.

Playing in harmony with Laughton's picture book pitch, the real, scummy, dirt-of-the-world viciousness Mitchum would later wallow gloriously in as Max Cady in *Cape Fear* is for the most part held at bay, sheathed. Still it sometimes lashes out: when he hisses at little Sally Jane Bruce 'tell me you little wretch or I'll tear your arm off'; when he turns to Billy Chapin in the dark with 'speak or I'll cut your throat and leave you to drip...'; when he humiliates Shelley Winters, standing foolish in her nightgown: 'You thought, Willa, that the moment you walked in that door that I'd start a-pawin' in that abominable way that men're supposed to on their wedding night.'

In these moments, he ruptures the fabulous surface, like the blade of the switchknife that leaps phallically up ('No, little lamb, don't touch it! Now don't touch my knife! That makes me mad. Very, very mad'), and tears through the heavy black cloth of Preacher's pocket as he sits in a burlesque joint, testing himself hatefully against the temptations of 'perfume-smelling things... lacy things... things with curly hair' as a blonde grinds listlessly before him in a brassy keyhole of light.

Mitchum's performance is unique in another respect. In this movie, this actor, who habitually rendered his acting invisible, plays a man constantly giving a performance: he's acting acting. On one level, he's performing because he's a preacher and he plays his sermons to the crowd, as in the fantastic 'Tale of Left hand Right hand' scene, when he replays the eternal conflict between darkness and light on his fingers – 'Hot dog! Love's a-winnin'!' But more fundamentally, Preacher's whole performance is a performance, as he goes about weaving the sheep's clothing to blind his prey, constantly trying to pull the wool over others' eyes, peering out from behind fake smiles, fake blubbing tears, fake righteousness to see how well he's doing.

In keeping with the childlike perspective, Laughton never tries to look behind that mask and see the sickness seething in there, listening to God's voice. Grubb's psychotic Preacher, as well as being meaner, is never so sure and so blithely relentless as Mitchum's. In the novel, he sometimes gets weary and cries in his sleep, the killing making him tired, and with a whole world still to kill.

In the starry-night opening to the movie, Gish reminds us and the little floating heads of the children how the Bible has warned us to beware those who come in sheep's clothing and 'inwards they are ravening wolves.' Oozing fake charm and pulling himself up straight in his black suit and flat hat, smiling, his eyes sliding slyly to the side as he watches the effect he's having or gauges the secret thoughts of others, eyebrows popping up like hot toast when he knows he's on to something, Mitchum is the wolf, of course, an animal from beyond the black woods of ancient parables. Also, though, jazzed up and angular, he's like the wolf from Tex Avery's fast screwball fairy tale cartoons of the 1940s come to weird, scary life – the creature whose eyes blare out on stalks in *Red Hot Riding Hood* and *Swing Shift Cinderella*.

Mitchum puts his wolf through slapstick routines: down in the cellar that hangs in a frame of blackness like a section taken through the world, as the children escape, he's hit on the head by a collapsing shelf filled with pickled fruit, and sits dazed for a second, face collapsing in a poor-me groan, then springs after them, only to stumble Oliver Hardy-style on a discarded jar and fall flat on his face. Then he's Frankenstein's monster, lumbering up the steep rickety stairs after them, both arms stretched out, hands grabbing – when his fingers are slammed in the door, the cartoon starts again and he shrieks like Stan Laurel and sucks his hands.

Out in the night, though, he's that rioting Karloff creature: we hear the doom-Doom-DOOM-CRASH as he busts down the cellar door, then see him appear as a shadow over the crest of the river bank, rampaging his way down through the thick tangle of undergrowth, an unstoppable thing programmed for destruction, smashing trees aside.

Sinking in the sandbank and wading into the water, just too late, as the little stern of the skiff the kids are in drifts out of his reach, he's far gone in fury, a wounded animal baying out a rising howl of frustration.

Elsewhere, there comes strange, murderously precise grace, as when he sets about killing Shelley Winters in their tiny bedroom that floats like a sick white chapel in the night: as she lies smilingly awaiting her end, he reaches his hand strangely skywards, tilts his ear to heaven to take in the news from on high, then stretches over her in the bed, his foot coming up in a straight, almost dancerly line behind him, raising the knife delicately, almost tenderly above his head.

With someone else as Preacher – Laughton had at one point wanted Gary Cooper for the role – *The Night of the Hunter* might exist, but it would be utterly changed from the movie we have. Mitchum is like the lead violin in Laughton's magical orchestration – his deep, haunting renditions of *Leaning on the Everlasting Arm*, a slow, sing-song hymn resounding from far away in the dark and secret world of the night to interrupt the children's sleep, is the defining sound of the movie. Laughton held him in high esteem:

"He has great talent. He'd make the best Macbeth of any actor living… He's one of my favourite people in the world. I can't praise him too much."[4]

The film Laughton made is a surprising, odd, haunting, endlessly inventive, courageously artistic and a boldly pared-down one, entirely true to itself and enough to make clear that cinema suffered a tragic loss when its failure dissuaded him from directing again. But it's unimaginable without Mitchum's keynote performance, without the sight of him barrelling along the back-projected road in his stolen Model-T, blood on his hands, tipping the wink to God.

Thunder Road

Director: Arthur Ripley, United Artists, 1958

Synopsis

After fighting in the Korean War, Luke Doolin (Mitchum) has returned to his home in the hills of Harlan County, Kentucky. Luke's father, and the rest of the men in the area, operate moonshine stills in the backwoods, and Luke works as a transporter, running illegal liquor along the highways at night from the hills to the point of distribution in Memphis, where he dates a night club singer. Luke's exploits behind the wheel as he evades the law have made him a local legend and agents of the Treasury department are staking out the area, hoping to catch him and end the illegal trade. Simultaneously, a powerful criminal syndicate headed by Carl Kogan (Jacques Aubuchon) is tying to muscle in and take over the moonshine operation, and has started intimidating and killing the moonrunners. Luke's younger brother, Robin (Jim Mitchum), hopes to follow in his footsteps, but Luke is determined the kid will never become a transporter. Kogan offers Luke the chance to work with him – Luke's response is to beat Kogan up. The Treasury men apprehend him and offer him the chance to co-operate with them in ending Kogan's campaign of terror but Luke isn't interested. Treasury agents swarm the hills of Harlan and begin destroying the mills. Luke's father prepares a final batch for Luke to take to Memphis. The roads are filled with treasury agents and hoodlums looking to stop him – Luke learns that Carl Kogan has tried to set up Robin by promising him the chance to become a transporter and he vows to kill him. Kogan is arrested by Treasury men; meanwhile, out on the highway Luke smashes his way through a trap set by the authorities, loses control of his car and crashes into an electricity substation.

"Nothing, really. Just keep moving."

That was how Mitchum once answered an interviewer who asked him why he had hit the road and started hoboing back and forth across the country during the 1930s, what it was he had been looking for. *Thunder Road*, the most personal movie Mitchum ever made and an exemplar of fast, cheap, disreputable, dirty, sub-rosa, night-filled roughneck film-making is a movie conceptualised around that philosophy of reasonless movement.

Mitchum is the *auteur* who was behind *Thunder Road*. He wrote the story – about a doomed, cynical, picaresque outsider setting himself against both the underworld and the agents of law and order – as well as playing the central role. He produced the film, controlling casting and hiring the technicians. He cast his son, Jim, as his younger brother. He wrote the songs heard in the movie and would later record his own hopped-up version of the title song as a single, and have a hit with it. He picked the locations for filming, in Transylvania county, North Carolina. He didn't direct, but he did pick the director and he designed the shots. It's the ultimate Mitchum movie, his own statement, and demonstrates that the fated, wandering outsider current that runs through all his work is no coincidence. At the same time, it exists at a ragged, flat, raw, strange gutter level far removed from any Hollywood vanity project.

The tale of a solitary moonshine transporter, threatened, shot at and chased by both the law and the mob as he makes an endless, lawless circular run along dirt roads and highways, transporting his father's illegal liquor from the backwoods of Harlan County to the big city lights of Memphis, *Thunder Road* isn't about running away from something or running to someplace, but just about running, or specifically, driving, fast and furious, bombing down empty roads in a car alone at night.

The recurring shot in the movie is just that – Mitchum, alone at the wheel of a fast moving car, a dim, back-projected night world jerking behind him. He enters the movie as a shadow in a shadowy car that evades capture by pursuing Government men by, incredibly, turning, skidding, rolling over on its roof and righting itself again in a cloud of moonlit dust. At the wheel, his face is obscured, turned away or hidden behind the stanchion of the side windows, until, when the moment's right, he finally strikes a match and leans into the flame to suck his cigarette awake, letting his face hang in the juddery light. He's extremely adept with matches in the movie, with a penchant for striking them off the seat of his pants.

Cigarettes, cars, night, lonely roads, speed and danger amalgamate in an equation that creates indelible actions and moments: Mitchum, rock 'n' roll hair shining, eyes heavily lidded, tearing along through the night alone in his car, engaged in a noisy shunting, scraping metal duel as a smug hoodlum in a roaring black jalopy tries to run him off the narrow road, pulls up level with the other car, takes a draw on his cigarette, takes it from his mouth, then leans over and calmly flicks it out the window right into the other guy's eye, shunting him off the road and over a cliff as the mobster loses control.

At either end of the road there are decisions that could be made – Mitchum is unable to commit to the girl who waits for him in a night club at the urban end of the line and remains unable to fit back into the little mountain community he once had to leave to fight a war across the world – but he knows that those decisions don't mean anything anymore. The car, the dangerous road and the night are all that matter, making their own pure sense.

This is a film of delinquent existentialism, about a profound loneliness that resists authority and digs chrome, the smell of burning rubber and the sounds of overworked engines, tortured tyres and twangy jukebox music. Both strands proved fertile for other film-makers. The speeding, low-trash backwoods outlaw hero mayhem movie was picked up by low-grade Z-movie makers who, after Mitchum's film came to dominate fleapit and drive-in theatres on double-bills across the 1960s and early 1970s, started supplying the market with more car-thieves and moonshiners, tearing up roads and cars to the strains of fast-plucked banjo in films like *Gone in 60 Seconds* (1974) and *Moonrunners* (1974) – the latter of which starred Jim Mitchum and ultimately birthed the *Dukes of Hazzard* TV series. Noting the popularity and profitability of this liquored-up reprobate chase-wreck strand, studios with

more cash wrecked more cars in their own versions, keeping Burt Reynolds busy from *Smokey and The Bandit* (1977) to *The Cannonball Run II* (1983).

Meanwhile, though, more cerebral film-makers explored *Thunder Road*'s tough-poetic presentation of the perpetual American road as existential parable, charting variously chill, hermetic, alienated and relentlessly furious destinationless journeys in *Two Lane Blacktop* (1970), *Vanishing Point* (1971) and, along Canadian motorways at the far, mutated end of the line, David Cronenberg's adaptation of JG Ballard's *Crash* (1996).

While Mitchum's movie acknowledges the impulses, it ignores the excesses of both these strands, and shoots down the middle. *Thunder Road* understands the excitement of night, speed and metal, explosions and pop trash and liquor, but still sees something deep, obsessive and melancholy behind all these things. Simultaneously, it isn't concerned with big ideas, it follows a philosophy built on the lack of philosophy.

The film is completely unconcerned about anything going on outside its boundaries, but, still, burying deep into itself, *Thunder Road* knows absolutely everything about the rough-hewn backcountry world it describes. Mitchum's movie bubbles up from a secret, shadowy, folksy, outlaw America. It understands bare garages and pay phones, the windows of cosy rooms slick with rain at night when you only have a little time together, ashtrays and rifles, men with guitars, the blare of tinny radios, meetings in backrooms and talks in forest clearings while the wind makes a hiss among the trees, cheap, clean houses, small bedrooms, little white churches, a lazy horse standing in a field, beer bottles at night, the way a shining dirt track leading down from a black hill looks when the sinking evening sun behind creates a corona around the ridge, the way a fast forest road curves, pressed on from the sides by leaves catching moonlight and shadow, how cars look in the dark.

Both Mitchum and his son, Jim, had had brushes with car crime – in the winter of 1953, after a night chase through the streets of Los Angeles, Mitchum had been stopped for speeding, then driven away from the motorcycle

Delinquent existentialism.

cop during questioning. A charge of escape from lawful custody was added to the speeding and he was ultimately fined $200. In 1956, Jim Mitchum, then aged 15 and in the company of Johnny 'Tarzan' Weismuller's son, John, had been picked up with a couple of other boys after stealing a car from a hospital car park, joy riding it around LA and pushing the car over a cliff into a canyon.

Mitchum had spent some time in shackles in Georgia while roving as a teenager and *Thunder Road*, set amid the hills and forests of Kentucky, also comprehends the laid back but proud sociology of the ornery, isolated backwoods communities of the rebel South it sings about. The film describes a place haunted by history. The backwoods and backroads of Harlan County are filled with the strange ghosts of older countries, and with the ghosts of the Civil War and its aftermath. Stubborn independent pride is mixed with, even strengthened by the memory of guilty defeat and poverty.

Although they sell their liquor for a good price, the woodsy folk of *Thunder Road* are poor people living by Bible-schooled old codes, generally supporting themselves by traditional agricultural means, ways of life brought over from Ireland and Scotland. They cherish family ties and community bonds and, after centuries of farmland isolation, they are wary of outsiders. They still see the rights of an individual state as of prime importance and believe that what a man gets up to on his own property is nobody's business but his own. The moonshiners form a loose democracy of independent operators that meet only occasionally to discuss business that affects them all – like a scaled-down version of the sort of United States the South once wanted.

They are suspicious of centralisation, above all, whether this is represented by the forces of the Government, who are seeking to shut their stills down and talk about liquor taxation, or the businessmen-like mobsters with their more powerful technology – faster cars, bigger guns – who are trying to muscle in, looking to take over the stills and amalgamate them into one big streamlined, mechanised operation.

But neither the Treasury Agents nor the gangsters understand or have time for their values, and they reject the overtures of each. Mitchum distils the attitude when he talks to Keely Smith, his night club singer girlfriend in Memphis, about his father and why they won't give up the moonshining way of living:

> "Granddaddy had done it before him, his daddy before him and so on clean back to Ireland. They held that what a man did on his own land was his business... they fought for the country, scratched up those hills with ploughs and skinny old mules, they did it to guarantee the basic rights of free men. They just figured whisky-makin' was one of them."

The movie, with its background jukeboxes, radios, night club groups and country-rockin' front-porch bands throwing, as Jim Mitchum neatly describes it, 'a twistification' for the local jitterbugging teens, also inhales the folk-cultural currents in the air. With its confluence of black and Celtic influences, thrummed to music, the South had been the birthplace of the blues, jazz, country and, only recently, with a lonesome 19-year-old truck driver called Elvis Presley's visit to the Sun studios in Memphis, rock 'n' roll. The thin, unhinged alleycat electric noise of skinny rock 'n' roll guitar twangs and noodles often on the soundtrack, vying with lazy acoustic strums and banjos.

That music points up another aspect of the movie – while steeped in history, the film captures the South at the point where tradition begins fading into something else, under assault not only by the forces of the Government and the syndicate desires of the gangsters, but by a new consumer culture of cars, speed, loud music. Mitchum sees the change coming, knows he's out of time. His young brother in the movie is an ingenious mechanic who maintains his car for him, fits it out with gimmicks to outwit pursuers – detachable bumpers, oil-sprays, quick release switches to dump the moonshine if he's caught – till it resembles a muscular, roaring hillbilly James Bond vehicle. The kid idolises him and his lifestyle, but Mitchum's sole concern in the film is with keeping him out of that life, urging him to head into the future and study, pursue his engineering skills. Maybe someday work on aeroplanes and rocketships.

The newly born rocket-fuelled punkish rock 'n' roll was a vital element in the movie's conception. Mitchum had, for a while, hoped that Elvis might agree to star in it – Mitchum understood the raw, lonely rebel sound of Elvis' music, where it came from and what it meant. He went to Graceland to talk to the singer and Elvis came to Mitchum's place. A Mitchum fan, Elvis was keen to make the film. He had just finished his second picture, playing a delivery driver in *Loving You* (1957), and the movie industry still hadn't quite worked out how to neuter and mess him up completely.

At that time the Elvis on screen still projected a presence that was simultaneously insulting, decent and bruised, a surly mask worn over raw emotions and deep, desperate uncertainty, somewhere nervous and dreamy between Brando and James Dean. Elvis, though, was getting a lot of cash per movie, and *Thunder Road* was a resolutely low-budget affair. The singer's management, reckoning the kid should stick to pictures that gave him some songs to sing so they could stick an album out, nixed the deal. Elvis went on to make a few films that almost got the idea – *Jailhouse Rock* (1957), the noirish *King Creole* (1958) and Don Siegel's *Flaming Star* (1960) – before disappearing into the candy factory and drowning in the sugar.

Mitchum knew what sort of movies Elvis should have been making all along, ones that were cheap and fast and quick and of the night, that were lonely and hopeless and torn, that were outside the law where folk heroes live, and that, most important of all, ended in flaming, metal-twisting death.

When Elvis faded out of the picture, Mitchum stepped in himself. Still, he constructed a film that's like a song. Between the chases and smashes and fights and explosions, come odd lulls, quiet spells. The camera, steering clear of art, occasionally frames an odd, modest, awkward beauty among the cheap, quick cardboard and the script steps toward an honest, simple poetry. Like when Mitchum, still explaining his family's way of life to Keely Smith in her cosy room, remembers following his father up into the hills to the still on wintry mornings as a child:

"I don't remember anything dark and shameful, I just recollect the dogwoods and laurels with little tags of ice at the end of them, just snipped off clean, like that, when you brushed past 'em…"

Thunder Road is like a mixture of the strange, ancient and eerie mountain moonshining ballads of the South as recorded by Bob Dylan – songs like the traditional *Moonshiner* and AF Beddoe's *Copper Kettle*, which contain lines and imagery that echo through the movie:

"My daddy he made whisky / My granddaddy he did too / We ain't paid no whisky tax since 1792 / We just lay there by the junipers / While the moon is bright / Watch them jugs a-fillin' / In the pale moonlight…"

And the reprobate, hot-rodding, death-lusting, electric-gangfight black-leather violence rock of

Gene Vincent, songs that fetishised the shapes and colours of cars, and, as in *Race with the Devil*, released the year before the movie was made, celebrated the unerring belief that a souped-up hot-rod could outrun any problems:

"Well I led an evil life / So you say / But I'll hide from the devil on judgment day… / Goin' pretty fast / I look behind / here come the Devil doing 99…"

Or, as Mitchum says to the Treasury Agent, Gene Barry, who is threatening him:

"I believe you can do all that you say – but you've got to catch me."

Barry gets second billing after Mitchum and, after Mitchum, is the closest thing to a recognisable face in the film. A former big band singer, Barry had forged a career as the stiffish lead or supporting player in a number of modest, mediocre mainstream movies, gaining by far his biggest exposure as the straight-laced scientist in *The War of the Worlds* (1953).

In his next movie as a producer, the Western *The Wonderful Country* (1959) – in which Mitchum also staged what amounted to a deconstruction of his wandering derelict persona – the casting would be lively and unexpected; in *Thunder Road*, however, it's not just energetically offbeat, it's right off the map. The movie is filled with strange, unfamiliar faces, many of whom would seem to be acting for the first time, putting a weird wooden quality to a few scenes. Partly this is to do with the picture's low budget – but it's also a function of how that low budget is confidentially absorbed by the movie, to become not a hindrance, but an integral element of its raw, unlit aesthetic. The weird, flat, depthless unreal back-projected exteriors that crop up from time to time to cover the gaps of scenes someone forgot to film while on location, the cardboard bareness of some of the sets, the uncertain acting of certain cast members – all of this becomes part of the dense texture of the movie, like the grain and slivers of wood in a cheaply produced pulp paperback, designed only to be consumed and discarded.

After Barry, the most famous face is the jazz singer Keely Smith, who plays the roadhouse chanteuse patiently waiting for Mitchum in Memphis and never making any demands beyond idly explaining how she just wants to be 'normal people'. Smith, prettily angular, sporting her trademark severely fringed black bob, was best known as the singer with her then-husband Louis Prima's band, swinging along through wild nights at the Sahara in Las Vegas then cooling things down with ballads. There her audiences had included Frank Sinatra, Dean Martin, Howard Hughes, Robert Mitchum. Here, she leans her head on Mitchum's shoulder, looks dark-eyed and wistful, and slowly breathes her way through his composition *Whippoorwill*, a tune he'd written as a love song for his wife.

Then comes a host of mysterious stiff, odd, jerky half-familiar or completely new faces. There's Jim Mitchum, trying to be like his dad but not getting it, which is perfect because the character he's playing is trying to be just Mitchum, but not getting it; there's Jacques Aubuchon, soft-faced, pale, corpulent and corrupt as the pudgy gangster who's trying to take over and keeps sending faceless men with hats and guns after Mitchum; there's a wired, fidgety moonrunner with shifty eyes, wearing black denim and eventually going over to the other side and joining with Aubuchon – he's played by Peter Breck, in his first film role, five years before he would gain lasting underground fame as the lead in Sam Fuller's ferocious insane-America tabloid-noir *Shock Corridor*. There's another briefly-glimpsed fellow young moonrunner, with a happy, rubbery face, one of the first to get killed, his car ambushed by gunmen out along the woodland road – this is the first film appearance by Jerry Hardin who, 40 years later would gain cult fame as the Deep Throat aiding Mulder and Scully in the paranoid sci-fi series *The X-Files*. Then, playing Mitchum's father from behind a moustache and under a hat, Trevor Bardette, who had turned up at the corner of the screen in countless Westerns from the 1930s on, and had briefly stuck his head into Mitchum's universe before, in the background of *Macao*.

Around Bardette, in one of the weirdest, stiffest, most interesting scenes – as the moonshiners of the valley debate whether or not to take up the gangster's potentially profitable offer – gather an oddball Mount Rushmore of other unknown faces, the screen all about whiskers and noses and watery eyes, odd clothes, odd hats, a old thin face chewing on an enormous plug of tobacco, so big that his words come out as an indecipherable wet hum while a fly lands unnoticed on his hat brim.

To frame all of this, Mitchum turned to the veteran director Arthur Ripley, who had been in movies in various capacities since 1908. Then 63, this was the last film Ripley directed. In keeping with the quick, subterranean, anti-studio mentality, Mitchum hired Ripley for his reputation of working extraordinarily fast and with low budgets, his history of getting into trouble through shunning studio conventions.

As well as directing, Ripley had been an editor, a director of photography, and, during the late 1910s and 1920s, a gag writer on the insane silent comedies of Mack Sennett, collaborating with Frank Capra and writing for WC Fields. Mitchum admired Ripley's scriptwriting and also the film for which he received his biggest notices as a director, the quickly-shot *Voice in the Wind* (1944) an unusual shoestring picture, independently produced as an experiment and a demonstration about what could be done without stars, money or formula, about a pianist hounded by Nazis.

Some of the shots Mitchum had Ripley shoot are mighty strange. There are some images of startling, unpretentious beauty: a twice-recurring shot from high up on a ridge at night, the camera looking down on the darkened valley floor as the distant moonshiners slowly bring their dead home in an eerie processional convoy of far-off car headlights. The film often pauses, the soundtrack falling silent, simply to observe real time events: in a garage in Memphis, a man goes about working with pipes and machines to empty a tank of moonshine while, behind him, bleakly haloed by a bare overhead light, Mitchum dials numbers on a telephone and waits for answers. Later, another scene that waits patiently, silently, as Mitchum feeds coin after coin into a clanging payphone out on the highway at night, calling the big city to warn Aubuchon that he's coming in to get him, to pay him back for trying to corrupt his kid brother.

One of the strangest shots in the film matches up with one of the strangest lines in the script.

When Mitchum is sheltering in that sweet, warm Memphis room with Keely Smith on his shoulder and the black rainy night hammering outside, explaining himself to her, he talks about why he can't fit back in among the folk of Harlan county – going off to war, he saw all sorts of things, all the big cities, all 'the pretty people'. He tells her of his reluctant new sophistication, how now he can read 'expensive restaurant menus' – and then, this bizarre line: 'I know what a mobile is.' Sure enough, there's a cut to a mobile hanging in the corner of the room, a weird, spindly thing showing home-made cardboard planets and shooting stars dangling from awkward wire, exactly like an artefact from a David Lynch film.

Although he says little about it, his head, these days, is 'full of so many things.' And that's what's at the heart of this furious, tough, melancholy proletarian melodrama about a man alone refusing to compromise, seeking out oblivion on the road at night, what's powering all the speed and the violence and the loneliness. This guy went away to war, to fight in Korea, and then found he could never go home again – the film explicitly injects that history into the story twice: first, following Mitchum's come home bone-weary after outrunning the Federal revenuers who attempted to ambush him at the start of the movie, he enters his small bare bedroom and prepares to catch a few hours sleep, and as he twists his wrist free of his watchstrap, he turns and half stares at the pennant of his old infantry battalion pinned above the bed. Then, as the old moonshiners debate their problems with Government and gangsters, one of them blames Mitchum's behaviour for bringing down the big heat in the first place: he has the pace set at a such lunatic level it's attracted the attentions of every lawman in the territory, and the other, lesser young moonrunners, in awe of his legend, are going similarly crazy trying to keep up with him. The difference between them and him, however, is, as the old guy describes it:

"He's got a machine-gunner's outlook and death doesn't phase him much..."

This Luke Doolin character, nursing a calm fury throughout, has the same problems that left the ambulance driver Mitchum played in *Angel Face* a misfit dreaming only of engine oil and speed. It's behind everything he does. When a man won't shut up during Keely Smith's night club act, it's why Mitchum wanders over and begins strangling the guy with his necktie. When the gangster has him in his office with his gunsels outside and lays out the way it's going to be when his mob muscle in on Harlan County, telling Mitchum he can be a part of it or be crushed by it and then asking 'How rough do you want it?', it's why Mitchum's answer is to karate chop him in the neck, smash his hat, then jump out the window and take off. It's why, when the Treasury man offers Mitchum the chance to co-operate, to ensure that the mob gets crushed, it's why Mitchum refuses point blank, furiously explaining himself to his brother when the kid suggests it might be a good idea:

"I don't make no deals with nobody... I don't fix, I don't buddy up with one livin' soul..."

Instead, what he does is he jumps in his car, bullet holes in his mirror, heads for the murkiest stretches of highway, hoping there might be someone in a powerful vehicle there to chase him, attack him, shoot at him, to shunt him close to the precipice. Hoping there might be two cars across the road ahead trying to block his way, so he can gun himself up to 100 and smash straight through them to the other side. Just keep moving. He won't stop, not until somebody stops him – and every night he thinks, hopes that, maybe, tonight's the night, tonight's the night...

Finally, they do stop him, at night, about the break of day, by laying spikes and oil slicks across the highway, near an oblivious little roadside house pale in the twilight, so he rips his tyres and skids and loses control, flipping his car, still loaded with 250 gallons of pure moonshine, over and over, rocketing off the road and smashing into a conveniently placed electricity transformer, going out in a mangled, romantic auto-death apocalypse, a pure conflagration of crackling electricity, oil, raw gut-rot alcohol, night and legend.

Home from the Hill

Director: Vincente Minnelli, MGM, 1960

Synopsis

While duck shooting, Captain Wade Hunnicutt (Mitchum), the boss of a town in East Texas, is shot at by the husband of a woman he's been sleeping with. He's saved by his right-hand man, Rafe Copley (George Peppard). A legendary hunter, Wade is also an infamous womaniser, and his wife (Eleanor Parker) has long since stopped sleeping with him. She's also demanded that he play no part in raising their son, Theron (George Hamilton), whose effeminate manner has made him a local laughing stock. Wade determines to make a man of the boy and pairs him with Rafe, who teaches him about the woods. A wild boar is plaguing local farmers and they demand that Wade, their landlord, get rid of it. He asks Theron to kill the animal and, after a treacherous hunt, he succeeds. Theron falls for a girl, Libby Halstead (Luana Patten) but is turned away by her father (Everett Sloane), who judges the boy by his father's reputation. His eyes opened, Theron discovers Rafe is actually his half brother, a result of Wade's past dalliances. He confronts his father and demands that Rafe become part of the family. When Wade dismisses him, he leaves home. Meanwhile, Rafe has discovered that Libby is carrying Theron's baby – she hasn't told Theron. Mr Halstead knows his daughter is pregnant but doesn't know who the father is. Rafe proposes to her and they marry. When the baby is born, Libby's father overhears a group of locals speculating that Wade is the father. Outraged, he goes after him with a shotgun and kills him. Theron chases Mr Halstead into the swamps and kills him, then wanders into the woods alone. On Wade's headstone, his widow has Rafe's name inscribed alongside Theron's as his son.

Home from the Hill unfolds in a small, stifling, sticky Texas town, a place filled with eager, lazy whispers, where energies are soon sapped and things quickly curdle and go off. The whole place is snarled up with sex. It comes pouring viciously out of the biggest house in town, where Mitchum, the local landed potentate, is engaged in a protracted war with his wife, turned frigid by his incessant, flagrant, philandering – which has in turn only escalated as a reaction to her locked bedroom door.

The open secret of their battle leaks out and infects the whole town: sex as a punishment, sex as a reward, sex as a brief oblivion, sex as a guilty secret – the possibility of it hangs in the air like the smell of the marsh gas drifting in from the swamps, and its consequences litter up the streets.

Vincente Minnelli's Southern movie is like a moneyed, manners-minding *Thunder Road*, turning away from the folk in the backroads valley to concentrate on the sick family up on the hill in town, but not so far away that they can't smell the swamps and the graveyards. In this film the cheap, quick, rickety black-and-white interior B-movie aesthetic is replaced by long, slow, expensive colour, Cinemascope, painstaking attention to composition and a sweeping, strange choreography of actors and camera.

Best known for his vivid, vigorous, dream-like, almost expressionistic musicals – from *Meet Me in St Louis* (1942) and *The Pirate* (1945) to *An American in Paris* (1951) and *The Bandwagon* (1953) – Minnelli approaches this twisted, soapy melodrama like a weird, sour ballet of Americana, scored to the simmer of shifting hothouse emotions. A frantic hunt for a wild boar through the swamps plays out like an awkward, jerky, forward-flowing stop-start dance.

There's a lot of location photography – parts of the movie were shot around Oxford, Mississippi, William Faulkner's stomping ground – but just as much studio work. Whether indoors or out, Minnelli abandons realism for a heightened, stylised world, where elements such as the throne-like, glaring red armchair Mitchum sits on in his study, surrounded by hounds and shotguns and the heads of the animals he's killed, blare from the screen like sudden shouts of sickness and danger.

Still, as in *Thunder Road*, in this place Mitchum is still a 'grown man still playing guns 'n' cars' and is once again a local legend. The rest of the men want to be like him. He has the most money, he owns the most land, he's the best hunter, the best shot and the most legendary lover,

treating the female populace – wives, tramps, wild and woodsy girls who hide behind him like animals – as his own private harem, to be dipped into whenever he feels like it.

Above them all, he sits untouchable in the centre of the community, regarded by the locals as a combination of warrior king and ongoing soap opera, *Dallas* scripted by Faulkner. A group of the men, middle-aged but still loitering the sultry streets at night in the same formations they first struck as teenagers, still giggling like teenagers, tag after him like his pack of hunting dogs, but when he's not around they snigger and whisper to one another about his exploits, his conquests and the unknown battalion of his bastards wandering the town: 'How many do you think he's fathered?'

For them, one of the most entertaining sub-plots in the ongoing saga comes in the less than manly shape of George Hamilton, Mitchum's one legitimate child and the butt of their practical jokes. A Tennessee lad, Hamilton was then 21, and his future of tanning salons and self-parody was nowhere in sight: he had just played an arrogant teen psycho in the weird, stark Dostoevsky adaptation *Crime and Punishment USA* (1959). Here, as the nervy momma's boy realising he wants to be something more than the cow-licked stamp collector he is, he skulks around as though he could be Anthony Perkins' brother.

Hamilton is the result of bizarre pact that Mitchum agreed with his wife when the kid was born: having found him with his paws on some road trash girl in a shabby dress, she made him swear he'd never touch her child, never interfere with his upbringing, so she could avoid raising another man like him. But now he's determined to make his kind of man out of the boy. Mitchum introduces Hamilton to his other, unacknowledged son, George Peppard, a proper, dirty, hard-drinking guy who lives in a shack, sweating in denims and dreaming of being James Dean in *Giant* – that's how the whole can of worms that will leave Mitchum lying dead in his house from a shotgun blast busts open.

Through it all, Mitchum struts lazily around the place with utter, spiteful confidence, cocksure and duded-up in shining pointed leather boots, spotless big hats and pristine menswear. Playing this son-of-a-bitch patriarch he goes whoring and ties on a four-day drunk, he intimidates his family and lords it over all of those around him without straining a muscle. What is so extraordinary about his performance, though, is that never once does he slip over into caricature.

All through the movie, as he tries to do what he thinks is best by his boy, come fleeting flashes of a hard tenderness, hints that he's burdened down by the guilt of his life, is haunted by regret and the look in his wife's eyes, wants to make it all better. Ultimately, though, for better or worse he's compassionate only on his own terms. He knows he's chosen to be alone in his arrogant mannish nightmare of guns, hounds, drink, women and money, and wants to be left alone, making his own mistakes.

Battling Eleanor Parker in the biggest house in town.

The Sundowners

Director: Fred Zinnemann, United Artists, 1960

Synopsis

Sheep-drover Paddy Carmody (Mitchum), his wife Ida (Deborah Kerr) and their son Sean (Michael Anderson Jr) live an itinerant existence in Australia. Paddy has landed a job driving sheep across the outback to the town of Cawndilla. Getting drunk in celebration, he hires Rupert Venneker (Peter Ustinov) a snobbish ex-sea captain to help. En route, they nearly perish in a raging bush fire. Resting with an ex-droving family who have settled, Ida and Sean gaze at a nearby farmhouse for sale. They're both tired of travelling and want to settle but Paddy won't hear of it. In Cawndilla, Ida persuades Paddy to take a job at the sheep station, which is preparing for its annual shearing. Paddy is unwilling but is eventually persuaded; Ida and Sean have hatched a plan to use the money they earn as a down payment on the farm. As the weeks on the station pass, Paddy gets restless and feels left out as his wife and son form friendships with people around them. When the shearing is complete, during a coin-tossing contest, Paddy wins $200 and a racehorse Ida names Sundowner. They leave the station and tour racetracks. With Sean riding, Sundowner wins race after race. Finally Ida has enough money to put down on the farm – she and Sean reveal their plans to Paddy who is put out but reluctantly agrees. That night, however, he gets drunk and gambles away their savings. Ida weeps. At a race the next day, Paddy secretly agrees to sell Sundowner if he wins the race, so he can buy the farm for his wife. When the horse wins, Ida refuses to let him sell the animal. While they argue, umpires announce that Sundowner has been disqualified, freeing Paddy of his obligation to sell. The Carmodys hit the road.

Fred Zinnemann's sprawling shepherd's odyssey runs for well over two hours but a lot of that screen time is given over to shots of sheep. Sometimes kangaroos come bounding across the road (though no boxing ones) or koalas climbing a tree – this is Australia after all, and what's the point of filming in Australia if you're not going to include koalas and kangaroos – mostly, though, sheep. Sheep moving, sheep standing still. Sheep running, sheep jumping. Sheep escaping a fire. Undignified close-ups of a surprised sheep as it finds itself being unexpectedly shorn. Bald sheep frolicking in a pen. There's also a lot of decidedly Disneyish cartoon music gambolling and prat-falling about,

courtesy of the otherwise often-great Dmitri Tiomkin, and maybe just a little too much of Peter Ustinov's beard.

Underneath it all, though, if you cut away the wool, there's a very fine, very human little movie going on between Mitchum and Deborah Kerr, in their third film together, about a husband and wife who love each other but whose hopes for their future are diametrically opposed.

Paddy Carmody, the character Mitchum plays, is a completely different patriarch from the Wade Hunnicutt he played in *Home from the Hill*, but both men have in common the desire to be left alone to make up their own minds. It's up to the families around them whether they let that destroy them all or not.

This Paddy has no hopes and no dreams, and he lives in an eternal present. His unwillingness to get stuck in one place, his predilection for self-destruction, seeking oblivion in gambling and booze, and his unwritten, jealously maintained credo of independence, makes him another permutation of the regular Mitchum protagonist, and a character, you suspect, close to the actor's heart, too. In life, around the period the film was being made, Mitchum had just started breeding horses at his farm in Maryland, and when late on in Zinnemann's movie he reverently regards the extraordinarily beautiful white horse they call Sundowner, the line between actor and character evaporates.

In fact, he seems incredibly in touch with the stuff of Carmody's life – very comfortable singing, drinking, fighting, galloping around on a horse, wrestling sheep. He makes all this look natural, not as if he's mounting a display of his own athleticism or versatility. After a while, you don't even notice that he and Kerr are speaking in Australian accents.

Zinnemann's film is specifically concerned with the misfit, wandering, futureless aspect of the

The healthiest picture of marriage, with Deborah Kerr.

Mitchum persona, and the toll it can take on the people around him. After years on the move, setting up home by the roadside wherever they happen to be when the sun goes down, taking whatever transitory jobs they can get, Kerr is tired of all the dust and sweat and road, all the back breaking work that leads only to more uncertainty and another few miles rattling along the flat red earth in their carriage.

She gazes longingly after the women she sees from time to time in the pages of magazines and in the windows of passing trains and even in a tumbledown little house beside an empty dirt track; women who get to wear make-up if they feel like it, sit on chairs, own little things they can put out on shelves. Just like Keely Smith in *Thunder Road*, her fervent desire is to be 'normal people'. She wants permanence, settling down, stability – the safety and security that Mitchum's *Holiday Affair* character maintained were impossible if two people really loved one another.

The eternal Australian–Irish rover, Mitchum still holds with that thinking, continues his suspicious rejection of conformity. Career, house, garden, bank account, none of these holds any interest. He just wants to drift, keep moving, think free. Although he loves his wife and kid, he doesn't particularly need any friends, and is disturbed when they try to bring other people into his life. Paddy Carmody has the wanderlust and the code of self-reliance that runs through Mitchum's characters like a plague. Without thinking about it, his philosophy is that there's no point in planning for a future, because the future may well never come. If it ever does, he'll deal with it then.

The difference this time is that he's dragging a wife and child who don't subscribe to his pure loner thinking but are forced to live with its consequences. Years ago, miles away, in the frosty New York of *Holiday Affair*, he told Janet Leigh:

> "I want a girl that'll drop everything and run to me, no matter what the score is."

Often – in films like *His Kind of Woman*, *Macao*, *Blood on the Moon* – the implication was that, when he finally got his kind of girl, his drifting would come to an end. But in this movie he doesn't ever let her stop running.

Yet somehow, the love between Mitchum and Kerr, keeps them together in the face of everything. That love, and the incredible rapport between the two actors, is really the whole film. Immediately before *The Sundowners* was made, Mitchum and Kerr, along with Cary Grant and Jean Simmons, had acted in Stanley Donen's movie *The Grass Is Greener* (1960), a stagy, cut-glass drawing-room comedy. Zinnemann's movie, with all its movement, dirt, sweat, sheep-smell and work, resembles a reaction to Donen's static, and also to the exquisite restraint of Huston's *Heaven Knows, Mr Allison*. As with Huston's film, Mitchum's performance here is incredibly physical but it's allowed to spill over into his relationship with Kerr.

Zinnemann had made the actress an icon of tempestuous passion seven years previously when he had her rolling in the foam with Burt Lancaster in *From Here to Eternity*, but here, aged 39, with little make-up and wearing dirt-smeared sweat and grimy thrift-store clothes, she's sexier than ever before. Even more than when she dressed as a nun.

In the way in which Mitchum and Kerr look at each other, in how he drapes an arm around her during a sing-song, and, particularly when, on the exhausted night after his first day working at the sheep station, she leans over him in her slip and rubs lotion into his aching muscles, there's a real, common, decent carnality. Despite the director's *National Geographic* leanings throughout, despite the sheep, and despite the battle between hopeless-existential-vagrancy and sheltered-flowers-on-the-windowsill-domesticity, in the work of the actors this movie presents one of the finest, healthiest pictures of marriage ever to be found in a Hollywood film.

Ryan's Daughter

Director: David Lean, MGM, 1970

Synopsis

1916. As WWI rages and the troubles between the British and the Irish rumble in Dublin, in the tiny village of Kirrary on Ireland's west coast, widowed schoolteacher Charles Shaughnessy (Mitchum) marries a much younger girl, Rosy (Sarah Miles) a former pupil, and daughter of the landlord of the village pub, Tom Ryan (Leo McKern). Where Rosy has a passionately romantic imagination, Charles is shy and uncertain, and, as Rosy learns on their wedding night, impotent. A wounded young British officer, Randolph Doryan (Christopher Jones) arrives to command the garrison nearby and he and Rosy begin an affair. Charles knows about their relationship but elects to say nothing, hoping it will blow itself out. Tom Ryan blusters revolutionary anti-British sentiments loudly in the pub but it transpires he is an informant for the British Army. The affair between Rosy and the English soldier becomes public knowledge and the village turn against her. Meanwhile, IRA man Tim O'Leary (Barry Foster) has arranged for a shipment of arms to be delivered by a German ship and the villagers risk their lives bringing the weapons ashore in a raging storm. When, however, they are intercepted by British soldiers, they believe Rosy has informed on them. Back at the schoolhouse, Charles tells Rosy he knows about her affair, which she has broken off. They agree to leave the village together and then separate. The mob of villagers break in and accuse Rosy of colluding with the British. Among them, her father, the real informant, says nothing. Holding Charles down, the villagers assault Rosy and hack off her hair. They are halted by the intervention of the fearsome priest, Father Collins (Trevor Howard). Charles and Rosy leave the village the next morning, intending to stay together.

Sometimes, all there is to do is keep your head down and do the work. So it was for Robert Mitchum when he went to the bleakly beautiful Dingle peninsula on the west coast of Ireland to spend 10 months on David Lean's strange, mistily over-inflated *Ryan's Daughter* – a weird big chocolate box of a movie, dripping out at treacle pace.

Lean had asked him to do the picture and Mitchum was intrigued by the script – but put off by the infamous length of time it took Lean to put a film together. He declined. When the scriptwriter, Robert Bolt, then phoned and asked him to reconsider the movie, Mitchum said he couldn't, because he'd planned committing suicide. Bolt offered to stand the cost of his funeral if Mitchum would make 'this wretched little film of ours' before he did himself in.[1] Impressed, he signed up.

Lean had already decided that the part of the mild, decent, impotent, cuckolded village schoolteacher was a pretty dull one and he therefore needed an actor with powerful presence to prevent it from fading into the film. It was presumably by this logic that the director had cast Christopher Jones – the part of the romantically crippled, orchid-like British officer with whom Sarah Miles has her calamitous fling was in danger of being a fairly exciting role, and therefore needed Jones to make it seem as uninteresting as possible.

Lean held Mitchum in the highest regard:

"He is a master of stillness. Other actors act. Mitchum is. He has true delicacy and expressiveness but his forte is in his indelible identity. Simply by being there, Mitchum can make almost any other actor look like a hole in the screen."[2]

As it was, when Mitchum reported for duty, the director was suddenly fearful that he was, in purely physical terms, too much, and had the costumes of other actors padded out and lifts built into their shoes in compensation.

But the padding didn't stop there. At the heart of *Ryan's Daughter* is a sad, strange, small trashy love story in keeping with the paperbacks Miles reads early in the movie but you need to hack back through three hours' worth of Quality Film-making to get at it. Where Fred Zinnemann had his endless flocks

of sheep clogging up the outback tale of *The Sundowners*, Lean stuffs and supercharges *Ryan's Daughter* with symbolic fauna and weather: waves, clouds, towering storms, copses full of bobbering flowers catching the light, glinting spider's webs, seagulls, wind-driven sand on a stretching white beach. Beautifully photographed by Lean regular Freddie Young, it looks exquisite, but drowns the fragile narrative in a swamp of portent and faux-significance.

The protracted circumstances of the film's making, however, would themselves have provided enough material for a truly epic satire on the movie business. Trevor Howard and John Mills, as the village idiot, were nearly drowned during filming, as was Leo McKern. While incessant rain repeatedly called a halt to the production and while Lean waited patiently on hilltops for waves of a specific shape, the

right sorts of seagulls to fly by and certain types of sand formation, the cast cooled their heels. Mitchum tried to avoid fights with the locals and took to hosting regular, boozy gatherings of cast and crew in the cottage-hotel he had been assigned for the duration.

In his back garden there, according to Sarah Miles, he tried to grow grass. One night, he was planning to cook lobsters for everyone, but Miles, confronted by the forlorn sight of them in a tank in the kitchen, returned them to the sea without his knowing. Back in the kitchen, Mitchum met her with a cheery greeting:

"What the fuck am I going to give everyone tonight? I'll get you for this Miles. Yes, one day you'll pay for this. So beware."[3]

Some seven years later, Mitchum happened to mention, very much in passing, during a round of interviews, that Sarah Miles was given to drinking her own urine, which set the tone for her own interviews for the next few years.

"The story ran in enough British newspapers for journalists to contact me to hear it from the horse's mouth. I didn't think to deny it. How could I deny it and spend the rest of my life living out a daily lie? Drinking your own pee is one of the most harmless, and some would say beneficial of daily activities."

Despite all the drawn-out, off-screen carnival, Mitchum goes to work on camera. Once more, he's playing someone who just doesn't fit, with a wounded past – the young wife he buried on the hill years before. The villagers have an unspecified resentment toward him, and he has little to say to them. The portrait he paints of a retiring, diffident soul is entirely believable. There are looks of confusion and pain, uncertain movements during his nightmarish wedding celebrations – the way he disappoints Miles with his reticence in the bedroom an inversion of the domineering put down of Shelley Winters in *The Night of the Hunter* wedding night, wearing the same night shirt.

Although there's a briefly easy, relaxed manner about him with the kids in the school, the only place he feels at home, in general, as in *The Friends of Eddie Coyle*, he wears his body as though he's trying not to offend anyone with it, seems as though he's still not quite used to steering it around.

Lean throws unnecessary gimmicks at him to deal with throughout – the script has the teacher listen constantly to Beethoven to show he's operating on a higher plane than the peasants frolicking in the mud, and spends his quiet Sundays pressing wild flowers – but Mitchum handles this stuff with graceful aplomb, ignores all the symbolism and keeps in line with the truth of the man. Somehow, the flower pressing looks as natural to him as loading a rifle did when he was Wade Hunnicutt, as instinctive as crushing a beer can was for Max Cady.

Charles Shaughnessy was the centre panel of a triptych of weirdo teachers Mitchum played. Two years prior to this, he turned up in another symbolically overloaded film, *Secret Ceremony*.

As a university lecturer, he gave one of the most whacked-out performances of his career. Directed by Joseph Losey, the movie was set in a run-down London, where ageing prostitute Elizabeth Taylor, whose daughter drowned years before, is stalked by insane girl-woman Mia Farrow, whose mother, the spitting image of Taylor, has just died. Farrow, 23 going on 14, is loaded with cash, and Taylor moves in with her. They play house, and have baths together until Mitchum turns up as Farrow's wicked stepfather, kicked out years before because he'd started fooling around with the kid.

The teacher he plays here, a groovy, bitter, nasty satyr described by his in-laws as a 'randy bastard,' is Charles Shaughnessy from a negative universe. He looks incredible, striding around in tweed hat and raincoat, sporting a bushy goatee. The film is overblown, hysterical pseudo-profound 1960s junk, but, again, he ignores that, cuts through it and finds a truth to stick with. The truth this time is that of an utterly reprehensible, utterly jaded cynic. His playing is lively, perverse, dripping contempt. Sizing up Taylor, he calls her a cow, then moos at her. He asks Farrow if she likes his beard, then gives its biography:

"It's my sheep's clothing. All the little sophomores think I'm just a benign old poof from England... until we get to the parking lot and I grab 'em, plough into the groves of academia. The wretched lecher they call me."

Despite his protestations that he 'couldn't rape a randy elephant', Taylor blames him for Farrow's suicide and kills him in a funeral parlour.

In *That Championship Season* (1983), he was in the halls of learning again – or, at least, in the gym hall to the side, playing a retired but still overbearing high-school basketball coach. The film was written and directed by Jason Miller, best known as the priest who jumps out the window and breaks his neck at the end of *The Exorcist* (1973). Miller's movie is even more disturbing than that demonic-possession flick, in that the opening scene features a whole crowd of people running around wearing cardboard Bruce Dern masks.

Dern, a right-winger, is struggling to be re-elected as a Pennsylvania town mayor, and is

FILLMORE HIGH
1957 PENNSYLVANIA STATE
CHAMPIONS

Paul Sorvino, Stacy Keach, Bruce Dern and Martin Sheen take lessons: That Championship Season.

helped out by his back-scratching buddies Stacy Keach, a repressed head teacher, and Paul Sorvino, a coke-snorting businessman. Twenty-four years previously, this trio, along with Keach's brother Martin Sheen, were part of a basketball team who won an against-all-odds state championship under the leadership of coach Mitchum. Every year since, they celebrate the anniversary at the coach's house – it's apparent that they still can't break away from the old guy.

This year, things become maudlin and nasty. The coasting on former glories has soon given way to four bleak, conservative American mid-life crises: ambitions were never fulfilled, Dern is being soundly whipped in the election – he only won the last time because

Mitchum stepped in; Sorvino has been having an affair with Dern's wife; Sheen is a washed-up alcoholic; and Keach is blubbing because his daddy didn't love him.

Mitchum, meantime, wanders around spouting reactionary and generally racist cant, gives winning-is-all-that-matters pep-talks, rips some stitches in his gut where he's had an ulcer operation, throws boxing moves, then retires to his office to talk about the French teacher he used to date, who wore silk stockings and baked honey biscuits. He tells the boys to buck up, then, looking at Sheen passed out on the sofa, delivers a heartfelt verdict on the younger generation:

"You drink like women."

Chapter Eight
Westerns

In noir films, Mitchum found his own hazy world, a place he recognised and which, in turn, recognised him back. In war pictures, he did his duty convincingly and made 'his name', gaining his only Oscar nomination. However, he was born in the west.

At the age of 26, Mitchum entered movies by riding past the camera at the rear of a galloping group of no-good cowboys, headed for a saloon. The last film of his to be released while he was alive, *Dead Man*, saw him, aged 77, still out there on the frontier, a very different kind of Western heavy, toting a shotgun and bent on weird revenge. Although he never became a Wayne-like icon of the genre – he would never play mythic Western archetypes such as Wayne portrayed, essaying instead a line of smaller, troubled individuals – across his career Mitchum appeared in over 30 Westerns, making the prairie his most habitual habitat. As he put it:

> "I have two acting styles: with or
> without a horse."[1]

He arrived on a film set for the first time in the summer of 1942, when the producer Harry 'Pop' Sherman sent him out to the desert location of Kernville, outside Bakersfield, California, where Sherman's unit proficiently cranked out the *Hopalong Cassidy* series. How Mitchum came to the Hoppy movies is fuzzy; in one version, the actor was sent along to audition by his agent and William Boyd – Hopalong Cassidy himself – gave him the nod because he figured Mitchum looked shifty enough to play a good for nothing cowpoke; in another, Sherman's daughter was driving Sunset Boulevard one afternoon, saw Mitchum trying to bum a ride, and took him straight to Pop as a potential cowboy.

By then the Western, the paternal American movie genre, was just about 40 years old; there are quibbles, but, even though it was filmed in New Jersey, Edwin S Porter's one-reel epic, *The Great Train Robbery* (1903), with its bad men and chases and shoot outs and open air, can be seen as setting out the basic formula every subsequent cowboy flick fed on. If film noir was America's erupting subconscious, then the Western was the trick mirror in which the country regarded itself, able to alter the features it didn't like. Here, history was not simply rewritten but created anew. In the process of telling these frontier tales the country's founding myths were established: man against nature; civilisation against savagery; the dirty, sad job of progress. The archetypal hero of North American popular culture was born: a decent but dangerous, independent man of few words and decisive action, someone who comprehends the wilderness and is capable of rendering it safe for communities he himself could never join.

Consolidating through the 1920s and 1930s, by the early 1940s the Western had reached its classical state, but it was also beginning to reveal itself as a far more flexible form. While traditional movies were still being created, the Western started to fracture and in some cases, eat itself. The genre took to calling itself a liar. Films began interrogating the versions of history presented by previous movies. The standard approach of representing Native American peoples as evil savages was, albeit slowly and reluctantly, taken to task. The driven, lonesome cowboy was now revealed to be a dysfunctional, antisocial psychotic, his ascetic, immutable will an anti-democratic impulse, close to misogyny and fascist mania. The Western communities that he rejected, meanwhile, were beginning to look rotten, too, filled with weakness and corruption.

A long way from myth:
El Dorado (1967).

Eventually, the form became not only about looking back but about scrutinising the present, changing from a mirror to a microscope, under which were passed issues from race to ecology to generational conflict. In the rock and rolling 1950s, delinquent cowboys began appearing, through the 1960s more black range hands and cavalry men were glimpsed and, by the end of that decade, the prairie was littered with film-makers dragging debris from Vietnam.

Forgetting history, sociology and psychology, however, the Western was, of course, always about something else, too: unpretentious, fast-paced action and adventure, big-kid stories about – as the title of one of Mitchum's most easy-going oaters had it – *The Good Guys and the Bad Guys* (1969).

This was the disreputable, energetic, unadorned dime book milieu in which Mitchum first started out. According to legend, when he arrived at Kernville to be fitted out with bad-man's duds, he was handed a hat encrusted with the still-damp blood of a stunt rider who had been killed that morning when he was dragged beneath a four-horse stagecoach. Mitchum went to work in the dead man's headgear.

William Boyd had been playing Hopalong Cassidy exclusively since 1935, when he brought paperback novelist Clarence E. Mulford's character to life in Paramount's picture, *Hop-a-Long Cassidy*. Mulford's Hoppy carried a bullet wound in his leg but, following that movie's success, Boyd and producer Sherman eliminated the limp, removed the hyphens and cleaned up Hoppy's act – unlike the man in Mulford's books, Boyd's Hoppy neither drank, cussed, nor smoked – for a series that eventually ran to 61 films. The pair took Hoppy with them when they broke from Paramount after 41 movies and, after Sherman quit the series, Boyd became his own producer. Eventually, he obtained sole rights to the character and made a fortune in the early 1950s when the old movies were sold to television and, on the back of their renewed popularity, a new TV serial was born.

On his tall, beautiful white horse, Boyd cut a memorable figure – straight-backed and dressed always in black, he was 40 when he started to play Hoppy, with a head of prematurely snowy hair and an enormous hat. With the hero flanked usually by a cantankerous, foolish old timer and an over-eager young buck, these films helped promulgate one of the most popular Western heroic structures: Howard Hawks tinkered with the same three-ages-of-man style trio in *Red River* (1948), then reworked it for *Rio Bravo* (1959), and *El Dorado* (1967).

Quick, cheap to make (while enjoying a much higher budget than other serial horse-operas) and happily ridiculous, the Hoppy flicks were formula Westerns, but efficiently-crafted, turned out on time to a certain standard and crackling with Saturday-morning energy. The Kernville set was the perfect training ground for the Mitchum who would later go to such lengths to duck any allegations of art. He made seven Hoppy movies in total, all released in 1943. The first film he shot was *Border Patrol*, but the first to be released was *Hoppy Serves a Writ*.

Here, then, is the birth of the screen Mitchum. The world of *Hoppy Serves a Writ* is a day-lit place of humour and action, big Californian skies and leafy trees, and it stirs to the busy, chattering sound of square heroic music – dun-da-da-da-duhn! The acting in the main is straight and rigid and to the point. There's no time and no call for shading, because there's a lot to get into 66 minutes. In the film, as he would be in all but one of them, Mitchum is a low-rung rowdy. He inhabits Oklahoma Territory, a place across the river where, as Hoppy's cantankerous old sidekick, California (Andy Clyde) says: 'there ain't enough law… to put under your hat.' Hoppy elucidates that, over there, a lawman's star is 'not much good, except as target for gunmen' – a line Hawks would later appropriate for *El Dorado*.

Hoppy goes into that lawless country to capture a rustler cum stagecoach robber, by posing as a gambler posing as a travelling salesman. He tracks his quarry to a saloon. Outside, a posse of the villain's henchmen ride into town. Mitchum, playing a character called Rigney, is enormous among them. Tethering his horse to a tree he walks into the bar with the other roughnecks while, in the foreground, his boss and Hoppy size one another up over a poker table.

Clad in filthy jeans, a plaid shirt, greasy waistcoat and sporting a five-day beard, rambling across the barroom just as lazily as he ever would pace the length of a movie screen, Mitchum calls attention to himself by his very ease, is, already, recognisably Mitchum. He props himself at the bar, pours himself a drink and regards proceedings with the same casual, silent watchfulness he would later bring to the pauses of *Out of the Past*. His first words, delivered in a distracted manner, are: 'You mean the one that took our guns?'

Mitchum never shook off this badman's blood. It was the taint of his original sinning as a big ugly hooligan, pacing the wild frontier and looking a little shifty around the eyes, that in part led to the ambiguous resonance of his later portrayals. He set another precedent here, too, in that *Hoppy Serves a Writ* recognised him as someone marked out for death. Hoppy, as a straight-shooting good guy, preferred in general to capture his opponents alive – the movie ends with him rounding up most of the bad guys with his trademark lasso skill – but Mitchum is the first man the film sees dead, killed off in a shoot out. He dies very well, losing his hat, and spilling off of the boulder he's been hiding behind, crumbling onto the smaller rocks beneath it, his body left lying alone as the film rushes off toward the climax.

Such was Mitchum's usual fate in the wide open Hopalong land – his first non-Hoppy Western, *Beyond the Last Frontier* (1943) saw him dying, too, on a bar room floor. In one of them, though, *Bar 20*, he did play the young, decent rancher to whose aid Hoppy and his pals ride when bad men steal from his fiancée. *Bar 20* proffered the notion that Mitchum could fill the generic romantic hero role and, after making his last Hoppy movie, *Riders of the Deadline*, and drifting as actor for hire through a rapid series of war pictures, it was as a square-jawed, clean-cut cowboy hero that RKO first signed him.

Mitchum's debut RKO movie was *The Girl Rush* (1944), when he played the love interest action man opposite Frances Langford in a dum-dum comedy Western directed by Gordon Douglas and intended as a vehicle for ex-vaudevillians Wally Brown and Alan Carney, a kind of poor, poor man's Abbott and Costello. It's limp stuff, but the funniest section of the movie grows funnier with time: at the climax, for no particular reason, the good guys have to dress up as women and Mitchum, in full face powder and lipstick, is crammed into a silky, spotted prairie-style dress, a blonde wig just showing from beneath his polk bonnet.

Resembling a nightmare Goldilocks, relishing the fact he looks that way, rolling and flickering his eyes and making no attempt to disguise his baritone voice, he daintily adjusts his hat and pulls at his dress in a saloon, as a hairy old prospector tries to pick him up:

PROSPECTOR: "You're for me, ma'am. I like 'em big."

MITCHUM: "Well, now, they don't come too big for me either, bud."

PROSPECTOR: "That's good – got a voice to match your figure. I'm buyin' you the first drink sweetie-pie… I got a feelin' you and I are gonna have a lotta fun, big girl."

MITCHUM: "We-ellll, you never can tell."

After uncertainly shoe-horning him into this oddity, RKO, noting the continued popularity of B-Western serials, decided to try Mitchum as lead in a projected series based on the novels of Zane Grey, whose cheerfully adolescent tales of romance and adventure under big skies had made him by far the most popular author of Western fiction. Two films were made, both tidily directed by Edward Killy and photographed by Harry J Wild: *Nevada* (1944), in which Mitchum played Jim 'Nevada' Lacy; and *West of the Pecos* (1945), in which he played 'Pecos' Smith.

Both movies were played out against a quite majestic backdrop of distant, endless pale mountains rising heavenward from flat white plains in a hazy heat. Against this magnificent vista, Mitchum played the part of a rootin'-tootin' two-gunned, two-fisted roustabout like kids dreamed of being. In a white hat and black neckerchief, he got to gallop a handsome horse at a fearsome rate, save runaway buggies full of women, teach young kids the dangers of gaining a gunslinger's reputation, round up bad guys who had done him wrong and, in the second movie, get romantic with a young Barbara Hale, even though he'd spent most of the film thinking she was a boy.

Happily paying bills and playing cowboys and Indians, Mitchum might have ticked along in Zane Grey land indefinitely. Just after the appearance of *West of the Pecos*, however, *The Story of GI Joe* appeared in murky blood and mud, and Mitchum's performance in it made it clear that he was more than just another big, smiling bright cowboy. Re-examining those lonesome eyes, film-makers saw the glow of something calmly uncertain, something tortured and, perhaps, the glint of something capable of torture. Mitchum's disillusioned ambiguity reared up along with the restless traces of the sceptical Blackfoot blood his father bequeathed him, and branded him for the rest of his frontier career. His next Western, made on loan-out to Warner Brothers, harsh home of the Gangster picture, would definitively hammer out his aloneness, and take place in the darkest, most haunted prairies the studio could find.

Pursued

Director: Raoul Walsh, Warner Brothers, 1947

Synopsis

In turn-of-the-century New Mexico, Jeb Rand (Mitchum) hides in a ruined cabin. His wife, Thorley (Teresa Wright) arrives. Jeb's awaiting gunmen but doesn't know why they're after him. He recounts his troubled life: the first thing he remembers is hiding under floorboards as a child, seeing spurs, flashes of light and a strange woman. That woman, Thorley's mother, Ma Callum (Judith Anderson), raised him as her own, along with Thorley and her brother, Adam (John Rodney). When Jeb was 10, someone tried to shoot him — he never knew who but it was Thorley's uncle, Grant Callum (Dean Jagger). Years later, Jeb fought in the Spanish–American war. Before leaving, he confessed his love to Thorley and she revealed she felt the same. Jeb returned a wounded hero. Adam's resentment of him had grown in his absence; he forbad Jeb and Thorley's marriage. After leaving the ranch, Jeb was shot at, and killed his attacker — Adam. Years passed. Thorley, hating Jeb over Adam's death, planned to marry grocery-clerk Prentice (Harry Carey Jr). At a dance, Jeb forced Thorley to dance with him; Grant Callum persuaded Prentice to defend her honour. Prentice tried to shoot Jeb and Jeb killed him. Soon after, he started courting Thorley. She went along, planning to murder him on their wedding night but at the final moment realised she loved him. Outraged by the marriage, Grant Callum arrived with a mob to lynch Jeb. He escaped to the ruined cabin. Realising it was his original home, he now remembers: as a child, he watched Callum's men massacre his family. Callum arrives with his posse and Thorley's mother; Callum reveals the feud started when she had an adulterous affair with Jeb's father. Thorley's mother shoots Callum as he prepares to hang Jeb. Jeb and Thorley embrace.

Raoul Walsh lost an eye one night in 1929 when he was driving through the desert after a day's work on his movie *In Old Arizona* – the first significant talking Western. His headlights startled a jackrabbit badly enough to make it come flying at him through his windscreen. Still, eye patch and all, he retained an uncanny ability to see what was what. Two years later on, Walsh spotted a lanky ex-college footballer who was gracefully waltzing props around a movie set and, recognising the sort of movement that should be in pictures, cast him in the role of the slim, buck-skinned lead in his epic westward-ho! movie, *The Big Trail*. The prop hand went on to became famous as John Wayne. Ten years later, in 1941, it was Walsh who turned Humphrey Bogart into Humphrey Bogart, making him a star in *High Sierra* by showing him he should have been doing the anti-hero thing all along, playing a good bad man hitching up his trousers and rushing to death in the mountains.

In *Pursued*, a fantastic, cruel, relentlessly murky movie that crams obscure childhood trauma into flashing Freudian cowboy boots, Walsh became the first director fully to expose and to begin to explore the hunted, equivocal gloom in Mitchum's gaze. The film had a dark current of action but also called for a kind of uncertain paralysis; Mitchum had to exercise his most subtle restraint, be seen to chase ambiguous thoughts through the deep parts of his skull and feel the twinge of uncertain emotions. He also had to sing *The Streets of Laredo*, confessing:

> I'm a poor cowboy / I know I've done wrong…

In this, the first noir Western, concerned only with the interior life of its anguished protagonist as he tries to avoid the thundering hooves of fate and make sense of a planet of misery and his place in it, Mitchum came together. Walsh has the actor look at his life and confess what had been obvious in those eyes all along, that there has been 'a black dog riding my back…'

In the movie, Mitchum's life has been full of dread. The first thing he remembers is being a small child, hiding alone and scared at night beneath the floorboards of a house, looking into a confusion of darkness and seeing, close-up, anxious, shuffling feet with jagged, shiny spurs, sourceless flashes of light, a woman lying on

The sickest wedding night, with Teresa Wright.

the floor reaching out toward him, with other, more indeterminate shapes lying dim and inert beyond her. Next thing, he's pulled urgently out from that safe, horrific dark by the woman, bundled through the cold night outside and put into a strange bed, observed in lantern light by other children with suspicious eyes.

Grafted on to this other family like an awkward limb, he grows knowing he's different, suspecting that there's something wrong with him, aware that he can't love like the other kids. When, years later, he asks the woman he now calls Ma about the way he feels, her muttered words of comfort are:

"We're alone, each of us, each in our different ways."

Like so many of the films Mitchum made, *Pursued*, with its restless hero hounded through the treacherous world by half-seen phantoms and the events of long ago, could just as easily have been called *Out of the Past*. In common with the later film, it's constructed around Mitchum's soft narration of extended flashbacks as he relates his history of dim trouble to a girl he thinks he's going to lose. The crucial difference, and the element that pushes this cowboy picture deep into the anxious noir heartland, is that, for all his obsessive raking over of yesterday, this hero has no idea what happened back then, doesn't know who's hunting him, or why. He hardly even knows who he is himself.

All he knows is that he's alone, an outcast in the only family he's ever had, that his brother hates him, that he doesn't love Ma and that he feels shameful things about his sister. That wherever he goes the people he meets are already hating him and that, sometimes, as he rides along by himself through empty places, shots come firing at him out of nowhere.

"I've always got the feeling something's after me, a bad feeling…"

Mitchum emerged here as the most burdened, haunted, luckless and uncertain cowboy to ever ride the range and – with his incestuous wedding to the girl who, for all intents and purposes, has been his sister since he was three years old – one of the most screwed up.

Walsh established another precedent here. Across his career, Mitchum went through some of the most incredibly twisted marriages movies had seen: in *Where Danger Lives*, half paralysed and fading into a coma, he's forced by drunken, small-town officials into marrying a psychotic, who tries to kill him; in *Angel Face*, before a psychiatric ward filled with addled old women, he unwillingly marries a lunatic who succeeds in killing him; in *The Night of the Hunter*, he himself is the psycho, marrying a woman only to humiliate her on their wedding night, then slit her throat; in *Ryan's Daughter* he's a teacher who marries one of his young pupils, only to disappoint her afterwards by being so clumsy in the marriage bed that she subsequently goes off to sleep with the enemy, becoming an outcast, almost killed by her own community.

This *Pursued* marriage is among the sickest, though. Not only is Mitchum marrying his sister – played, with a happy face falling into tight, scrubbed bitterness by Teresa Wright, then-wife of the movie's screenwriter, Niven Busch, who also concocted the delirious, psychologically overloaded flashback Western *Duel in the Sun* (1946) – he's marrying her in the full knowledge she's planning to kill him on their wedding night.

Their courting is gruesome: Mitchum comes a-callin' on Wright after having killed both her (his) brother and her previous, ineffectual beau (both of whom had tried to kill him, for reasons he can't fathom). Her hatred of him has grown quickly, twined itself around her guilty old love and festered, and the unhappy couple trot grimly, primly around town together like listless ghosts in their surrey, going through rituals of mannerly romance in their Sunday best, faces set in death-mask repose.

On night of their wedding, after Mitchum has carried her over the threshold into the house where they grew together up as kids, Wright takes herself off to prepare to consummate her feelings. In the bedroom, removing her virgin-white dress as music curdles weirdly on the soundtrack, she arranges herself in her night gown, perfumes her neck, fixes her hair and puts a gun within reach of her side of the bed. A knock at the door and Mitchum enters silently, wrapped in shadows and carrying a silver tray bearing wine, dainty sweetmeats and something wrapped in a napkin. He leaves her the tray and takes his glass languorously to a lightless corner, sits in the dark and watches her. She peels back the napkin to find another loaded revolver; he's brought it as a honeymoon present for her to use on him, and he stands and waits as she takes her aim.

Her love–hate becomes too much, though, and, as she starts to shake, Wright misses him as he approaches. They collapse into a clinch, just as the man who, unknown to him, has been orchestrating the persecution that's fallen down on Mitchum all his life, arrives with his posse to prevent this union from taking place. All Mitchum sees, though, are yet more vague, sombre figures transpiring with guns out there in the night, coming after him the way they've always come after him, in dreams and empty plains and in the unlit wooden alleyways of the little town, for their own arcane reasons.

As the gunmen move in on the house, and Mitchum prepares to flee, Walsh – who learned about film-making under DW Griffith in the 1910s – leans back into his silent training and there follows a superb segment of escape and chase. Following Mitchum in close-up and running five minutes without a single word spoken, it's plain, poetic action, tense and fluid, prefiguring the similar voiceless hunt Josef von Sternberg would create as a centrepiece to *Macao*.

Escaping the house, Mitchum runs, vaults the corral fence and gallops off toward the desert astride a spooked horse. Reduced to a ridiculously tiny figure scurrying ant-like along the bottom of the screen beneath a towering moonscape of cliff faces, this final run takes him all the way to the present, coming out from his flashback at the place where we found him at the beginning of the movie. The opening shots surveyed this same vista, defining the psychogeography that Walsh would go on to explore succinctly: shot in Monument Valley, Walsh and James Wong Howe, the cinematographer who was responsible for the remarkable, ominous black wash of the film, manage to transform scenery familiar from John Ford Westerns and *Roadrunner* cartoons into a bleak cosmic stage, the odd butes and rocks looming like massive chunks of solidified fate, conspiring to crush and imprison Mitchum.

Alone in this desolate place stands the central location of the movie, a derelict, burned-out cabin, collapsing gradually in on itself. This is where he runs to, where we found him at the start of the film. Like an animal, he hides in a hole in this old house, waiting for his killers and realising that this devastated building is where it all began, where he hid once before, beneath the floor. His sister–wife gets there before the gunmen do, and Mitchum steps out to meet her and recite his tale of woe.

Around him, the wrecked cabin, its charred stone walls, splintered planks and rafters jutting out almost like picked bones, begins to resemble a projection of his soul. Walsh had a knack for making metaphorical, yet unpretentious use of environment – the end of *High Sierra* with Bogart incarcerated in the mythic frame of the mountains, the apocalyptic crescendo of *White Heat* (1949),

with James Cagney's raging psychosis framed against the hard steel and erupting flames of the exploding gas cylinder – here, without the movie getting arty about it, this ruined place, with the corpses buried in unmarked graves in its back yard, is Mitchum's mind. He's been hiding in that hole in the floor ever since he was a kid and he watched his family get slaughtered.

That is what he now, finally, remembers: watching gunfire strobing the dark as his folks were killed that night long ago by the one-armed man who's coming at him now with a hemp lynching rope (three years on from playing the dubious husband in *When Strangers Marry*, the vengeful killer is Dean Jagger, giving a great, straight-backed performance of cold, controlled, driven, petty nastiness). The woman crawling on the floor that night was the woman who took him in and raised him as one of her own – but it was she who caused the trouble in the first place; she cheated on her husband with Mitchum's father, provoking Jagger, her righteous brother in-law, into the feud that has dogged Mitchum ever since. Jagger has sworn to stamp out every trace of Mitchum's bloodline. That's what the black dog was: the primal image of his father and this woman, his counterfeit Ma, fooling around, the way it birthed a night of slaughter that's still not over.

In the pale morning of the movie's end, his hands are bound and the noose is around his neck, the other end of the rope tied around the bare branches of the hanging tree. Just as Jagger is about to complete the execution, though, a shot rings out; Jagger dies, shot in the back by Ma who had been brought along to witness the lynching. Mitchum is cut free, walks into the arms of his sister–wife.

The film finishes up here, as if this was a happy ending: leaving this sick, outcast couple, standing together in a stark, stretching dismal land with their carnal, joyless Ma sitting behind them, silently nursing her smoking gun, their only inheritance the ground they stand on, a bitter field of their families' corpses. Mitchum is still wearing the loose, grimy white blouse-shirt he wore to his wedding. Longish hair pushed back, confused black eyes at once apprehensive, hunted and battered by ghosts and memories, he looks like the Hamlet of the prairie.

Rachel and the Stranger

Director: Norman Foster, RKO Radio Pictures, 1947

Synopsis

Big Davey (William Holden) is a farmer on the frontier of Ohio around the mid-1820s. His wife has recently died and, although still grieving, he ventures into the nearby stockade hoping to find a new wife to help raise and school his son, Davey (Gary Gray). At the stockade, he hears about Rachel (Loretta Young), a bonds woman working to pay off her dead father's debts. Buying her out of bondage, Big Davey marries her and takes her back to the farm. While he treats Rachel with casual indifference, regarding her as little more than a housemaid, his son is overtly hostile to her. One afternoon, Big Davey's friend, Jim Fairways (Mitchum), an itinerant mountain man and trapper, wanders in from his travels in the woods. Noticing how his Big Davey ignores Rachel, Jim decides to hang around the place and takes practically to courting her. Big Davey, meanwhile, feeling the stir of jealousy, comes to regard Rachel in a new light and begins falling in love with her. Eventually, the two men come to blows over her and, disgusted, Rachel leaves the farm, heading back to the stockade. The men follow after her and Jim proposes. Just then, however, they see fire in the sky over the farm and hurry back to find the place under attack from Shawnee Indians. They manage to fight the attackers off but the cabin is burned to the ground in the process. A group of soldiers arrives from the stockade to go after the Indians and, while Rachel and Big Davey pledge their love for one another, Jim decides a domestic life is not for him, and rides off with them.

The ragged edge of civilisation. It's some time in the 1820s, someplace in the American north west. After the titles mount a tour through bright, unsettled big country vistas, the film opens on a lonely, sunny hillside dotted with the stumps of felled trees, serving as broken markers to indicate where the tip of the civilising push ends and the wilderness begins. The skies are big and spotted with slowly scudding cotton clouds. Visible over the crest of the hill rise the sharp dark shapes of nearby treetops, the tall, lightless forests of undiscovered territory.

A strange sound fades up, becoming gradually louder and clearer: ambling happily over the brow of hill out of those unknown wild woods, where he has obviously been pursing his own leisurely liberty, comes Robert Mitchum, dressed in Indian-style long-fringed buckskins, strumming a guitar and singing softly to the horse he's leading on a slack rein, a song about wandering the country, eating lunch in Can-a-dee and suppering in Mexico, making a night cap of Capricorn and snuffing out the northern lights before he sleeps, remembering a girl as he goes:

"Oh-he, O-hi, O-ho / there's a girl I used to know / I don't think much / but when I do / I think about that girl I knew..."

Rachel and the Stranger had been filmed in the summer of 1947 but it sat on the shelf for months. One of the main reasons for the delay in release was that, meanwhile, Mitchum had gotten himself busted for conspiracy to possess marijuana. Columnists were baying for his head. Across the media his name was sprayed with evil-depraved-corrupting-degenerate-reefer-madness-stink. According to the papers and the radio his career was through, and good riddance!

Mitchum's trial had still to be heard though and, perhaps figuring, what the hell, they'd made the movie and might just as well put the damn thing out, RKO released the film in early 1948, shortly before he went to court. Curious crowds turned out to see the sort of picture an immoral rampaging dope fiend would make and what they saw was a man looking like the roving free maverick spirit of their nation's childhood, leading his horse in from the untamed parts of history, singing to the world, dressed like a frontier Robin Hood, rejecting civilisation with a smile and going his own sweet rebellious way. Before long, audiences were applauding whenever Mitchum – taking third billing after Loretta Young and William Holden – appeared in the movie.

Rejecting the society of William Holden and Loretta Young.

of the film. Foster's lushly photographed 'Bonito' footage[1] had a tender, moody charcoal beauty that was new to his work and, shot in and around working Mexican bull ranches, a tremendous sense of place. Similarly, watching *Rachel...* it gets easy to lose the foreground action and become beguiled by the variously dappling and gritty bucolic backgrounds.

Out where Holden has built his isolated pioneer's cabin, Foster is intensely aware of the untold surrounding miles of natural beauty: the textures of wood and grass, blossoming trees, the play of light and shadow among leaves, the glistening cold rapids of the river. He understands the contour of the land, the quality of the air, the scale and place of this valley, where the river is in relation to the homestead, what the unseen land across the river might be like, what it might be like to sit out the night up on the ridge, listening to the forest. While horses and cattle walk their extraordinary shapes around the farm, the cabin also plays house to an expanded family of hounds and pups, and these dogs scrabble and snuffle interestingly all around, drinking from barrels of water, enlivening the frame.

Holden's homestead is a vulnerable probe satellite, flung tentatively out into the wilds from the nearby fortress-like stockade town, on constant alert against raids from Shawnee Indians. The stockade, too, when the young widower Holden visits to find himself a wife, is brought to extraordinary, very tenderly observed and meticulously cluttered background life. Around Holden in detailed layers of action move soldiers and wandering trappers, more kids with dogs, horses and cattle, men leaning on tethering posts, people about their business, women at work in vegetable gardens laid out in rows.

Shooting in longish takes, the lyrical fluidity of Foster's camera as it explores these various spaces intensifies the feeling of a real, breathing environment wrapping around the players: that fine opening tracking shot, the camera waiting for Mitchum to come over the hill, then travelling along with him as he strums his guitar, stepping through the long grass, effectively merges his character with the landscape, establishing a wilderness connection.

Gazing fondly on this character's anarchic autonomy, Norman Foster's film unwittingly turned out to be the most sympathetic, folksy frame Mitchum could possibly have been given at this point. A former actor, Foster had been directing ever since 1936, when, specialising in Oriental detectives, he worked at Twentieth Century Fox studios, turning out entries in both the *Charlie Chan* and *Mr Motto* movies. In the late 1930s, he became a friend of Orson Welles and joined Welles' working circle. As well as co-directing *Journey into Fear* (1943) with Welles at RKO, he had travelled to Mexico, a country he loved, in 1941 to shoot the a-boy-and-his-bull story *My Friend Bonito*, intended as part of Welles' planned Pan-American portmanteau documentary *It's All True*. The project was shut down by RKO but, receiving guidelines from Welles, who saw rushes in Hollywood, Foster completed most of his segment.

After shooting a couple more movies in Mexico, *Rachel and the Stranger* was his next solo Hollywood outing. While, in the well-assembled Indian raid that closes the film, some of his experience on those efficiently entertaining detective serials is felt, Welles' tuition can be seen infecting his general direction

Holden is engaged in the hard project of taming the country, building civilisation, but he needs reminding from this straight-talking, to-the-point woodland spirit to look up from his work and take stock of what's really important – why it is he's working in the first place. Holden prizes the notion of civilisation, and along with schooling and bible-learning, the thing he prizes most of all is music. The dead young wife he mourns used to play elegantly at her spinet after a day's toiling, sending abstract thought in its most beautiful expression defiantly out into the desolate nights surrounding their little home. But Holden himself doesn't understand music. It's Mitchum who, for all his wild and woodsy ways, is connected to that higher sphere, knows his way lazily around a guitar, a ballad handy for every occasion.

"I guess someone's meant to sing the life, and others to labour it..."

The same way he can appreciate music, Mitchum can appreciate the elegance of Holden's new, paid-for bride, Loretta Young, as she totes a milk yoke around the farm. Part of the appealing folksiness of Foster's movie is its offbeat, gentle, but sardonic sense of humour. Mitchum plays this earthy rover with a laid back, knowing mischievousness and as he and Holden's straight-laced pilgrim argue over Young's affections, their arguments degenerating into a flailing knockabout fist fight, they come almost to resemble a rustic Hope and Crosby, never quite misplacing the underlying affection that ties them together.

Mitchum appeared before the inquisitive public here as a mountain man, a Kit Carson-ish hero who has consciously shaken off the constricts of civilisation to move off beyond the frontier, a solitary man who perhaps even resents the intrusion of society. Alone yet again, he's gone impatiently out into the wilds, to break new paths through tangled forests, work out the secrets of the land, fighting and observing and

learning from the Indians he travels among to the extent he's practically become one – returning after a spell out alone charting the wilderness, Mitchum, hidden from sight among the trees, startles Holden and his kid by gabbling the turkey-squawks that are the Shawnee's trademark call at them.

The sight of Young, playing at her spinet, tending to laundry and helping to wash the dishes after dinner, gives Mitchum pause for thought – a home life, a family, a warm soft bed every night, a safe roof overhead rather than edgy cold nights alone beneath a canopy of leaves in some perilous wasteland place. At the end of the movie, though, he realises domesticity isn't his destiny and he's eagerly off, his Sunday clothes all tattered and torn, leading the troops from the stockade into the woods after the Shawnee war party, off to point out secret trails and signs.

He's cheerfully rejected law and a life of regulated toil to become a voluntary outsider, working his own ways for his own reasons – but he's not quite an outlaw; when he reappears every now and then, it's to bring back news or act as a guide. Just as Holden needs Mitchum to open his eyes to what's right before him, so the fledging society needs men like him, men who reject that society, if it's going to develop.

Presented as a nonconformist trailing pleasant, itinerant anarchy across the breadth of a country that's growing smaller and smaller around him, the character he plays, Jim Fairways, chimed faintly with the pre-Hollywood hoboish figure of Mitchum, the kid who grew up on a farm, ran off from home to follow a hard, but Huck Finnish existence through the Depression, served chain-gang time, became a cowboy and then got busted. To the folks crowding the dark cinemas of 1948, watching this storybook about where their cities had sprung from, things started making sense. It only stood to reason that a Jim Fairways would have picked marijuana wherever he found it growing along his lonely trail.

Blood on the Moon

Director: Robert Wise, RKO Radio Pictures, 1948

Synopsis

Jim Garry (Mitchum) rides alone through the night, narrowly avoiding some stampeding cattle. Suspicious of the stranger, the cattlemen's boss, John Lufton (Tom Tully), questions him. Lufton had been supplying meat for the nearby Indian reservation but the new Indian agent, Pindalest (Frank Faylen), has rejected his beef and demanded the herd be moved. Lufton has been attempting to take the cattle to his old grazing land but is resisted by homesteaders who, organising under Tate Reiling (Robert Preston), claim the land is theirs. Lufton knows Reiling has sent for hired gunmen, hence his suspicion. Rejecting Lufton's offer of work, Garry heads toward town. Crossing Lufton's land, he is shot at by Lufton's daughter, Amy (Barbara Bel Geddes). In town, it transpires Garry has indeed been sent for by Reiling. Reiling has conned the homesteaders into believing they're fighting for their land; in reality, he's in cahoots with Pindalest, planning to break Lufton and buy his herd cheap. Garry is unhappy with the set-up but, needing cash, agrees to help. Reiling's men stampede Lufton's herd, scattering the cattle so Lufton will be unable to regroup before the deadline. During the stampede, Fritz, son of ageing homesteader Kris Barden (Walter Brennan), is killed. Garry decides to quit. In town, he fights off Reiling's thugs when they assault Lufton and Amy. He leaves, followed by Reiling. Reiling and Garry have a vicious fight, after which Garry joins Lufton. To buy the cattleman time, he kidnaps Pindalest. Reiling and his men come after him, and Garry is knifed in the stomach. He escapes to Kris Barden's place. Barden sends for Amy, who arrives just as Reiling's men surround the house. In the stand-off Garry kills Reiling. Lufton, the homesteaders and Pindalest arrive, and Garry reveals Pindalest's duplicity. Amy and Garry plan to be married.

Rain hammers down, ceaseless, biblical black sheets, the whole valley filling up. The deliriously, inexplicably, titled *Blood on the Moon* opens on a scene that looks like the night before the flood or the night after apocalypse. *Pursued* was the first Western to chart the dark prairies but Robert Wise's range war noir picked up where Raoul Walsh's neuropathic picture left off and, feeling its way through the murk, began excavating the land. Photographed by RKO's resident poet of the shadows, Nicholas Musuraca, save for a sequence set among blinding mountain snowdrifts,

where Mitchum drags the kidnapped, perfidious Indian agent, the relentlessly dark movie could almost be taking place underground, describing some dim subterranean kingdom into which sad cowboys wander and get lost, sunlight receding into rumour.

Exemplified by the mythic *Shane* (1952), the battle over land between cattlemen and homesteaders was a standard of the Western genre. The battle speaks of the changing country: often in these movies, cattle-kings are depicted as feudal tyrants, homesteaders as the decent, hard-working citizens of the new society. Wise's film however, was less certain. Neither side seemed better or worse; the bad men were in the middle, stirring up conflict to line their own pockets. The movie explored an unusually complicated network of shifting emotions and conflicting loyalties, the struggle personified by Mitchum as, pricked by his conscience, he reluctantly opens his eyes to see himself how others see him, and recognise that Robert Preston, the closest thing to a friend he has, is actually a mean, conniving, murderous, back-stabbing son of a bitch.

While, for all its anxious confusion, *Pursued* had a grand haunted classicism, Wise's bad mood film had frenzied pulp at heart. *Blood on the Moon* is a smaller picture in conception, alive to smaller details and urgent, localised brutality. When Mitchum, playing the eternal, ambiguous outsider, comes walking his horse between the raindrops into that great opening, riding in alone out of nowhere along a smudged charcoal brow of hill beneath an oppressive sky, the scene has the grim charge of an existential metaphor. It quickly shifts focus, however, to become a scene about a specific man riding through bleak, specific rain, by showing Mitchum, stopped to set up camp in the muddy night. Stretched out by a pale, tiny fire in filthy caked chaps, sipping thankfully

at hot coffee, he pulls off his boots to reveal thick socks saturated with watery dirt. The cold, bone-weary way he does it, the way his socks look, starting to dry and stiffen, feels right. The movie shifts from myth into urgent, tired reality.

Mitchum sits gazing at nothing, until a curious thunder starts up. Suddenly, he hauls himself up into a tree, clinging to the branches as, inches beneath him, a rampaging herd of cattle stampedes across his bedding. The beleaguered cattlemen who own the beasts, warily awaiting the killers Preston has hired to run them off the land, lead Mitchum into their camp at gunpoint and attempt to interrogate him: who is he, why is he here, why didn't he follow the usual, well-travelled trade routes?

With the huge night blowing wild around them, these men are wired enough to do anything, they could club him into a shallow, muddy grave and no one would be any the wiser. In the face of this, realising that, if that's what they decide, there's nothing he can do beyond choosing the manner in which he meets his end he adopts a calm, almost polite insolence uttering little more than this statement of philosophy:

"There's no law says a man has to stick to the wagon road, is there?"

(Following the success of *Rachel and the Stranger*, *Blood on the Moon* was rushed into cinemas at the height of Mitchum marijuana madness – this blasé facing-down of his inquisitors was exactly the sort of thing audiences wanted from him at this point, fitting with that court room photo, another illumination of the Mitchum credo *You can never win, but you can choose how you go about being defeated, if you can be bothered.*)

The abominable *Sound of Music* (1965), has done much to obscure all the fantastic films Wise directed. Schooled by the finest tutors to pass through the RKO university – he was Orson Welles' editor, then started directing under the instruction of Val Lewton – in his early career, Wise turned out a series of incredible movies focusing on small underground happenings. The same year he shot *Blood on the Moon*, he made a blistering, superbly nasty little noir, *Born to Kill* (1947), starring Lawrence Tierney as a murdering ex-boxer who marries a rich girl but can't keep his mitts or mind off the glorious Claire Trevor.

In that explosively sleazy cocktail, in which everybody murdered everybody else, Tierney and Trevor were like rabid rutting dogs. The love affair in *Blood on the Moon* between Mitchum and cattle baron's daughter Barbara Bel Geddes – in the last movie she made at RKO before being fired by new boss Howard Hughes, who decided she didn't move him the way girls like Jane Russell did – is entirely more wholesome, but Wise injects a touch of that same fever into it, nonetheless.

Mitchum first encounters Bel Geddes as he's riding along, alone and oblivious, and she starts shooting at him from the riverside bushes. Clad in perky buckskins, she keeps on cocking and firing, until, dismounting, Mitchum starts unloading his own shotgun back at her, the two of them blasting away at each other until he's driven her into the water. Courtship in hot lead.

Blood on the Moon is driven by low emotion, paranoia, hate, greed, disappointment and herds of steaming cattle stampeding uncontrollably through the night. The black heart of the movie is the most brutal thing Wise ever filmed: sickened by the way Preston is using everyone – including Phyllis Thaxter, the cattleman's other daughter, whom Preston ruthlessly romances solely to extract information about her father – Mitchum quits his crew, heads back into the wilderness. Along the way he stops for a drink at a dim commissary, where Preston tracks him down. Mitchum spells out to his former buddy just what he thinks of him:

"I've seen dogs wouldn't claim you for a son…"

And they launch at each other. The following brawl is astounding. The end of a friendship, Mitchum rejecting something in himself, trying to beat up his past, it's an entirely graceless scuffle, powered by frustration, brute dumb anger and the numb hurt of bonds being severed.

Throughout the movie, Musuraca, lighting from the basement, carves darkness with precise, delicate splinters of light – during the climactic evening siege of old timer Walter Brennan's little forest cabin, every pine needle and twig seems individually lit. In this bar room fight, Musuraca lights the struggling figures in hellish silver; the cramped commissary started out gloomy but as they go at it, Mitchum knocks out the single lantern, so their scuffle develops in flickering light from the fire in the hearth.

The battle goes on for an age and has an artless realism. Along the way, Mitchum gets knocked to the floor and gashes his hand open on broken glass. The best moments come when the two men, exhausted, hang off and pause, regarding each other for a few seconds, panting, before springing at each other again. The battle ends with Mitchum kneeling on the unconscious Preston, pummelling wildly at his face. He looks lost, set to literally beat the other man's brains out.

Long after he had forgotten that kind of savagery, Wise directed Mitchum again, in *Two for the Seesaw* (1962), an autumnal love story with Mitchum as an out of town lawyer who has a sad fling with oddball Greenwich Village girl Shirley MacLaine, then decides to return to his wife in Nebraska. By then, Wise was making slow, inflated movies and, although excellently played, the film is bogged down, shackled by stage-bound origins. Several years before *Ryan's Daughter*, however, it gave Mitchum the chance to play a diffident, weak man in retreat.

His indecisive *Seesaw* character is lost to himself, cripplingly self-regarding, uncertain how to reach the people he sees living interesting-looking lives around him. This wavering inertia could easily be extremely disagreeable but Mitchum elicits sympathy, delicately maintaining a difficult balance. For all its flaws, the film has a beautiful overture, following Mitchum's lonely man on a tour of a Panavision New York, crossing the boardwalk of a melancholy Brooklyn Bridge into a monochrome Manhattan then wandering its canyons, feeding soft grey clusters of pigeons in abandoned afternoon squares.

Two for the Seesaw and *Blood on the Moon* couldn't be further apart. They look like the work of different directors but there are connections, in that, in both, Mitchum is a man alone, beat down by the world, a stranger, who slowly realises he's become a stranger to himself, too.

In *Blood on the Moon*, he's 'come over the peaks' for reasons unknown to him. He's been sent for, promised work and money, and, with nothing better to do – there are clues he had been building his own herd, but lost all his animals – he's come, wandering into other people's danger.

At the start of the movie, listening to the cattlemen's tale of bitter land disputes and hired guns, recognising the name of their enemy as the friend who sent for him, Mitchum knows he's somehow involved but he doesn't recognise himself in the description of the assassins Preston has hired. In town, when Preston fills him in on the deal and Mitchum realises he's been bought as a thug, hired for his gun, he's puzzled, a little hurt. When they look at him, it would seem, all these other people, both the homesteaders he's supposedly fighting for and the cattlemen he's fighting against, see a killer.

Eventually, of course, Mitchum rejects this notion; however, he takes his time about it. Like

Preston says, Mitchum's always had a conscience breathing down his neck but, although he feels twinges, he isn't so badly bothered by his conscience that he rejects the idea of being a mercenary out of hand. That he might be a bad man hadn't occurred to him before but he tries it on anyway, goes along with Preston's scheme in full awareness that the set-up stinks. The whole movie is about Mitchum working out which way he wants to go: good man or bad man.

It takes him a long time to decide. Finally, wishing he'd never got involved, he tries to simply leave rather than make the decision, wishing he'd remembered to never get involved in other people's affairs. When he finally chooses to do right, he does so reluctantly, loathing that he has to make the choice at all. In *Pursued* Mitchum's perplexity had been the result of squinting into the enormity of things and comprehending his own lost littleness in the face of it. In Wise's far more claustrophobic movie, the uncertainty and wearied despair glimpsed behind his uncaring facade are more to do with his becoming aware of the way the world can close in, cutting off escape.

The eternal outsider, reluctantly choosing to do right.

The Lusty Men

Director: Nicholas Ray, RKO Radio Pictures, 1952

Synopsis

Jeff McCloud (Mitchum) is a veteran rodeo rider, a world champion several times over, but penniless. After being badly wounded in a competition, he returns to his childhood home to find it's a run-down place, up for sale by its current owner Jeremiah (Burt Mustin). He meets a young couple there who are hoping to buy the place, Wes Merritt (Arthur Kennedy) and his wife, Louise (Susan Hayward). Wes follows rodeo and recognises Jeff. He gets Jeff a job on the ranch where he works and persuades him to start teaching him how to become a rodeo rider. Louise, conscious of Jeff's injuries, is dubious, but when Wes wins his first competition she agrees to support him, so long as he stops when they've made enough money to put a down payment on the house. Wes's continued success on the rodeo circuit, however, goes to his head and, enjoying the attention – and the girls – he attracts, he shows no signs of wanting to quit. Tensions between Jeff, Wes and Louise build. Jeff has fallen for Louise and asks her to leave her husband and set up home with him instead. Louise still loves her husband and pleads with Jeff to straighten Wes out before he injures himself and destroys their marriage. At a party, Wes tries to humiliate Jeff, accusing him of being too scared and too past it to still ride. The next day, Jeff enters a competition and proves himself the better rider – when his foot gets caught in his stirrup, though, he is thrown and dragged by his horse, puncturing a lung with his ribs. Jeff dies in Louise's arms and Wes, startled to his senses, quits the rodeo. He and Louise leave to buy the old farm and set up home.

We Can't Go Home Again was the name of a determinedly experimental movie Nicholas Ray, by then lecturing at New York State University, made in the early 1970s with the help of his students. Really though, mapping out a big, lonely ghost America drifted by stray, alienated souls, he had been making movies to fit that title ever since his first picture, *They Live by Night* (1948), in which two sweet, brutalised kids tried to make up home on the run as they fled the law. None of Ray's movies, however, is so explicitly about trying to make the journey home again than the movie that – with the exception of his Jane Russell gypsy flick, *Hot Blood* – bears the most baroquely trashy title in his entire oeuvre, *The Lusty Men*.

The opening section of this film about the modern last cowboys, cut-off escape routes and the sham of the cowboy myth, is among the most poetic, low-key evocations of loneliness in American cinema. Through the credits come glimpses of parades, stars and stripes, a tinny, popcorn fanfare, the blare of loudspeaker announcements, the whole yee-haw hoopla of the show. Then we see Mitchum, a veteran rider, already battered by his years on the rodeo circuit and now badly injured by a bull, nursing broken ribs. The injuries would appear to have put an end to his career and he's facing up to his end in this life. After more years than he can remember, he's reached the end of the road and he's realising that he hasn't brought anything, or anyone with him. The carnival's over and the crowds have all gone home and Mitchum walks gingerly through the deserted arena, accompanied only by the rest of the trash the spectators forgot and left behind, blowing around him sympathetically, mockingly in dusty twilight.

In a sense, he's lived the sort of life that his Paddy Carmody character in *The Sundowners* so doggedly maintains – Paddy, living by the strength of his arm, refuses to face up and plan for the future because he figures the future might never come. For the Mitchum of *The Lusty Men*, though, the future's here. He's made it to 35, so he begins to realise, with something like fear, that he might just as easily make it along a long dimming road to 70, but he's got no idea how.

With no clue about where to go from here, he tries to start over, to do the thing he knows other people living normal lives do when the rodeo is over and they file away through the exits. He heads for the only place he can conjure up when he hears the word 'home'.

Mitchum hitches a lift back to the house where he grew up. Instead of the boyhood home he had floating in his mind, however, what this tall figure in denims and cowboy hat finds is a run-down tumble of a place, the wood of the walls about ready to start rotting, the chimney falling in on itself, mean, weedy bushes reaching up to claim the place. It's no kind of home, just a house where nobody lives, with a door that's locked.

Then, in a scene that could have been sheer cornball but is tough and heartbreakingly poignant, with his head filling with memories that have been hidden away, he drops down and crawls underneath the house, into the secret place that was his kingdom-den, back when he was a kid who didn't know about broken bones and wasting money and time in bar rooms.

Down there, among the cobwebs and the shadows, he searches the joists above his head and finds what he's looking for, something that's been held safe and forgotten these past few decades, a time capsule containing the last breath of his childhood. It's an old tobacco can and he pops it open to find treasure, archaeological proof of life: a couple of coins, a toy gun, a folded-up flier for a rodeo. That creased and fading piece of paper is where the bronco-busting dream first started for him as a kid – a dream that's just ended with him rediscovering the programme again. All the years in between are just gone in a wink, for nothing, leaving nothing except, as Mitchum soon explains:

"What I started out with – a strong back and a weak mind."

Except now his back's not quite as strong.

The roots of *The Lusty Men* tangle in the ball of studio confusion that seemed endemic to RKO under Howard Hughes' regime. One of the definite origins of the story was an article about the life of rodeo cowboys in *Life* magazine by a writer called Claude Stanush, which, with Stanush's input was worked into a screenplay by hired scriptwriter David Dortort.

When the project was finally passed to Ray, however, the director, a former researcher and connoisseur of America's folk outsider communities became intrigued by the world that he caught a glimpse of in the script and commenced his own investigation of the bronco-busting lifestyle. In the end result, the film gets to know the transient rodeo circuit community as thoroughly, and as intimately, as Mitchum's *Thunder Road* understands its Appalachian moonshiners.

Ray wrote to Claude Stanush about the project and received a seven-page letter back. He then hired the hard boiled novelist Horace McCoy, on whose novels a few movies, including the ferocious, relentlessly harsh Jimmy Cagney prison-break noir *Kiss Tomorrow Goodbye* (1950) had been based, to put a script together from Stanush's *Life* article and letter, and Dortort's screenplay.

The names of Dortort and McCoy appear on the finished movie and much of the magnificent opening sequence is McCoy's, but he was working concurrently on another project and soon faded out of the film. It was also felt by the studio that his script had to be altered in order to play up the star presence of Susan Hayward, playing Louise, Arthur Kennedy's wife, who dreams only of settling down. Hayward was on loan to RKO from 20th Century Fox, and so shooting had to commence without delay.

So, as they had on *Macao*, Ray and Mitchum had to turn to making the movie up themselves as they went along, filming by day, they wrote by night. Like Mitchum, Ray had travelled the breadth of America during the Depression. Both men had a feel for the sweep of the country and, crucially for this movie, had seen the anxious faces of families forced on to uncertain highways looking only for lost safety and security and a place to settle and call their own again. *The Lusty Men* was about demythologising the figure of the free-rovin' cowboy to show the pit of loneliness beneath that image, but equally about taking the romance away from the road.

Shot with a sparse but sensuous glory by the great Lee Garmes, when, under Mitchum's tutelage, Kennedy begins making it as a rodeo rider and the trio tour the circuit, the movie paints a picture of America as a land of dusk and dawn, creeping with long shadows, consisting almost solely of dusty arenas and tent-filled trailer parks filled with the transient armies of young hopefuls and breaking-down old timers, the faces of men who are kidding themselves, the faces of the hangers-on who kid along with them,

and the more anxious faces of their women, who know that time's running out.

In this movie Mitchum, yet again, turns the most haunted eyes to America. He looks like the tall cowboy ideal: wildly proficient on horseback, decent, brave – but he's also confused, close to terror and melancholy and aching from head to foot. He's not lusty anymore, just lonely, more alone than ever, and getting scared. While Kennedy has his head full of boyish fantasies of buckaroo glory, Mitchum dreams only of settling down with Hayward – he gazes after her with a veiled, solemn, desperate longing – and rediscovering the security he left lying years ago beneath that beat-up ranch house. That dream of getting home is all that matters and, when he realises that Hayward shares a similar dream, but wants her home to be with Kennedy, he respects that, bows to it and then sacrifices himself to it. It's as close to her as he can get. In his final exit from the movie, Mitchum maybe realises that the empty, futureless arena had been his home all along.

Track of the Cat

Director: William A Wellman, Warner Brothers, 1954.

Synopsis

The Bridges family live in a remote, snowbound cabin in the Nevada mountains circa 1880. Years of isolation have taken their toll: the father (Philip Tonge) is an alcoholic; his wife (Beulah Bondi) bitterly puritanical. They have four children: Arthur (William Hopper), a gentle soul; Grace (Teresa Wright), nursing her own frustrations; Curt (Mitchum), an arrogant, dominating figure imposing his will on the others; and the timid Harold (Tab Hunter). Harold's girlfriend, Gwenn (Diana Lynn) is visiting — they intend to marry but Curt is constantly running Harold down in front of Gwenn, making it clear he intends to have her for himself. The farm is being terrorised by an unseen big cat which has been killing the cattle. The ancient Indian handy man, Joe Sam (Carl Switzer), believes the beast is the fabled 'black painter' a marauding evil spirit. Promising he'll be back to finish his business with Gwenn, Curt goes with Arthur to hunt the thing. When Arthur is killed, Curt goes on alone, following the track of the cat deep into the snowdrifts. Back at the cabin, Arthur's death has thrown the family into despair. Out in the wild, Curt continues his hunt, never seeing the animal and gradually realising he has become utterly lost. Not wishing to lose another son, Ma Bridges orders Harold to build a bonfire, to act as a beacon to guide Curt home. Miles away, he sees the glow on the horizon and begins running for it — in his panic, he falls to his death down a deep ravine. The next day, Harold and Joe Sam hunt the cat. Harold kills it and prepares to marry Gwenn.

Suddenly, he turned strange and bad. The snowy Nevada mountains could sometimes be glimpsed on the horizons of Mitchum's films. When he sat by a lakeside murmuring hopeless plans for the future in *Out of the Past*, those glacial peaks mocked him from afar. Earlier, when he galloped after clean-cut cowboy adventures across the prairies of *Nevada*, the distant white summits provided his kids' game heroics with a picture book backdrop. Always, those mountains looked unreachable, the far-off foothills of the edge of the world.

Set among those same ranges,[1] *Track of the Cat* was like gazing through a telescope at that faraway perimeter, seeing what strange sort of people would live at the wintry edge of the world and what living there might do to them. The ultimate cabin fever movie, William Wellman's frozen film was the frontier story gone profoundly wrong; it told of a little pioneer family who had trekked into the deep virgin wilderness with nothing but each other and faith in The Lord, looking to forge a new life. They started messing with the land in the American way and built themselves a hopeful little farm in the snow, constantly fighting off the blizzard elements, the Indian raids, the animal attacks.

Lonely years passed and, slowly, instead of their taming the land, the country started beating them down. The constant low whistle of the wind began to whisper about how small they were compared with the colossal, unchanging blank distances around them. Cowed and weary and tasting all their failures, the family gradually retreated inwards, holing up inside their little house and the confining rituals of family. Gradually, they went even further in, disappearing inside their own heads, inverted pioneers now, exploring unknown psychic terrain.

In there, they each found other whispers and before long they were lost, disconnected minds trapped in that little wooden house, looking suspiciously out at each other, snapping and hating but unable to imagine leaving or changing.

This is how the film finds them: the defeated father (Philip Tonge) has crawled into a whisky bottle and the mother (Beulah Bondi) into the twisting black and white words of the Old Testament. The eldest son (William Hopper) has grown himself a Christ-beard and flipped into some weird New-Age mysticism of his own devising and is not-so-secretly lusted after by his frustrated, spinster sister (Teresa Wright again; strange how movie-makers saw her programmed for incest, harbouring passions for her brothers in this and *Pursued*; keen on

The baddest seed.

second son, just as trapped as the rest but able to see their pathetic situation for what it is and taking twisted pleasure from that. He knows the bloodline has gone off and, seeing this fresh new girl, has determined to simply take her for his own, knowing there's no one around able to stop him. When he looks at her, there's an amused psychotic gleam in his eyes. He seems perversely nourished by his relentless mocking of his family, laughing himself sicker with scorn, his potential for violence a constant presence in the house.

Track of the Cat was like a Mitchum western pulled inside out. Here he was a villain settled into a nowhere land with a family around him, not planning on moving. This was an inversion of almost every other cowboy picture he made, films that presented him alone, with neither home nor family, always wandering, drifting in from somewhere else, reluctantly helping out.

Occasionally, those films would conclude with him still alone; sometimes they ended with him settling to build a family of his own. The latter had been the case with the film he made directly before Wellman's weird nightmare, *River of No Return* (1954). That movie reunited him with *Angel Face* director Otto Preminger, *Out of the Past* co-scripter Frank Fenton, and Marilyn Monroe, the Norma Jean he'd known from his Lockheed Aircraft days. The plot involved dirt farmer Mitchum, saloon singer Monroe and Mitchum's son, Tommy Rettig – most famous as the kid in Dr Seuss' surrealistic atomic-age parable *The 5,000 Fingers of Dr T* (1953)[2] – going on a deadly raft ride down the rapids of the titular waterway, as Mitchum seeks revenge on Monroe's lover, the man who stole his rifle and horse.

Preminger's movie started with Mitchum alone on the Cinemascope frontier, maintaining another isolated farm against marauding Indians. He was playing the pioneer role William Holden had played in *Rachel and the Stranger*, and, similarly, his character's wife was dead. The difference was that Mitchum had already lost her, and their son, Rettig, long before. Holden was out there building the new world; Mitchum was in self-imposed exile, his back turned to society. This was a man haunted by his past. He'd lost his family because he'd been jailed for the worst violation of the storybook Western Code: he'd shot a man in the back. Finally, despite almost raping Monroe at one point, Mitchum comes through, and is

her deranged Uncle Charlie in Hitchcock's 1943 small-town noir *Shadow of a Doubt*). The youngest son (Tab Hunter) is just a weak afterthought, ineffectual and nervous, quietly feeding birds in the yard, scared to cause a stir.

Somehow, though, his bland prettiness has attracted a girl (Diana Lynn) from the community at the foot of the mountains. She's agreed to become his fiancée and is visiting. Her presence rouses the household like fresh blood in a long-starved shark tank. Sluggish emotions are writhing. The mother regards her with barely disguised loathing, holding tight to her Bible; the father can't keep his hands off her, rubs at her as he passes; the mystic brother seems unconcerned, attuned to a higher plane, but the thought of the impending marriage bed brings Teresa Wright's suppressed mania passions bubbling up and she flutters feverishly.

Standing tall and cruel in the middle of them, dressed in black, is the baddest seed, Mitchum, the

Seeking revenge on the Cinemascope frontier: *River of No Return*.

rewarded with a new family, little Rettig by his side, Marilyn in the kitchen. What lingers, though, is his character's undercurrent, the way he goes through the movie implacably bent on murder, a serene, matter-of-fact mania.

Track of the Cat managed to bring that latent psychosis to the fore. Mitchum was a monster here, and Wellman dispensed with naturalism for the movie, to create a haunted universe fit for monsters. The place is crawling with dreams. While the physical reality of the location confers great, stark natural beauty, *Track of the Cat* was painstakingly stylised. The film represented the fulfilment of a cherished ambition for Wellman: carrying a secret penchant for Art, he had long envisioned making a black and white film in colour. Filming under these enormous grey skies amid endless, blinding snow, a cold vapour hanging constant in the air, the trees like sharp pencil marks against the frozen hills,

was as close to black and white in colour as he could get it.

Wellman purposefully eliminates all colour from the film, with the exception of the symbolic, violent red of the coat Mitchum wears and the sliver of silky yellow scarf Lynn has around her neck. All other clothes are black or white or grey. The studio-built cabin is austerely bare, with white wooden walls, white floorboards, white cupboards and white shelves, black wooden chairs, a black stove, a black table. There's a strange, piercing quality to the environment, intensified by the way that skin tones are recorded in their natural colours. The actors appear trapped in a stark nightmare.

Wellman adds a further layer of perversity with the character of Joe Sam, the ancient albino Indian whom, although he's well over 100 years old, Mitchum blithely kicks and beats; wandering voicelessly around, he's already an unsettling figure, but becomes even more bizarre when you realise he's played by former child actor Carl

Switzer (then still only 28), who had found freckled fame during the 1930s as 'Alfalfa' in the *Our Gang* shorts.[3]

The unseen black mountain cat that's stalking the farm, spooking the big black horses and killing the cattle is explained as being related to Joe Sam somehow, representing the avenging spirit of the Indian tribes run off their land by the whites. It's that – or it's the spirit of the land itself, revolting against the men trying to claim it; or it's all the repressed thoughts and feelings of this soured family combined in one ravenous black force, come to tear them to shreds.

For the vehemently unsuperstitious Mitchum, however, it's just one more thing that needs to be killed. He intends to hunt it, skin it and then drag its pelt back as a blanket for the wedding bed, onto which he'll throw the girl he plans taking from his kid brother. When the cat kills the mystic Hopper – unimpressed by his hippy vibration – Mitchum goes after the beast alone. The film splits in two: back inside the stifling cabin, the family fuss and fret, but without the electrifying jolt of Mitchum's aggression the movie begins to feel stagy around them; meanwhile, in the other film set out among the icy power of the real wild world, he tracks his cat.

Wellman's biggest mistake was in not sticking more fully to Mitchum's solitary quest; in the original novel by Walter Van Tilberg Clark, the Curt Bridges character eventually realises that, far from stalking the cat, the animal has started hunting him. This never happens in the movie – here the animal simply leads Mitchum further and further out of his depth, until this would be king of the mountain realises he's lost, doesn't know the direction home.

There are great little scenes, though, as Mitchum takes refuge at night in natural shelters at the bases of towering pine trees, with the cold darkness bearing down outside. By now he's wearing his dead brother's coat, and finds a book of poetry in the pocket. It's gloom-ridden Keats:

"When I have fears that I may cease to be…"

And, with no time for such nay-saying, he builds a pale, pathetic little fire and indulges in constructive criticism as he huddles over it, tearing out the pages and using them to feed the flames:

"Only time any good came of your moaning boy…"

Talking to himself as he scuffs along in his snowshoes, Mitchum is involved in a one man show, just him, the snow and the idea of that vengeful cat. Acting is exposed out here: intimately scrutinised, with no place to hide, no other actors to hide behind and the camouflage of dialogue at a minimum, Mitchum calls up a performance that's restrained, yet detailed and alert, suggestive of his character's shifting interior life as his customary arrogance slowly gets eaten away by the constant presence of that invisible black tiger – Mitchum calls the thing into being, just out of sight, just beyond the frame – finally degenerating into blind panic as he cracks up, wanting only to get home.

He dies stupidly, spectacularly. Lost and crumbling, close to tears, he suddenly sees a glow on the horizon where his family have built a fire to guide him. Emitting an animalistic yelp of delight, he runs blindly toward it, ground crumbling beneath him as he falls into an enormous gorge, dashed to pieces on the rocks, beaten by the weather, by the mountain, by the cat.

While the character was beaten, the actor wasn't. Mitchum had learned something here, something he would revisit, refine and resurrect. He had played bad before but his sidekick villains in the Hoppy Westerns were regular baddies, all surface, there only to be cleaned up. In this film, freed from his RKO duties and collaborating again with the director with whom he had created his only Oscar-nominated performance, he was allowed to cut loose and plunge inwards, to be evil, sick and degenerate for the first time since *When Strangers Marry*.

His wickedness here had unprecedented depth, confidence and vigour. He's plugged into sex and enjoys scaring the people around him, taunting them, laughing at their aspirations. He takes obvious, arrogant pleasure from his loathsome deviancy, almost swaggering, but cold to the bone – here, out among the snowy wastes of the edge of the world Mitchum broodingly drafted the blueprint for the unthinkable monsters he would build in *Cape Fear* and *The Night of the Hunter*.

Man with the Gun

Director: Richard Wilson, United Artists, 1955 (aka *The Trouble Shooter*)

Synopsis

Clint Tollinger (Mitchum), a gunslinger with a notorious reputation as a town tamer, drifts into Sheridan city, looking for his ex-wife, Nelly (Jan Sterling). Sheridan is being terrorised by a local cattle baron and the city fathers hire Clint to go to work and clean the thugs out of town. Clint installs himself as temporary sheriff and goes about his job, imposing martial law and killing handfuls of the rancher's men. He discovers that Nelly now runs the local cat house and demands to know what became of their daughter. She refuses to say. In the meantime, a stranger in town notes Clint's every move. Clint plays a tense waiting game, hoping to lure the rancher into Sheridan. One night, he demands an answer from Nelly and she reveals that their daughter is dead. Going berserk, Clint starts a fire in the saloon the rancher owns, almost burning the whole city down. The town turn against him but he refuses to leave. It transpires that the stranger is the rancher's lawyer and has set a trap for Clint. Finally, the rancher arrives and almost kills Clint but, with the help of a decent local, he prevails. Announcing that he's quitting his gunslinger's life, he's reunited with Nelly.

One of the strangest aspects of his journey through the West was the way Mitchum kept encountering members of the Orson Welles diaspora scattered throughout the prairies. Norman Foster and Robert Wise, both former members of the disbanded Mercury unit Welles assembled at RKO, had directed him in *Rachel and the Stranger* and *Blood on the Moon*. Now, in desolate Sheridan City, he ran into Richard Wilson, the man who had been Welles' right hand since the radio days of 1937. A very bleak film about a world gone wrong, *Man with the Gun* was Wilson's first attempt at directing. He keeps his style simple and to the point, as bare as the branches of the blasted trees on the edge of town.

The opening scene establishes the story: a man wearing a black hat rides into Sheridan, the afternoon main street empty before him, with the apprehensive townspeople looking on from doorways and darkened rooms. He pauses to shoot a little kid's dog dead, just for the hell of it, then rides on to the saloon.

Cowering in the shadow of a rogue cattle baron living beyond the town perimeter with his lawless ranch hands, the town is scared static. The cattleman has the place sewn up, making sure no one gets any ideas about expanding into the free land he sees as his domain. Anyone trying to build beyond town limits winds up shot. There's a paranoid charge; until the final scene, the cattleman, whose corruption permeates the town, remains unseen, orchestrating events from afar. When he arrives in the final reel, he's a toad-like monstrosity, crammed perversely into a tiny one-seat buggy with a fringe on top.

Filmed in plain black and white, Wilson's movie has a visual starkness, a sharp grey look that fits the tense, unusually grim mood and emphasises the emptied feeling of this depressed little city. Sheridan is a well-realised locale but conceived as a beat-down, joyless place; backgrounds are frugal, often – as in the case of the little cemetery on the edge of town with its clustering bouquet of white and black crosses – so spare as to resemble a kind of symbolic shorthand: 'graveyard', 'saloon', 'Sheriff's Office'.

There's an echo of Welles' *The Magnificent Ambersons* in Wilson's approach to the citizens of the borough. Used as a chorus to comment and push narrative along, they gather in little gossiping compositions, complaining, but never seem actually to do anything themselves. Scared and petty, their bitter, prattling laziness, as much as the villainous cowboys, is responsible for the sick state of their city. As someone comments:

"The town's rotten ripe."

SAMUEL GOLDWYN Jr. presents

ROBERT MITCHUM
The Trouble Shooter 'A'
co-starring
JAN STERLING

with KAREN SHARPE · HENRY HULL · EMILE MEYER · JOHN LUPTON · BARBARA LAWRENCE · TED DE CORSIA · JAMES WESTERFIELD · LEO GORDON

Screenplay by N. B. STONE JR. and RICHARD WILSON   Produced by SAMUEL GOLDWYN Jr.   Directed by RICHARD WILSON

AKA Man with the Gun

The cure for what ails the place comes riding in from the wilderness on a tall, pale, dappling grey Appaloosa. Mitchum was yet again playing the eternally drifting stranger. Wilson stages his entry to Sheridan as a practically shot-for-shot replay of the way that dog-killing louse entered before him, adding a dubious inflection to his ambiguity. It's unclear whether he's here to do good or bad, but he comes in a bad man's footsteps.

As it happens, he's here to do neither. The carcass of that luckless hound is still lying dumbly in the street, but, beyond noting its presence, and the mean look of the cowboys riding slowly past him, Mitchum pays it no mind. He's not looking to get involved. He's here for one reason only, following the trail of his ex-wife, wanting an answer to a question.

The local doctor recognises him. A notorious gunslinger, he's built a fearsome reputation as a town-tamer for hire. All over the country, settlements plagued by outlaws have paid for his

baneful services. The doctor mutters about the slaughter he's seen this man carry out elsewhere:

"…A mighty sick town. Clint operated on her. Patient lost a lot of blood – but lived."

Convinced, the city fathers hire him to clean up their mess.

Mitchum had built his career on playing men with pasts but this Clint Tollinger character had a more bleakly baroque background than most. Just before this movie, Mitchum had made *Track of the Cat* and *The Night of the Hunter* and, even though here playing the nominal hero, the same fluctuating malignancy that animated those films lingered in him. Playing a man hired for his strength by weaker men, his performance illustrates how close his preternatural casualness could be to an expression of contempt for those around him.

There's madness in this man. We learn that, as a kid, he watched his father, a peaceful fellow who refused to carry a gun, shot down and burned to death. That trauma set him off along a lonely path, hunting down all the bad men in the world and dishing out retribution; pretty soon, guns were all he knew (Mitchum gets in tune with the stuff of this character's life in his easy, but very careful way of handling his weapons).

Like many of the gunslingers seen in the genre, a super-vigilante, he's particularly clothes conscious, has invented a costume for himself: an ascetic dandy, he's famed for always wearing grey, head to toe. Part of his dementia expresses itself in this mania for rituals – his punctilious time-keeping plays a part in the final trap that the cattle baron sets for him.

Wandering the west, dampening the dust down with blood, killing his father's killers over and over again, this grey man has become a fabled, terrible phantom. He married a woman once – Jan Sterling, a pinched blonde beauty with a slight turn in her eye – and they had a baby daughter. The things he did for a living were so unremittingly gruesome, however, he scared his bride off. Once she was a churchy girl, unwilling to even dance for the sin of it; now, when he finds her in this Godforsaken town, he discovers she's the madam of the locale brothel (the sparkiest among her girls is Angie Dickinson, in her second movie), as if she's flung herself into the dirt as penance for knowing him.

Killing the men sent against him almost as an afterthought, all Mitchum wants to know is what has become of their little daughter, but Sterling won't tell him. So he waits. As he goes on killing, the place starts getting more civilised. A stalemate sets in between Mitchum and the rancher in his remote stronghold, tense lull time descending. Mitchum paces the town in the way of a caged cat. A little tea dance for 'the strawberry festival' rolls around and he reluctantly attends, quiff piled up like cowboy Elvis, letting a distracted grimace flit across his face when one of the local ladies hands him her 'green tomato pie'.

Finally, one night he confronts Sterling and demands his answer. Ready to hurt him, she tells him a truth he hadn't bargained on: their little girl has been dead for years. Mitchum does a tremendous piece of split-second acting as he adds the revelation that his baby is dead to the fact that his wife is the top whore in

town, then multiplies it by all the death he's seen. His face falls into a decisive set and he stalks rapidly away.

There follows an amazing but straight-faced sequence as he loses his mind. He storms the saloon, clears the place out, all except the owner, Ted De Corsia in a fine, ridiculous part as a Cajun smoothie whose most cherished possessions are the Bowie knife he kills with and the huge Parisian crystal chandelier he hangs in his place. Mitchum provokes him into a fight by smashing that treasured light fitting on the bar room floor. With flames from the broken chandelier catching spilled alcohol and beginning to lick around them, De Corsia goes for his knife and Mitchum executes him, then starts dementedly feeding the spreading fire. He clambers around, throwing bottles, falling over, pulling the bar apart, ripping paintings off the walls. He's had it now, you can see it in his face, he's far gone. Head full of flames and dead children, everything is vile and depraved and wrong, and he's determined to burn the whole town down, building the same fire that took his dad.

After he's got the white flames going good, Mitchum then throws De Corsia's corpse across his shoulders and walks outside. The place is all lit up like a party. In the jerking, sharp white firelight, townsfolk are throwing water around, in an attempt to stop the inferno from spreading. Mitchum dumps the body like a sack of dirt and stalks past, takes refuge in the shadows between two buildings, leans against the wall, watching the saloon consume itself, fiery light playing over his face.

In the charred morning, the little community, outraged by this attempted Armageddon and suddenly protesting Mitchum's campaign of extermination, have turned against their hired killer. He's had his fill of them, too.

Here, again, Wilson's 1955 film was a little ahead of its time. In classical pieces, like those exemplified by *Shane*, gunslingers had been presented as unbridled but moral outsiders, men with a skill for savagery, whom the fledgling societies needed to protect their ideals, but whose executioner's ways rendered them unable to join those communities. By the 1960s, Westerns started presenting those pioneer societies as decadent, morally fraudulent, hiring gunmen to keep their hands clean, then treating them with contempt, because the killers exposed their own hypocrisy. Meanwhile, for their part, secure in their own kill/be killed philosophy, the gunfighters started regarding the complacent weakness of these settled, passive civilised folk with disdain.

This is the case in *Man with the Gun*: the town tells Mitchum to leave. But they're too late, by now, he's no longer working for them. He's risen far above the concerns of these little bland-faced men and their committee decisions, ignores them and carries on, engaged on his own private programme of eradication, determined to wipe out every last bad man. If that means laying waste to Sheridan City in the process, so be it.

Accordingly, in this final section the town becomes eerily empty – the citizens are now hiding both from the rancher and from the terminator unleashed among them. By the final shoot-out, the whole community seems to be cringing indoors, peering through lace curtains. Wilson stages the climactic battle as a tightly-strung, suspenseful affair. Mitchum, although wounded, prevails. As he lies in the street, Jan Sterling runs to him. Looking up at her, he renounces his life as a gunfighter and so – with his killing ways, her life of prostitution and the death of their daughter all forgotten – it looks like they're back together, ready to settle in Sheridan for a happy life. Maybe Mitchum will become sheriff.

It's unbelievable, though. The film never recovers from that night of fire. *Man with the Gun* ended in that inferno, as Mitchum went about constructing hell. The real closing scene of this story was that incredible close-up of him as he settled back and regarded his handiwork, a wild loner resting in the shadows, his face a rictus of blank psychosis, the ghosts of all his victims crowding his satisfied eyes, watching the whole damn world burn.

Westerns

The Wonderful Country

Director: Robert Parrish, United Artists, 1959

Synopsis

Around 1880, Martin Brady (Mitchum) is an American who years ago fled into Mexico after killing his father's murderer. He works as a gunman for the Castro brothers, Cipriano (Pedro Armendariz) and Victor (Victor Mendoza), who control northern Mexico. Travelling north to buy them rifles, he breaks his leg when his horse is spooked by a tumbleweed and stays in a Texas town while the break heals. Major Colton (Gary Merrill), who commands a local cavalry unit of Buffalo Soldiers, questions him about the Castros but Brady tells him nothing. Captain Rukker (Albert Dekker) of the Texas rangers recognises Brady and tells him the charges against him were dropped years ago – he can return to the States a free man. Brady begins an affair with Major Colton's frustrated wife, Ellen (Julie London), and gossip fills the town. When a friend of Brady's defends his name, he is killed. Brady kills his friend's murderer and flees south again. He discovers relations have soured between the Castros. Months pass. With the help of railroad money, the Major has come south hunting Apaches. Cipriano Castro orders Brady to kill Victor; Brady refuses and Castro men are sent after him. As he flees, he encounters the remnants of the critically wounded Major Colton's forces, decimated by Apaches. Brady guides the soldiers safely to a US camp but Colton dies. Brady finds Ellen and tells her. She returns north. Cipriano Castro is killed by Victor, who demands the US army turn Brady over. Brady flees again. At the river, he is attacked by one of Victor's assassins. He kills the man but his beloved horse, Lágrimas, is injured. Brady sadly puts the horse out of its misery, and wades into the river, heading for the US.

A silhouette land spreads out beneath enormous skies, big clouds bruised pink by unseen sunset, the only thing moving a solitary tumbleweed, skipping headlong over the plains, driven by desolate winds that blow the dust from south to north, then later from north to south again. The dust blows forward and the dust blows back and *The Wonderful Country* moves with it. Directed by Robert Parrish and produced by Robert Mitchum, the film is just as tangled and as plain as that rootless ball of brush, moving in patterns just as unpredictable, drifting one way then suddenly changing direction, going back over the same ground, never arriving anywhere, picking up interesting litter as it goes.

In this somewhat odd, tough, but romantically melancholy borderline movie, it's as if Mitchum consciously set out to define his equivocal, causeless, nomadic-outsider Western character; or rather, refine it to essentials. Nudged around by the gritty gusts of fate he is, of course, playing that tumbleweed, a man without a home drifting aimlessly, helplessly back and forth between the US and Mexico across a metaphorical Rio Grande. A perpetual immigrant with eyes that slide downwards, riding a big black horse called *Lágrimas* – Spanish for 'Tears' – trying to work out which side of the little river he belongs.

Parrish's film plugs into Mitchum's well-established Mexican connection. The bolt for the border had been such a recurrent motif of his RKO noirs that the imagined landscapes of the country beyond seemed his longed-for natural habitat. The idea of Mexico those films subscribed to – a land of wild hope and new beginnings; of refuge from law; of chance violence and dangerous freedoms; of escape from Americanism – had itself originally been developed, and would continue to be explored, across countless Westerns. As the titles of the earliest, such as *The Greaser's Revenge* (1914), made transparent, there was from the first a racist slant in the depiction of Mexico's 'exoticism'. In early Westerns, the country was predominantly a lawless adventure land with a running supply of lazy, dirty, no-good bandit thugs for busily clean-cut Yankee buckaroos to defeat.

By the 1960s, though, the imagined lawlessness of Mexico had come to be regarded through rose-tinted camera lenses. As film-makers continued to explore the idea of the increasingly civilised west outgrowing, or growing too small for, the gunslingers and other

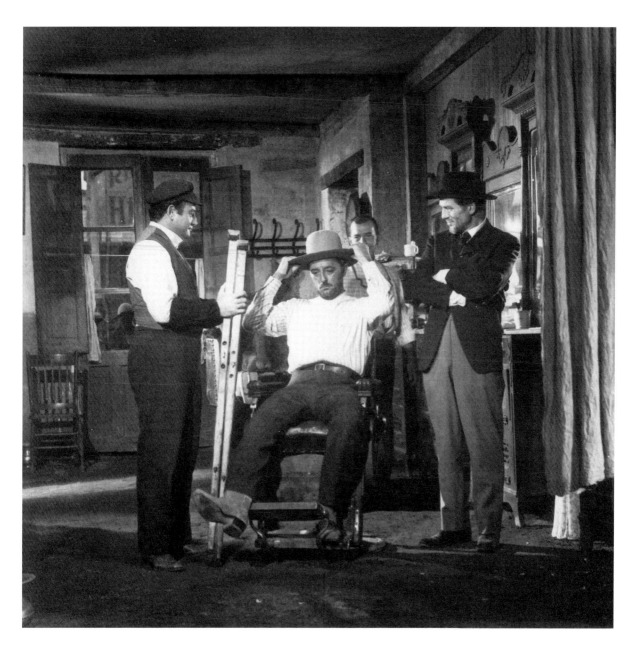

Shedding Mexican skin under the eye of Charles McGraw (right) and Tom Lea (behind chair).

dangerous men who had rendered it safe in the first place, a sub-genre of South-Westerns, or 'Professional Westerns' – so called because of the mercenary occupations of their protagonists – appeared. These out-of-time characters headed below the border into an unstable, anarchic, revolution-wracked land where they could still exercise their martial skills, partly as a way of making cash – mostly because it was a landscape in which they still made sense.

Down there, from *The Magnificent Seven* (1960) to *The Wild Bunch* (1969) – the latter a film Mitchum turned down – bruised, cynical, but ultimately idealistic killers found fresh fledgling societies needing saving, things to believe in and variously apocalyptic forms of spiritual renewal. For all their philanthropic bent, most of these films bought the supremacist line: the paternalistic gringos with their superior skills helped out lowly peasants, taught them how to shoot straight or fought their battles for them, were responsible for making their society safe.

The Western that was made by Mitchum before Parrish's movie, *Bandido* (1956), vaguely fitted this altruistic–mercenary mould. In that good-looking film, co-produced by Mitchum and briskly directed by Richard Fleischer, he played a soldier of fortune drifting through the Mexican Revolution, eventually shedding some cynicism, throwing in with the rebels and helping them defeat a gun-running Yankee who'd been supplying the forces of oppression. Later, in *Villa Rides!* (1968) – a disappointing movie co-written by *Chinatown*'s Robert Towne and Sam Peckinpah, poet laureate of the Mexico-as-savage-sunset-land genre – he'd play much the same part, helping Pancho Villa (Yul Brynner, with hair) further the revolution as a wandering aviator for hire.

The Wonderful Country, however, mounted a far more complex, self-contradictory exploration of Mexico and this American's relationship with it. Across his career, with his jail time and hip refusal, Mitchum had come to represent a shadowier America than most movie stars; Mexico meanwhile had been imagined as the United States' shadow. This movie merged the two. Mitchum became Mexico, affected and reflected by the landscape.

The title of the movie seems intended with little irony and certainly, the quite beautiful cinematography by Floyd Crosby (father of singer David, of Crosby, Stills, Nash and Young fame) makes a rhapsody of endless green grasslands and bare deserts, mountains, big skies and low clouds, hazy grey mornings and purple rivers at night. Crosby had started his career shooting some of Robert Flaherty's pioneering documentaries, and that documentary training informs the eye regarding this landscape, and, particularly, a vibrant fiesta, the restless camera exploring excited faces and skull masks, lit up by fire and fireworks and firecracker bulls.

In his noir films, Mitchum sought escape into a freer country hanging like a mirage across the border from the bankrupt States; this film – in which he played a man who snuck south to avoid being prosecuted for murder – picked up the story long years after, to see what might have become of him down there. For one thing, his memories of the States have faded into myth and the cycle has repeated; now he's imagining a land of freedom *north* of the border.

Unlike the professionals who came after him, he hadn't strutted into Mexico like a cocksure

executioner touting for work, and doesn't stride untouched through the country as an ambassador for US arrogance. Instead, partly overwhelmed by the place, partly in love with it, he 'went native'. Not only does he sport a gloriously outsized sombrero, he speaks like a Mexican: along with the slow healing of his leg, the movie signals the passage of time by the way that, the longer he spends north of the Rio Grande, the more his Mexican accent fades, and vice-versa.

He makes his living down there dejectedly killing for money, but he's not regarded by his Mexican employers as a specialist. They see him as just another lowly pistolero – lower than most, in fact, because, recognising desperate, stray-dog sadness in this man without country, they treat him with some contempt.

Meanwhile, when Mitchum reappears from his southern exile, his fellow Americans recoil from the sight. His 'Mexicanisation' is so complete that, when he lapses into a fever dream having broken his leg, his unconscious gibberish comes out in Spanish. Just a generation on from the defeat at the Alamo, this confusing, filthy figure appears to have rejected their civilisation and gone over to the other side, stirring lynching tendencies: 'What's a Mexican doing with a horse like that?' Both societies demand that he change – his clothes, his bearing – become more like them. His ability to see similarities through the differences, to almost, but not quite, fit either community leaves him outcast by both.

Importantly, though, not everyone he meets judges and rejects him. On his travels he sees bad and good, weak and strong characters on either side of the border; in other words, individuals: some lend a helping hand, some try to kill him, some have little to do with him at all.

As he covers the 200-mile sweep from Texas to Durango Mitchum encounters a lot of people – and continually along the sad countryside he finds people as lost as himself: the cavalry troop preparing to fight the Apaches is an all-black outfit, Buffalo Soldiers, who until recently would have been slaves and who have found that freedom and equality don't yet go together; the white Major who commands them and his wife move constantly because their loveless marriage has pushed her into a scandalous string of affairs (a gossip sneers, 'back in Missouri… she had everyone but the flagpole'); a mild, recently arrived German immigrant tries to make friends to cover his crushing loneliness.

Enumerating the subplots around Mitchum's drifter's dilemma would suggest *The Wonderful Country* had a truly operatic sweep: the Apache wars, gun running, revolution, homesick Germans, bandits, the coming of the railroad, an adulterous love affair, the Texas Rangers, Buffalo Soldiers, revenge killings, man hunts… Instead, however, the film has an almost jazzy approach. Familiar themes are established, only for the picture to glance off them, then drift away along its own path.

This deliberately inconsequential flow is particularly modern and is carried through to the smallest details. Moments are set up, then nothing is made of them: the doctor who heals Mitchum's leg is an alcoholic but his alcoholism isn't shoehorned into a plot point and, although presented like a major player, he disappears when Mitchum disappears from his locale. When Mitchum is alone in the little parlour the newly arrived Major's wife has set up at the fort, he's drawn to her piano, lifts the lid and is about to play, until, hearing someone approaching, he snatches his hand away. It's a privileged fragment, witnessed by no one, soon forgotten by the film – but not the viewer: when he reaches a finger toward that piano, an entire history is suggested.

Dialogue, too, follows this natural, awkward, unexpected drift: time and again – when Mitchum's affair with the Major's wife is about to become serious, when one of the Castros commands him to go on a mission to kill the other – suggested scenarios that look as though they could develop into major plot crises are instantly diffused, Mitchum muttering, 'I won't do it… I don't want to get into trouble…'

Mitchum's presence as producer of the movie may account for its confidently offbeat nature. The casting is particularly lively: that whiskyed-up doctor is Charles McGraw, the great, gravel-voiced, rough-hewn actor Mitchum had known from films like *Blood on the Moon* and *His Kind of Woman*; the despondent Major's wife is Julie London, the strangely sexy torch singer, her eyes so far apart as to be almost on the sides of her head; the town barber is Tom Lea, on whose novel the whole thing was based; and prominent among the Buffalo Soldiers is the ageless Leroy Robert 'Satchel' Paige, probably the greatest, most storied baseball pitcher to ever play the American game. There's an emphasis on interesting faces throughout – lots of close-ups, the camera particularly fascinated by dried-blood gunk leaking from Mitchum's nostril early on. This, coupled with the way in which the film plays constantly with symbols and archetypes, the casual humour cutting through the sadness and the way in which Mitchum's lonesome stranger has been pared down almost to abstraction, pushes the film to the verge of the stylisation of the Spaghetti style waiting to be born in *A Fistful of Dollars* (1964).

However, at heart there's an old-fashioned cowboy romanticism. At the fade, on the Mexican side of the Rio Grande, sadly shooting his beloved, wounded horse called Tears without a muscle in his face moving, laying down his sombrero and his gun and wading into the cleansing water, Mitchum manages to be simultaneously a symbol for everything lost and lonely seeking redemption, and a specific, lonely man, trying finally to head home. Had a Sam Peckinpah or a Sergio Leone directed this odd, half-forgotten movie, cineastes would cherish it as a masterpiece of a mess.

El Dorado

Director: Howard Hawks, Paramount Pictures, 1967

Synopsis

Ageing gunslinger Cole Thornton (John Wayne) arrives in El Dorado and is confronted by the sheriff, his old friend JP Harrah (Mitchum). An ex-gunfighter, JP wants to know why Cole's come – he tells him he's been hired by cattle baron Bart Jason (Ed Asner) to settle a dispute. JP informs him Jason is trying to force farmer Kevin MacDonald (RG Armstrong) off his land; if Cole works for Jason, he'll have to kill JP. Cole tells Jason the deal's off. Returning, he's fired on, shoots back and finds he's mortally wounded MacDonald's youngest son. Cole delivers the boy's body to the MacDonalds. As he leaves, MacDonald's daughter shoots him in the back, wounding him. Months later, in another part of Texas, Cole watches young gambler Mississippi (James Caan) triumph with his knife in a showdown with a man who murdered his friend. Among the dead man's companions is Nelse McCloud (Christopher George), a gunfighter who recognises Cole. McCloud is going to work for Jason, informing Cole the once-feared sheriff JP Harrah is now a drunk. Cole rides to aid JP, followed by Mississippi; en route, Mississippi discovers that, since being shot, Cole suffers paralysing fits. They find JP a pathetic drunk but, with the aid of his deputy, Bull (Arthur Hunnicutt), sober him up and fend off an attack by Jason's men, taking the cattleman prisoner. Their jailhouse comes under siege and JP is shot in the leg. Patrolling one night, Cole suffers an attack and is captured by Jason's men, McCloud among them. They exchange him for the cattleman. With the MacDonalds riding into town to confront Jason, a bloodbath seems inevitable. In a last-ditch attempt, Cole, half-paralysed, JP, on crutches, Mississippi, unable to use a gun, and Bull, armed with a bow and arrow, attack Jason and his men and triumph. The following morning, Cole and JP hobble around together on their crutches.

All through *El Dorado*, while John Wayne and Robert Mitchum look on bemused, James Caan, playing the young knife-throwing gambler who's useless with a gun and wears a goofy hat, recites from Edgar Allen Poe's 1849 poem of the same title. Poe's verse tells of a quixotic knight who spends his life seeking the fabled golden city never finding it, until '*He grew so old... and o'er his heart fell a shadow...*' and, strength failing, he meets a shade, '*a pilgrim shadow*', who points him in the direction he must now journey:

"Over the mountains of the moon / Down the valley of the shadow / Ride, boldly ride... If you seek for El Dorado"

Howard Hawks was 71 when he released the film, his penultimate; Wayne was 60 and Mitchum, although a relative spring-chicken, had just notched up his half-century. Filled with flaring sunset colours that echo the mythic picture-book paintings of the title sequence – purples, midnight blues, lantern-yellow golds, autumnal reds and oranges – Hawks' *El Dorado* is all about men considering that final, impossible journey, down the valley of the shadow.

However, although leisurely paced – the film finds the weary-boned negative of the famous machine-gun clatter of Hawks films like *Scarface* (1932) and *His Girl Friday* (1940) – and replete with allusions to the onset of age and infirmity, this old man's movie is not some mournful elegy. Here, as in all of Hawks' movies, it's not arriving, winning the game or fulfilling the hopeless quest that counts, it's the manner of the journey taken, the road-going getting there. Poe's pilgrim shadow captures the attitude, telling the tired knight not just where to go, but how: '*Ride, boldly ride*'. To which advice Hawks would add, 'And stop off and have a little fun on the way.'

As *El Dorado* exemplifies, the fun of a movie was of over-riding importance to Hawks. Working again with *Big Sleep* co-writer Leigh Brackett, he initially adapted the film from Harry Brown's cowboy tragedy *The Stars in Their Courses*, but soon realised something was wrong – in following Brown's book, they forgot to leave any room for fun to sneak in. As he put it, 'everybody got killed.'[1]

So, they went back into the thing, taking it apart, loosening it up and eventually throwing most of Brown away – except, perversely, one of

Fun, Hawks-style: the
boozehound awaits
John Wayne's
hangover cure.

the grimmest scenes, the early encounter that
motivates much of the action, when Wayne shoots
a young boy in the stomach and, rather than endure
the pain, the kid kills himself.

Hawks' *The Big Sleep* movie had its share of
meanness and killing, too; all his movies
contained tough stuff – enough to provide the
spice of action but not enough to sour things,
reconfirming how sweet life could be for
people good enough not to get killed, good
enough not to be too mean. As Chandler's
novel had provided a framework for a movie
in which a detective story was the last thing
on anyone's mind, the script Hawks and
Brackett came up with was less about cowboys
defending a jail, than an excuse for Hawks to
get on set with good actors and his usual parcel
of abiding concerns, to see what might happen.

Hawks had wanted Mitchum at least once
before, for *The Big Sky* (1952), but the actor
turned it down because of his friendship with
the author of the source novel, AB Guthrie.
Hawks had adapted Guthrie's book as he did
Brown's, by throwing most of it away, and
Guthrie had been less than pleased. Mitchum
appeared in another Guthrie adaptation, though,
The Way West (1967), the movie he made just
before *El Dorado*. The tale of a wagon train of
decent folk like Richard Widmark striking out
from Missouri to Oregon under Kirk Douglas's
authoritarian eye, that film had been Mitchum's
first Western since *The Wonderful Country*, a
gap of eight years, by far the longest he'd spent
out the saddle so far in his career.

Again, he played an unabashed outsider:
wearing buckskins that could have been the

remnants of his *Rachel and the Stranger* gear, he was a once-famous guide living alone in the wilderness, going slowly blind and mourning the death of his wife – a Blackfoot woman, part of the tribe he was partly descended from. He agrees to lead the pioneers west but ultimately rejects their new civilisation, opting to head alone for Blackfoot country to join people as sceptical about the new Americans as he himself. He left the film with his eyes failing, but seeing a fine old age:

"I got me a few dim years left – after that, I'll get myself a couple of young wives and a fishin' pole and make camp alongside a waterfall…"

Mitchum plays with a light, observant touch however, directed by Andrew V McLaglen, as

it rolls its starry cast through the magnificent scenery, *The Way West* trips over itself, self-conscious about being an epic. In this, it was exactly the opposite of *El Dorado*, which treats its stars as if they had wandered into a cheerful serial B-Western.

John Wayne, who did his first great acting for Hawks in *Red River* (1948) and would go on to make five films with the director, agreed to the new picture long before it was even written. Hawks pitched *El Dorado* to Mitchum by telephone, knowing he needed a presence strong enough to balance Wayne in order for the movie to work:

HAWKS: "Bob, I'm making a picture with Duke Wayne this summer in Old Tucson – are you available?"

Hawks did tell stories but he denied plot. From before *Scarface* (1932) to beyond *El Dorado*, his preferred subject was the band apart, a group within society, but not touching the sides, forming a society of their own: gangsters, newspaper reporters, cowboys ushering cattle from Texas to Abilene, isolated flyers piloting mail bags around Colombian mountains, misfit fighters defending a jailhouse. He used these professional cabals to examine the nature of professionalism itself but more particularly the relationship between men – always men, though if there was an interesting enough woman around, he would investigate what happened between the men and her – patterns of friendship and loyalty, of disappointment and of stoic acceptance.

His movies were less consequential strings of incidents than explorations of character. There would be electric flurries of action – here there's a fantastic shoot-out as the rag-tag heroes track down bad guys to a church tower, bullets hammering out a clamouring atonal melody on the bells – but far more time spent watching people talking, chewing over the actions just taken, or still to be made. Character was defined through action and reaction – one of the most eloquent passages in *El Dorado* comes when, with Mitchum's alcoholic hands shaking from the DTs, Wayne silently loads his gun for him, the way that, back in *Rio Bravo* (1959), the last Western he'd made with Hawks, Wayne had rolled a cigarette for the similarly afflicted Dean Martin.

Long before *El Dorado*, Hawks had started to revisit situations, types and gestures ritualistically in his movies. In revamping their abortive adaptation of Harry Brown's book, he and Brackett saw no reason not to simply drag out the skeleton of *Rio Bravo* – in which sheriff Wayne defended a jail helped by toothless old coot Walter Brennan, young gunslinger Ricky Nelson and Wayne's slowly recovering drunk deputy, Dean Martin – and hang the new movie on it.

This time, Mitchum would play the drunk; although being part of a group was anathema to the Mitchum persona, and the movie altered slightly because of that. Martin's very aware performance in *Rio Bravo*, with the actor exploring a hitherto concealed uncertainty as he painfully drags himself toward cocksure redemption to help Wayne, gave the friendship explored in that film a very different character to the more cantankerously even-footed relationship between Wayne and Mitchum in *El Dorado*.

Mitchum's booze hound was a meaner creature than the pathetic, shaking wretch Martin played so superbly, perversely enjoying his debasement and bitterly going out of his way to refuse the help his buddies foist upon him nevertheless. In *Rio Bravo*, Martin gets himself from shaking, bottom-of-the-barrel alcoholism to a point where he has calm-nerved courage enough to pour a drink back into a bottle without spilling a drop. In *El Dorado*, Mitchum's journey is somewhat different: from an utterly liquored-up state of quivering foul stupefaction, to the place where he can... pour a couple of whiskys and raise a glass with Arthur Hunnicutt to the fact that they've both managed to get through the film alive. This guy isn't going to swear off and start pouring drinks back into the bottle. Christ, he might have had a little bit of a problem there but there's no reason to go getting silly about it.

At the start of the movie, before he's climbed inside the bottle, he saunters the main street straight and sure, dressed in grey, toting his rifle like he's just wandered off *Man with the Gun*. Indeed, he could be the same town-tamer 12 years on, decided to settle down and become sheriff after all, but still eager for trouble to test himself against. As in the earlier picture, he's renowned as a gunfighter but, as befits the actor, it's a shadowy renown, secret knowledge shared among a few. He's a gunslinger's gunslinger, as is made clear when Wayne, as gunman Cole Thornton, encounters Christopher George, the rival shootist who will be sent against them:

GEORGE: "There's only three men I know with
that kind of speed. One's dead. The other's me.
And the third's Cole Thornton."

WAYNE: "There's a fourth..."

By the time of this exchange, though, the news that Mitchum's no good anymore has spread. He hasn't

been sober for months, binging because a woman made a chump of him, and Wayne, feeling the tug of loyalty, heads back to help him out. That's the whole movie: one guy looking out for another.

Arriving in Mitchum's town, Wayne is told the story by Charlene Holt, Madame of the local brothel, but interrupts her to say he's heard it before. We all have, in that it's easy to picture a Jane Greer in Wayne's description of the girls who messed up Mitchum before:

"She probably had big sad eyes and a long sad story: that's his type."

By now Mitchum is broken and downcast, crawled inside himself and not caring anymore. Drunk and hungover simultaneously, he's unshaven, sweating, stinking, with an unhealthily reddened face tinged grey, saddlebags beneath each eye with a big, bloated belly stretching his grimy long johns. A shiveringly detailed performance of a thick-tongued, thick-fingered, thick-headed state, it's Max Cady in the morning, with a slapstick twist.

Roused by Wayne, but still soused, Mitchum realises the town has been laughing at him. Stung, sucking in his gut and peering through an alcohol haze, he goes to the saloon where bad guys congregate and, falling into mean, sour madness, begins breaking heads with his rifle butt.

"…Let me hear you laugh…"

As he goes about his beating, there's a very real, sneering, ugliness to this scene; with echoes of

A grouchy cartoon cat in a too-small tub.

the grim movie that Hawks originally scripted play around it. Still bewildered in his fuzzy state, however, as Mitchum returns to the jailhouse from this confrontation, with the villainous cattle baron as his prisoner and roughnecks preparing to lay siege, he discovers that, instead of a tense, tragic *High Noon*, he's somehow become involved in nothing so much as a Hopalong Cassidy picture scripted by lazy angels: there's Arthur Hunnicutt gabbing away in the old coot role once filled by Andy Clyde; there's James Caan in a souped-up, cooled-down mod version of the greenish youngster; and there's John Wayne holding down the Hoppy role, but keen to share duties with Mitchum when he sobers up.

From here, an easygoing celebration of phlegmatic friendship claims the film. Hawks preferred building humour less from having people lobbing gag-filled dialogue than from the way they react to the situations they find themselves in, a straight-faced, odd, sneaking-up kind of comedy Mitchum was extremely adept at: consider his gut-running hangover; the look on his face when he's shot in the leg and the doctor leaves him sitting with his finger plugging up the bullet hole while he examines an older, but more interesting bullet wound in Wayne's back; the moment when Mitchum and Hunnicutt are hiding in the bar room at the end of the movie, awaiting the final shoot-out, and start discussing how bad the saloon's piano player is.

Hawks made a rule of regarding the script as simply a place to start. When he had actors good enough, he encouraged them to mess a scene around, throw stuff in, make it more fun. Because he considered Mitchum 'a pretty good singer',[3] he included a scene where everyone gets together in the sheriff's bare little house for a sing song – he subsequently cut the moment, deciding the sheriff shouldn't sing, but he left the edges of the scene in, and Mitchum can still be seen sitting at his piano, flanked by a couple of guitar players for no particular reason. Later, waiting for the gunmen to come after them, he noodles a skimpy melody across a few keys, the sort of little half-tune he might have picked out on Julie London's piano in *The Wonderful Country* if he hadn't been interrupted.

Hawks teased out the quick writer in Mitchum, who composed the great sequence when he sits in

the tiny tin bath in the sheriff's office, trying to scrub off his months-long bender. A grouchy cartoon cat huddled in the too-small tub, still sporting the battered, unclaimed hat he'd found in the jailhouse, his bad leg sticking out, he's plagued by a stream of chirruping visitors, all bearing bars of soap, and when one of them, Charlene Holt, has to go out the back door of the place and comes walking past his tub, Mitchum improvises a fine turn-around bit of business, putting his hands over *his own* eyes to cover his modesty.

The director called on Mitchum again on the last day of filming to write their way out of a continuity glitch: the crutch Mitchum had been using after taking the bullet in his leg had switched from being under his right arm to his left throughout the picture (though the wound stays put, in the right leg).

Mitchum's solution was deft and obvious, spinning a little gold from the mistake: by the end of the film, Wayne, too, has a leg full of buckshot, courtesy James Caan's poor aim. As Wayne props himself on his own crutch, Mitchum scolds him – the two relate like a happily bitching old married couple throughout – that he's got it under the wrong arm. Wayne throws back:

"Well how would *you* know, you've been usin' it first under one arm then the other…"

That's how it ends, Wayne and Mitchum, both leaning on their crutches, walking main street together – Wayne has a date with Holt, Mitchum is waiting for another sad-eyed girl to blow into town. Around the movie they're in, all manner of new waves were breaking: 1967 was the year Arthur Penn's *Bonnie and Clyde* brought hip new violence to the American screen; the year before, with *The Good the Bad and the Ugly*, the Spaghetti Western reached a radical crescendo Sergio Leone would soon follow in 1968 with his sad, savvy *Once Upon a Time in the West*. Meanwhile, out beyond the edge of town, Sam Peckinpah was gearing up for his apocalyptic cowboy death-trip, *The Wild Bunch*.

The prevailing message was that the age of innocence was over. Ambling amiably along with its ageing stars and Hoppy rhythms, *El Dorado* seemed to ignore all that. However, Hawks' movies had been hip to post-modernist moves for decades. He made his films fun to

watch by expressing the fun of making them, incorporating the things thought up on set, teasing with his stars' images, toying with cliché. *El Dorado* retained the innocence of a dime book Western, while simultaneously displaying a self-reflexive playfulness – but the movie did this without making a big fuss of it.

Like his actors, Hawks didn't see the need for fuss. Some things were just obvious: that early scene, when the gut-shot kid kills himself rather than feel anymore pain, lays out a lesson about violence and its consequences that haunts Wayne for the rest of this film.

Another obvious thing: watching this movie, it's impossible not to notice the way in which John Wayne's breathing is already becoming painfully laboured. For a comment on the end of the Western, that's all you need. Showing Wayne

looking old, limping around half-paralysed and accompanied by sore-headed, shaking Mitchum in not much better shape, was in its way as radical as Leone's casting the perennially decent Henry Fonda as a sadistic killer in *Once Upon a Time....*

At one point in *El Dorado*, Wayne turns to Caan, the poetry fan, and jeers:

"'Ride, Boldly ride'? Well, it don't work out like that"

That's the same message all the hotshot new Westerns were determined to put across – still, watching Mitchum and Wayne, grizzled cowboy knights hobbling along alone together and undefeated, you know that, deep down, they kinda like the notion.

Grizzled cowboy knights, hobbling, but undefeated.

Dead Man

Director: Jim Jarmusch, Pandora Film, 1995

Synopsis

Falling in and out of sleep, Cleveland accountant William Blake (Johnny Depp) journeys west by train, headed for the town of Machine where he is promised a job in the Dickinson Metalworks. As he travels he has an unsettling encounter with the train's fireman (Crispin Glover), and watches other passengers shooting buffalo out the windows. In Machine, he discovers his job has gone to another man, and is sent packing by John Dickinson (Mitchum), the factory owner. Dejected, Blake meets Thel (Mili Avital) an ex-prostitute selling paper flowers. He spends the night with her but they are interrupted by Charlie (Gabriel Byrne), Thel's fiancé. Charlie shoots Thel, the bullet passing through her and lodging next to Blake's heart. Grabbing a gun, Blake kills Charlie and flees. He comes to the next day in the forest, with a half-Blackfoot, half-Blood Indian called Nobody (Gary Farmer) trying to remove the bullet from his chest. Nobody tells Blake the bullet is lodged too deep and has already killed him. Learning the accountant's name, Nobody, who was captured by white men and taken to England as a child, believes him to be the reincarnation of the visionary poet and painter. Meanwhile, in Machine, Dickinson has hired bounty hunters to kill Blake – Charlie was his son – and simultaneously posts a general reward for the accountant's head. Tracked by Dickinson's killers and regularly triumphing over other would-be assassins, as Blake and Nobody head west, the dying accountant gains a reputation as a fearsome killer. Reaching the coast, Nobody procures a canoe from a Makah village in which to send Blake off to death. As he drifts off, Blake sees Nobody and one of the bounty hunters kill each other on the shore, then floats toward the ocean, falling in and out of consciousness.

Fields and forests give way to mountains, mountains give way to cold flat deserts under flat cold skies as a black train smokes hypnotically west. An abandoned covered wagon sits rotting in miles of wilderness as the train passes, noticed only by a young, silent, uncertain passenger nodding in and out of wakefulness as endless miles fall past. Hours or days or weeks later he sees a teepee and the skeleton of a teepee, huddled together, dropping behind him on a desolate plain. Around him, the other passengers in his rocking carriage alter with the landscape: their faces and clothes gradually shed layers of civility. City duds give way to prairie costumes, until, finally, he's surrounded only by wildmen in skin and fur. He reads a magazine. An article about Italian bees. A long way till the end of the line.

A movie about heading west towards death, Jim Jarmusch's *Dead Man* was the last Robert Mitchum movie released before Mitchum died. His part is vital, but in terms of screen time, little more than a cameo. Still, there couldn't have been a more fitting film for him to have finished with.

Jarmusch's movie unfolds with the slow, disjointed logic of a dream, or a nightmare. The film mirrors itself, it begins like it ends, with the same young man who enters the film dozing on that train, Johnny Depp, making another endless journey back out the movie again, the same, but utterly changed. With this elliptical picture, Mitchum, too, came full circle, going out the way he first came in, playing a bad man in a black and white Western, but an entirely different kind of bad man, in an entirely different kind of Western.

Mitchum had stayed away from the genre for a long time. In the years immediately after *El Dorado*, however, he made a few Westerns that revisited his past: first up had come two journeys back to Mexico, playing the uncommitted outsider joining the revolution in *Villa Rides*, then – turning down Sam Peckinpah's invitation to become one of *The Wild Bunch* – teaming up with his buddy Dean Martin and director Henry Hathaway in Durango for *Five Card Stud* (1968).

In that, a modest, semi-comic cowboy thriller revolving around Martin's bemused investigation of a string of killings, he played a no-good preacher, gently kidding memories of *The Night of the Hunter*, riding into town to commit murder and set up a little house of God.

Next came two amiable oaters with director Burt Kennedy, *Young Billy Young* (1969) and *The Good Guys and the Bad Guys* (1969), filmed back-to-back and released in quick succession. Kennedy had started out as a radio writer, specialising in comedy Westerns; as a director, he continued ploughing the same furrow. An artisan rather than an artist, he nevertheless had a thorough knowledge of the Western form, and a knack for combining action, laconic humour and outright slapstick. Both these semi-spoofs resemble slightly more parodic echoes of *El Dorado.*

The first had him playing a veteran wandering lawman, searching for the killers of his son and taking Robert Walker Jr under his paternal wing and steering him toward decency. At the end, Mitchum gets to carry off saloon gal Angie Dickinson – just like John Wayne did in *Rio Bravo* and like Mitchum had Marilyn Monroe in *River of No Return.*

The Good Guys and the Bad Guys was the tale of Mitchum, as yet another ageing sheriff, forming an uneasy alliance with his old enemy, ageing gunslinger George Kennedy, to thwart a train robbery planned by a hoodlum gang of young bandits. Mitchum is marshal of a town called Progress but gets forced into retirement by politicians who feel his two-gunned law-giving is outmoded. This was an out-of-time lament for the passing of an age, featuring the totemic arrival of an early automobile – but the elegy is tempered with broad-brushed humour, gently mocking each cliché affectionately invoked. In a way, it's a cross between *El Dorado* and *Ride the High Country* (1961), Peckinpah's earliest meditation on the fall of the West and the death of honour.

Then came *The Wrath of God* (1972). This weirded-out picture was, in fact, more of a pseudo-Western. Set in the 1920s, Mitchum once again went to Mexico, once again got caught up in the local revolution, and, once again, played a psychotic man of God. The movie's pervading, dumb, but entertainingly excessive comic-book violence bespoke the heavy influence the vividly stylised mayhem of the Spaghetti Western was having. Wading through the gristle, Mitchum played a mean, alcoholic, de-frocked Catholic priest, drifting Mexico extravagantly tooled-up: he had a revolver secreted in his Bible, his

crucifix doubled as a switchblade, and, if those failed, there was always his sub-machine gun.

Mitchum becomes involved in a scheme to overthrow local despot Frank Langella, going stratospherically over the top, and ends up lashed to an enormous stone cross by barbed wire, climactically pulling the thing over so it squashes Langella to death. The film marked a sad end to the career of Rita Hayworth, already suffering the effects of Alzheimer's disease, playing the mother of a neighbourhood rebel leader. Mitchum, who had starred with Hayworth 15 years previously in a knockabout Caribbean Popeye adventure, *Fire Down Below*, had talked her into the role. For his part, he seemed to be enjoying himself but after this he quit the West, steering clear of the territory for over 20 years.

His break from the horse opera was – very – briefly interrupted in 1985 with a fleeting part as a doctor in the star-chariot television Civil War miniseries, *North and South*. In 1993, he stuck a toe back in prairie waters by providing the narration for *Tombstone*, a fine, pared-down picture retelling how Wyatt Earp and Doc Holliday took on the Clantons at the OK Corral. As sceptical, ornery, and half-interested as any old-timer telling a saloon tale should be, Mitchum's voice rumbled over the opening scenes like the sound of the Old West itself.

Then, finally, came *Dead Man* a movie set beyond the end of the line, where the West comes to an end – and, as the cyclical zen vibration of the film connotes, begins turning into the East.

Jim Jarmusch's movie stirred with old ghosts for the actor. Jarmusch had started out nursing literary ambitions, originally planning to become a poet, studying literature at New York's Columbia University. Travelling to Paris toward the end of his studies, however, he discovered he was spending more and more time trawling the archives of the Cinematheque Française and, on his return the States, enrolled on the film course at New York University. There he became first a student of, then friend and assistant to a film-maker with whom Mitchum had had one of his most productive relationships, Nicholas Ray, then in the final years of his fight against cancer.

Tall, favouring punk-rock pirate black and crowned with a shock of white hair, Jarmusch bore a passing resemblance to Ray, and like the older director, he retained a hungry and

A different kind of bad man.

wide-ranging intellectual appetite, constantly stimulated by areas out with cinema. Where Ray studied architecture and toured the country in the 1930s recording raw-boned blues men, jazzers and strange backcountry folk balladeers, Jarmusch explored avant-garde writing and travelled with the bohemian New York punk scene of the late 1970s. He was no placid Xerox acolyte, though: when Jarmusch made his first feature, *Permanent Vacation* (1982), having discussed the script with Ray, who died in the summer of 1979, he proceeded to do the opposite to whatever Ray advised.

A Jim Jarmusch movie doesn't look like a Nicholas Ray movie, but the themes obsessing Jarmusch are the same ones examined by Ray: loneliness, alienation, the brief moments when those things fade. Their films are peopled with misfits: lost, misplaced characters, unable to go home again. While his earliest movies wore their hipster veneer proudly, Jarmusch's output constitutes an extended bemused, increasingly disenchanted, but still bewitched, meditation on the nature of the US, a nation of colliding immigrants. *Dead Man*, his most poetic film, pushed this meditation to its limit.

Traces of the amused urbanite remain but the film exhibited a strange purity new to Jarmusch. Robby Muller's luminous, silvery monochrome cinematography and the production design's meticulous recreation of the late 19th century make *Dead Man* visually reminiscent of the photographs of Edward S Curtis – the greatest photographer of Indians operating at the turn of the century – the pictures somehow coming to slowly life. Made up of near static, self-contained scenes, or stanzas, each bordered by lulls of black screen, with its mesmerically slow pace, it looks like the last Western ever made, and it looks like the first.

Set around the 1870s, the America Jarmusch's film considers is a young nation, contemporary with the cowboy country of all the frontier movies before it. John Wayne is unimaginable here. Here, you'd expect to find *Waiting for Godot* playing out. The country looks ancient, decayed and sick, a place blighted by some unimaginable disaster, and listlessly anticipating another. This America would explain the haunted eyes of the young Mitchum.

The young man this time, though, is played by Johnny Depp, the passenger dozing on the train traversing this desolate nation. Rejected by his lover, his parents both dead, Depp is travelling west from Cleveland (Jarmusch's original stomping ground), done up in a plaid dude suit, to take a job as an accountant at a far flung factory. He will soon have a bullet lodged in his heart and begin to die; simultaneously he will become a hunted man. Never entirely understanding what is happening to him or why – reminiscent of the Mitchum of *Pursued* – he will be shepherded safely through the movie toward his end by Gary Farmer, playing Nobody, a half-Blood, half-Blackfoot Indian. Neither one thing nor the other, Nobody is an outcast from both warring tribes – floating around in a predicament reminiscent of the Mitchum of *The Wonderful Country*.

The person Farmer plays is neither a wild man, a mystical Earth-spirit nor a sad noble savage – he's an individual, an incredibly well-realised character, decent, messed-up, irascible, as unpredictable as life. Jarmusch's film is committed to an exploration of the Native American experience that is unprecedented in the Western genre in its respect, detail and open-handed sympathy. The subtext of the movie, the buried disaster constantly pushing through the surface, is that this nation has been founded on a holocaust, the genocide of the Native Americans (it's worth noting that, like Mitchum, Depp has Indian ancestors – his grandfather was a Cherokee).

As Neil Young's isolated shards of electric guitar knock against the images like the bones of music, the movie is appalled by this country, a country of ghosts where, anticipating the axe, even the pale bare forests look like the ghosts of forests. The landscape has witnessed apocalypse and another apocalypse is coming. As the new Americans push west, as the mass murder unfolds, the terrified country itself is in the process of being raped as a new industrial frontier is established, an assault that will go on unchecked for a century and more.

This is what awaits Depp at the end of the train tracks. He's heading to the town of Machine, a rutted, muddy place that looks like a one-horse Western town of the late 19th Century, a decaying industrial province of the late 20th Century or a cold, eternally depressed hell. He knows little about the place where he's going to work, or the man he is going to work for – John Dickinson, who built and owns the infernal metal works Machine grew up around, a looming edifice perched at the end of the main street like a gargantuan, awkward bird of doom, belching Dickensian smoke.

The grimy fireman on the train, played by Crispin Glover, leaves his furnace briefly to scare the bejesus out of Depp with omniscient, prophetic, but incomprehensible mutterings, then asks him what he's doing all the way out in Hell. Depp tells him about his job, about the letter he received from Dickinson. Glover, with furious calm, seems to recognise the name:

> "I'll tell you one thing for sure. I wouldn't trust no words writ down on no piece of paper. Specially from no Dickinson out in the town of Machine. You're just as likely to find your own grave..."

Glover's right.

Mitchum, infusing the movie with history simply by making an appearance, plays Dickinson, the famed, feared, long-insane boss man. When Depp unwittingly kills his son, Gabriel Byrne, Mitchum will send killers after him – not realising Byrne has already killed Depp, even though he's still moving – just the way killers once were sent after him, movie after movie.

Fleeing the long reach of Mitchum's wrath, Depp will become a poet and a killer, traverse a hallucinatory, absurd strip of country and ultimately fall off the edge. One of the oddest things he will see along the way is a filthy trio of demented trappers sitting by a sleepy campfire telling fairy tales and Bible stories and discussing the atrocities of the Emperor Nero. In the centre, stirring up beans and reciting the tale of Goldilocks is Iggy Pop, the Van Gogh of outsider music – wearing a grubby dress and bonnet. The scene is there to show how far gone all these people are, crushed and crazed by the endless wild wilderness and trying to remember what folks back home do, but the sight of Iggy dragged-up also works as a bizarre echo of Mitchum's first RKO Western, *The Girl Rush*, filmed over half a century before, in which he crammed himself into a bonnet and frock and made small talk.

Before all this, comes Depp's encounter with Mitchum. Jarmusch postpones the entrance of the man whose influence has been pervading the movie. After his nightmarish train ride, Depp has arrived in Machine and makes his way to the factory up a filthy main street full of godless men, coffins and animal skulls. He arrives only to be told by Mitchum's foreman, John Hurt, speaking in his Shropshire accent, that the job he was promised went to another man weeks ago. Politely bristling, Depp demands that he wants to speak to Mitchum. This sends Hurt and the rest of the boys in the outer office into gales of laughter:

"No, I, I don't think you want to do that..."

Then, for his own entertainment, Hurt sends Depp through into Mitchum's inner sanctum. The office is empty and odd: on the massive desk sits a smoking cigar and a human skull. There's a tall oil-painting of Mitchum hanging on the wall. In the corner, the safe is lying open and there are little piles of cash on the floor in front of it. An enormous stuffed bear rearing up close

by and a horned deer skull on the wall heighten the impression that the open safe is a baited trap.

Suddenly, Mitchum's unexpectedly there, peeking over the top of the desk with a shotgun levelled at Depp's belly, as if he'd been hiding under there the whole time:

"Who the hell are you, and where'd you get that clown suit, – Cleveland? What the hell are you doin' in my office? The only job you're going to get in here is pushin' up daisies from a pine box. Now git out."

Aged 78, gaunt, white-haired, saggy-faced but tall and still looking fearsomely tough, chomping constantly on a cigar, Mitchum cuts an amazing figure, like a man made out of chalk and soot. The man depicted in that oil painting seemed unlikely at first, but he looks exactly as though he's just stepped out from it.

Once he's sent Depp packing, Mitchum's not seen again until after his son has been killed and Depp has stolen his horse. He sends for the meanest bounty hunters in the country to go and fetch this greenhorn's corpse back to him and leaves them waiting in his office. When he arrives to give them instructions there comes a quite beautiful Marx Brothers moment as he stalks past the motley killers and, rather than talking directly to them, stands communicating his wishes loudly instead to that huge stuffed bear, as if it was the only one in the room capable of understanding him, the only one worth talking to.

Jarmusch understood the appetite for the grotesque that had always existed in Mitchum as only a few directors – notably Charles Laughton – fully had before, and allows it full rein: this John Dickinson is completely deranged.

What Mitchum conveys in his brief time on screen is a man who came out west to the heart of nowhere so long ago, spent so many tough, unspeakable, lonesome, bare-handed years building his formidable reputation and his fortune, and then so many more years surrounded by yes-men, that he's long since crawled inside his head, cut the moorings loose and sailed away, forgotten how to hear anything but the increasingly addled conversations he carries on with himself. He's like Preacher Harry Powell grown old and successful – except he doesn't think he hears God talking to him; he knows that he's God.

The killers he hires are mean men – one of them, the stories say, raped both his own parents, then ate them – but when they start gabbing he makes them shut up quick, with a look – and his shotgun. He tells them that he will give them an exclusive contract to do the job, but as soon as they leave, he calls for John Hurt to take a wire, putting the job out to all and sundry. He's a bad man himself, after all, and he's been doing it much longer than any of them have.

That scene, sitting smoking and ignoring John Hurt by his side scribbling down his words, is the last sight of Mitchum. Going out like he came in, fitted out with bad-man's duds in a place where there ain't enough law to put under your hat, soliciting the company of outlaws. This is what he says:

"I want this out over the wires. Post a $500 reward from here to hell and back. Notify every marshal, deputy and possum-skinnin' lowlife in the goddamn territory. Bring everybody in. I want that bastard's head."

Then, almost as an afterthought as the picture begins to fade around him and younger actors take up the story, his voice rouses again:

"...And make sure you include a full description of my pinto. I want that horse back..."

Then, black.

Chapter Nine
That Man Sings

In 1973, John Wayne, American icon, belatedly released his debut album, *America, Why I Love Her*, a collection of misty-eyed, catch-in-the-throat pieces all about America and why John Wayne loved her. Set against a patriotic musical syrup, among the toe-tappers The Duke recorded were *The Pledge of Allegiance*, *An American Boy Grows Up* and *Taps*.[1] The cover showed Wayne, leathery in a white ten-gallon hat, smiling contentedly against the fluttering stars and stripes of Old Glory, ready for his Mount Rushmore close-up.

In 1957, some sixteen years earlier, Robert Mitchum – icon of a shadowier America – had sashayed into a studio belonging to Capitol Records in Hollywood to record *his* debut album. Similarly to the point, it was entitled *Calypso – Is Like So...* and collected together songs about the advantages of marrying ugly women, dancing, the advantages of beautiful women, drinking, being ugly, bad women, jitterbugging delinquents, strip-searching women pickpockets, digging Elvis, more dancing, more drink and more women.

Among the titles Mitchum laid down in this declaration of independence were *Mama Looka Boo Boo* and *I Learn A Merengue, Mama*. The cover showed him, with a hungover, frog-eyed, Max-Cady, ready-for-trouble face on, lounging across a table top in some abstract, shocking-pink bordello in the company of a half-empty bottle of rum, a cigarette and a woman in a strapless red dress cocking defiant hips expectantly at him.

Although it seems like something dreamed up for sale in a surrealist boutique, Mitchum's rollicking calypso album remains about his single most well-known recording. It was, however, far from his only interaction with music – or music's with him.

Unlike the USA's other most famous calypsonian, Harry Belafonte or, for that matter, John Wayne, across the decades Mitchum has been recognised and tacitly acknowledged by members of the musical vanguards of various counter-cultures – artists who explore multifarious forms of American sex and darkness and booze and drugs and life and death and electricity – as one of their own.

In 1970, Mitchum became the only actor ever to be mentioned by name among the songs of The Velvet Underground, the incredible, pale subterranean godfathers of dangerous, seductive, spooky, sleazy amphetamined rock and progenitors of all the negative, sunglasses-after-dark energy the punk subculture plugged into. On *Loaded* the band's final album, Velvets main man Lou Reed had Mitchum appear as a totemic presence wandering the streets of the urban hymn *New Age*, a song about a woman, just about over the hill, still thinking she's living in a movie world:

> "...and when you kissed Robert Mitchum, gee, but I thought you'd never catch him..."

Jim Morrison, sex, leather and death guru of The Doors, The Velvets' close contemporaries, though hardly their equals, was a massive Mitchum fan, too. The night he died in a Paris bathtub in the summer of 1971, Morrison had just returned from a screening of Mitchum's unlit Freudian Western *Pursued* in a local cinema. Ten years later, the legendary critic Lester Bangs, who functioned as poet laureate and messed-up Pepysian chronicler of the American punk scene, placed Mitchum among a pantheon of figures responsible for the genesis of punk, tracing a line from Iggy Pop back through Lou Reed, Gene Vincent, James Dean and Marlon

Robert Mitchum, happy in Nashville, 1967.

Brando to Mitchum – 'the look on his face when he got busted for grass.'[2] Meanwhile, Bruce Springsteen was opening his *Born to Run* album with *Thunder Road*, a song written in the spirit of, and lifting the title of Mitchum's outlaw movie. Jim Jarmusch recognised Mitchum's place in this current when, in crafting his darkest portrait of a haunted, ulterior America in *Dead Man*, he put the actor in the same landscape as the beatific proto-punk Iggy Pop and the wracked, shattering, ghostly old sound of Neil Young's outlaw guitar.

Mitchum had brushed against the UK punk scene, too, in its sweet, volatile infancy. In 1977,

while filming *The Big Sleep* in London, he tagged along with a young cast member – Simon Fisher Turner, who would go on to compose the soundtracks for Derek Jarman's movies – to see a show at the short-lived Vortex club on Wardour Street, where The Slits and an embryonic Siouxsie and the Banshees were playing. A few years later in Liverpool, the post-punk contingent doffed their caps when anarcho-Druid rocker Julian Cope included *Robert Mitchum* – an offbeat little eulogy with breaks for whistling, which Echo and the Bunnymen's Ian McCulloch has also claimed to have written – on his 'lost' 1985 album *Skellington*:

"Robert, Robert Mitchum

I wrote a song for you

Robert, Robert Mitchum

I love you, yes I love you, yes I really do

*the part in Ryan's Daughter when you lose
your wife*

*I've never seen a more dignified man in my
life*

Robert, Robert Mitchum

I wrote a song for you…

*…So cancel your objections to this song, don't
you weep*

You're such a dude, you're such a guy

You know you're so half-asleep…"

Mitchum travelled with musicians. He cast singers he knew from the night club scene, like Keely Smith and the torchy Julie London, in the movies he produced, and he was friends, of course, with Frank Sinatra, the singer who stood with his Rat Pack at the apex of the Atomic-Age, razor-edged good times representing the only time the square mainstream got cool, promulgating louche life with arrogance and who, in his own blue-bruised recordings of the mid-to-late 1950s explored a simple, deep, alluring poetry of solitude and disappointment, singing songs soaked in bourbon and exploring a boulevard close to the lonely streets of noir.

Sinatra's pallie, Dean Martin, whose drunken shoes Mitchum had filled when Howard Hawks' remade *Rio Bravo* as *El Dorado*, had been a Mitchum pal for years. Martin's uncle, Leonard 'Bananas' Barr, having met Mitchum's sister through the night club circuit and then become friends with Mitchum's mother, who enjoyed the company of eccentrics, artists and entertainers, had been a regular presence in the Mitchum household during the late 1930s. Barr made his living as a crazy-legs novelty dancer – when Dean made it, he would get his uncle work opening for him, doing

spots on his TV shows and playing bit parts in his movies – and would often sit at the Mitchum kitchen table drumming out ideas for tap routines with his fingers.

Mitchum's mother and his brother also loved music, and by his teens he was a confident singer and knew his way around piano, guitar and saxophone. During the late 1940s and early 1950s, he was well known for singing at parties and other gatherings around Hollywood and occasionally, joined by other celebrities like Danny Kaye, would take the stage with Martin and Jerry Lewis as the pair's legendary night club act played at Slapsy Maxie's. Mitchum and Martin had many points in common – they had both been boxers, they both had night club knowledge, they both had a taste for booze, they both sung baritone and they both projected an aura of distantly-amused-half-bored-not-giving-a-damn, like long distance brothers.

For his part, Sinatra – who took to sending Mitchum Mother's Day cards every year from 1953 through to the 1990s after Mitchum nursed him through a poison hangover on the riotous set of *Not as a Stranger*, a movie they made in the company of Lee Marvin – bowed down before Mitchum's musical knowledge. However, the same year that the Chairman of the Board famously issued his point-missing proclamation that:

*"Rock 'n' roll smells phony and false… It is
sung, played and written for the most part by
cretinous goons and by means of its almost
imbecilic reiteration and sly, lewd, in plain
fact, dirty lyrics… manages to be the martial
music of every side-burned delinquent on the
face of the earth… the most brutal, ugly,
desperate, vicious form of expression it has
been my misfortune to hear…"*[3]

Mitchum was issuing his calypso album, containing as its fourth track the State of the Union address, *What Is This Generation Coming To?*, siding with the teenagers who:

*"have the country in con-fu-shun / rockin'
rollin' all of the time / have the parents out
of their mind / parents likin' Liberace / kids
is likin' Elvis Presley / so they rockin' rollin'
night an' day, bouncin' up an' down in
the way they do…"*

And he was already writing his own debut delinquent backwoods hot-rod rock 'n' roll single, *The Ballad of Thunder Road*. Elvis himself – who, as a kid dressed in shocking pink and black, patting his careful greasy hair, had watched Mitchum movies while trying to work out his own path to cool – was a Mitchum fan, then a friend, visiting the Mitchum house to eat and talk and hear stories about moonshine and chain gangs, and play piano until the wee small hours of the morning.

Mitchum's rollicking calypso record came about after the actor had filmed two movies back to back on location on the island of Tobago in 1956, *Fire Down Below* and *Heaven Knows, Mr Allison*. Spending time in the Caribbean, Mitchum became interested in the boisterous ad libbed form he heard in the clubs and cafes every night.

He was drawn to a traditionally disreputable – sly, lewd, in plain fact, dirty – form of party music, with roots in secrets and street fighting. The style had its origin in the collision of European and African influences on Trinidad and Tobago during the slave period, when plantation workers were often only able to communicate news to one another through coded call and response songs. After emancipation in the 1830s, the form developed as the celebratory institution of carnival grew among former-slave communities; at these initially riotous events, an early form of calypso acted as the soundtrack to vicious running battles between rival gangs who fought each other with sticks, but by the early 1900s, calypso was in the form recognised today. The stick fights had been replaced by verbal jousts between calypsonian masters boasting of their verbal dexterity and trying to best one another with songs increasingly crammed with twisting, polysyllabic agglomerations of words. By the 1950s, however, calypso was still a kind of underclass living newspaper, with songs

The roots of calypso

COLUMBIA PICTURES present A WARWICK PRODUCTION

RITA HAYWORTH
ROBERT MITCHUM
JACK LEMMON

FIRE DOWN BELOW

Technicolor® A CINEMASCOPE

DIRECTED BY **ROBERT PARRISH** SCREENPLAY BY IRWIN SHAW PRODUCED BY RONALD KINNOCH EXECUTIVE PRODUCERS: IRVING ALLEN AND ALBERT R. BROCCOLI reporting and discussing topical events – visits to the island by noted figures, scandalous crimes, local political and global matters – as well as the singer's ongoing trouble with women, his face, drink. Whatever the subject matter, though, the music's mocking, lively, upbeat humour always remained paramount.

Between getting into fights with sailors, while filming *Fire Down Below*, Mitchum would tour the night spots with his co-star Jack Lemmon, listening to the calypso singers going around the tables improvising songs about the clientele. One night, Lemmon was witness to something unexpected:

"All at once this son-of-a-bitch Mitchum got up and began making up lyrics along with the professionals. He must have gone for 20 minutes, moving from table to table"[4]

Once back in Hollywood, Mitchum extolled the virtues of calypso and continued lapsing into improvised songs at any opportunity. When an executive from Capitol records – encountering the actor and asking him what he had been up to – found himself on the receiving end of an extemporaneous Mitchum calypso ballad, he produced a five-year contract and put wheels in motion, and so the actor found himself in Hollywood recording his debut album.

Capitol records were particularly keen to hustle Mitchum's record out because, in the same period the actor had been soaking up rum and music in the Caribbean, Harry Belafonte had released his album *Calypso*, a record which, selling in its millions, single-handedly sparked off a craze. The bandwagon was rolling.

Belafonte attracted criticism from many quarters during this period, for being a fake-folkist, for selling a watered-down, cleaned-up version of the music, and for promulgating an Uncle Tommish image – as in his single most famous recording, *Day O (The Banana Boat Song)* – of safe, happy, simple island black folk that was far removed from the political complexities of the Caribbean, let alone the US, where the civil rights battle was just beginning. For his part Belafonte was troubled and angered by these accusations and, as if spurred into reaction and feeding off of them, became increasingly politically active and more

musically adventurous. Around about the same time as Mitchum was cutting *Calypso – Is Like So...,* however, the black poet and author Maya Angelou, then 27, recorded her calypso album, *Miss Calypso*. Angelou's record, simultaneously cashing-in on the Belafonte wave and courting the kind of people who got a little snooty about Belafonte's discs, would seem to be an attempt to approach the form from a very serious, high-brow, folk-purist angle, with the poet giving careful, conspicuous and deliberate pronunciation to every syllable of every lyric. The result is odd, self-conscious, ponderous, po-faced and, despite the jazzy rattle-can background, almost dirge-like.

Bizarrely, in that he approaches it like happy, good time weightless trash, Mitchum's record, despite its blatant plastic aesthetic, is closer in spirit to authentic calypso. A collection of standards put through a mild Americanising filter – with a few personal touches, as a gal named Dorothy (Mitchum's wife's name) turns up here and there – the lyrics have, like Belafonte's, been cleaned up from their bawdy originals, but the tongue-in-cheek joy and the sly, shameless but straight-faced insinuation in Mitchum's delivery, is entirely in keeping with the sexed-up, boozed-up, eyebrow-cocked raggedly roughneck spirit of the calypsos he heard on Tobago. There's not a serious note on the record.

Liberally sprinkled with hep cat exhortations – 'man!' – and set against a ramshackle tic-toc cartoon party of happily bickering percussion, cantina piano, shrill brass, steel drums, incredibly busy flutes, mockingly polite backing singers and a strange, noodling banjo following its own themes around the songs, this a recording from the basement of culture, designed only to be knocked back and discarded, like a bottle of beer.

There's roguish, reprobate joy here – with every breath, Mitchum makes it clear how it's understood that it's utterly ridiculous for him to be singing this stuff, and goofs off on that. This out-of-time awareness, of the singer and the music being in on the joke, keeps the joke fresh and places the recording outside the kind of laughed-at kitsch that quickly envelopes so many other celebrity albums – most infamously exemplified by William Shatner's historical, hysterical, histrionic 1960s readings of The Beatles and Bob Dylan on his *Transformed Man* album – a record Maya Angelou's highfalutin calypsoing shares some common ground with.

There's also a fair bit of vocal skill going on in Mitchum's half-sung, half-spoken delivery. With the exception of Danny Kaye, an expert with tongue-twisting, it's difficult to imagine many other actors of the time being able to keep the joke and the beat moving and clatter so breezily, confidently through these forward-moving, narrative-unfolding accumulations of words as they wrap and snake around bustling bumps and kinks of rhythm.

Like this, from Mitchum's version of The Roaring Lion's *From a Logical Point of View*, as he explains why ugly women make better wives and runs through a check list of the features a man should look out for in his prospective bride:

> "...an ugly woman give you your meals on time / and try to make you comfortable in mind /.... cute-looking, barbarous and rough / with skin like alligator bumpy and tough / pigeon-toed, bow-legged a-cross in the eye / she got two lips that look like a big bow-tie..."

Or, playing the narrator in Lord Melody's *Mama Looka Boo Boo* as, fed up with his children's constant disparaging of his looks, he decides to beat them:

> "...I leave me own house and go / me children don't want me no more / joke about my face and everything / and when I start to talk they sing / 'Mama looka Boo Boo...' / ...I couldn't even digest me supper / due to the children's behaviour / John / 'Yes pa?' / come here a moment / bring the belt you're too disobedient / 'Daddy it's James who start off first' / 'No daddy, it's Joyce who say the worst' / Drag me belt from off me waist and run those kids right off the place / Mama looka Boo Boo"

Mitchum's effortless delivery bespeaks his comfort in front of a microphone. In fact, this wasn't his first time in a recording studio. That had come almost a decade previously, late in 1947, when the Decca label had him record a six-track EP of the songs his wandering woodsy vagabond character sung in *Rachel and the Stranger*, though only two of the tracks – *Rachel*

and *O-He O-Hi O-Ho* – were released, as a 78 single in 1948.

These are weird, funny, folksy recordings, pure slices of Americana. The musical setting is simple, spartan: just his low-boots voice and guitar, sometimes joined oddly by a harpsichord. Intended as frontier ballads, the best of the songs describe a hopeful landscape of taffy pulls, fiddler's wives, willows, fresh-baked pies, the moon and the stars, tired preachers, crickets whispering in jasmine, whipoorwills and blossoming orchards – yet are still haunted with a sense of the size of an empty country.

On the sly, sprightly and self mocking *O-He O-Hi O-Ho* – a monologue from a roguish, roving wanderer, thinking about the girl he loved, but ran away from to wander the length of the nation – Mitchum sounds like a backwoods Bing Crosby. On *Foolish Pride*, a skeletal song about a pair of headstrong lovers each growing old and dying as they wait for the other to apologise for an unremembered slight, his hipster's minimal note-bending delivery creates a slow, strange, bare and eerie kind of ancient back country jazz.

Mitchum's singing understood its own kind of America, and he recognised it when he heard it in other places. He followed country and he was, as the scandalised section of society might have surmised after his marijuana arrest, an avid jazz fan. He could often be sighted following that music around the night. Late in 1951, when Mitchum was filming *One Minute to Zero* with drinking buddies like Charles McGraw in Colorado Springs, the inspired clarinettist Pee Wee Russell was booked for a three-week engagement in a club called the Zanzabar in Denver. Russell's band was having trouble filling the place every night but:

"all of a sudden, in walked a whole crowd of people including Robert Mitchum. He took the whole crew of the movie he was making into the Zanzabar because he heard that his friend, Pee Wee, was playing there. We played for an extra hour for him and his entourage. After the place closed we went back to Mitchum's hotel and he kept us up telling jokes until 3.30 in the morning... the next day, we all went down and played for

The jazzer in Mitchum came out in his first ever appearance on TV, as guest host and singer of the CBS programme Stage Show in 1955 – among the acts he introduced were the Dorsey Brothers, Jimmy and Tommy, and Sarah Vaughan. As part of his bit, Mitchum sang *Blue Skies*.

A strange, fragmentary, forgotten demo recording from around this period exists,[6] showcasing Mitchum rehearsing with a tight, together little trio of bass, drums and an excellent pianist, swinging his way good style through a set of standards with a light and dreamy touch. Feeling his way into the songs as though he's trying out a new script for size, there are fluffed intros, false starts and forgotten lines:

Dream a Little Dream of Me

'Stars shinin' bright above you

Night breezes seem to whisper 'I love you'

Birds singin' in the sycamore tree

Dream a little dream of me

...Night breezes... what the hell is it? Naw, we lost it..'

Above all though, there's a relaxed, easy vibe, the half-heard conversations between singer and the band heard at either end of the songs – discussing approaches, releases, mistakes, lyrics, timing – showing how comfortable and conversant he is with musicians. When things click the result – a perfect, paired-down, dreamy rock through *What Is This Thing Called Love* with notes hanging, not an extraneous moment – can be sublime.

Mitchum's reputation for singing around town began to rub off on the movies he made: already in 1946, as a cowboy GI, back from the war with a steel plate in his head in *Till the End of Time*, he strolls suburbia, booming out a happy lament.

Pretty soon he was conducting his own private, unlikely musical, stretched from movie to movie across decades: singing in *Pursued* while gathered with his sick family around a music box and out on the lonely prairie; trying to win

Loretta Young's hand with his guitar in *Rachel and the Stranger*; as another soldier in *One Minute to Zero*, joining with Ann Blyth on *Tell Me Golden Moon* a song which, a few years later, in the hands of Nat King Cole, became *When I Fall In Love*; his proud, distant night time cries of *Leaning On The Everlasting Arm* becoming the chill keynote sound of *The Night of the Hunter*; a soldier again in *Heaven Knows, Mr Allison*, serenading Deborah Kerr on a lost South Pacific beach with his Bronx-inflected assault on *Don't Sit Under The Apple Tree*; in *The Sundowners*, as an Australian dreaming of Ireland, entertaining a crammed, dusty, thirsty afternoon bar with *The Wild Colonial Boy*; providing *Young Billy Young* with a rumbling theme song that in places sounds like Nick Cave's Bad Seeds tuning up for a matinee; in *Farewell, My Lovely* chiming in with the faded Vera Miles as she tries to remember how to sing Jule Styne's *Sunday*; encouraging a gathering to start singing in *Maria's Lovers*.

Then finally, over the credits of *Jake Spanner, Private Eye*, he negotiates a low, sleepy path through the Charles Aznavour ballad, *The Old-Fashioned Way*. This last, with its lyric about dancing to the ends of the earth, sets Mitchum's cavernous vocal sashaying, impossibly weary and delicate, against a chintzy, stripped down programmed haze of cheap, tinny keyboards and drum machines – the effect is incredibly similar to the recordings Leonard Cohen made on his 1988 album *I'm Your Man*, on which Cohen experimented with a similar Hotel-lounge sound.

Away from the screen, after the calypso record, Mitchum's next musical salvo came in 1958, in the 7-inch circular shape of the single he recorded for Capitol, his own hopped-up reading of his moonshining car-smashing composition *The Ballad of Thunder Road* backed with a version of *My Honey's Lovin' Arms*.

Mitchum composed the music for *The Ballad of Thunder Road*, based an old Norwegian tune he'd learned from his mother, and wrote the lyrics with the veteran lyricist Don Raye, who had previously helped him remodel the calypso tunes. Raye, a former dance-champion, had been writing songs since the 1930s, providing the likes of the Andrews Sisters with a bundle of hits – he wrote *Boogie Woogie Bugle Boy From Company B* and *Down the Road A-Piece*, a boogie ballad later hi-jacked by the burning rubber rock 'n' rollers. The song he wrote with Mitchum was a straight synopsis of the movie:

Let me tell the story, I can tell it all;

About the mountain boy who ran illegal alcohol.

His daddy made the whiskey, the son he drove the load;

And when his engine roared they called the highway Thunder Road

On the soundtrack of the *Thunder Road* movie, a laid back, lullaby-like version of Mitchum's tune had been sung by someone else, but Mitchum's recording, a banging, twanging thing drenched in reverb, with lunatic bass, slapping drums and drunk-cat guitar backed up by a white bread Jordanairesian vocal group, went for good, lazy, plastic rocking, reaching in the direction of Elvis and Gene Vincent, while still keeping one foot on the porch. A similar, but sleepier approach – guitar still like cheesewire, but slowly rocking, with backing singers all a-doodle-ee-wop, doodle-ee-wop, shoooo-bah – was adopted in customising *My Honey's Lovin' Arms*, a tune most well known in a college-boy version recorded by Bing Crosby in 1933.

With this single, his calypso album and the *Thunder Road* movie all released in the space of a year, Mitchum pulled off a triple whammy as a practitioner of reprobate, careless, suspect art. He stayed away from recording for the next decade, but when he finally breezed into a studio again, it was to record his most personal record, the album *That Man, Robert Mitchum, Sings*.

The genesis of the record came early in 1967, when Mitchum was driving to Oregon for location shooting on *The Way West* and heard a country tune he liked a lot on the car radio, *Little Ole Wine Drinker Me*. He contacted Dean Martin to suggest that Martin record it. Martin was busy filming and told Mitchum that, if he liked it so much, he should record it himself. And so Mitchum did, gaining himself a sizeable hit on the country charts.

To make the record, Mitchum headed off for Nashville, where he signed with the independent Monument label, run by producer and entrepreneur Fred Foster. A pop-country specialist with a particularly inventive ear, earlier in the 1960s Foster had produced the most startling recordings by Roy Orbison – including *Only the Lonely*, *In Dreams*, *Running Scared*, *Crying*, *It's Over* and *Pretty Woman* – and worked with then-unconventional country talents like Willie Nelson, Dolly Parton and the young Kris Kristofferson, whom he had encouraged to sing.

For Mitchum, he provided a palette of styles that were alternately growlly, boozy and rough, light, lush and wistful, roadhouse rowdy and pure pop, but which were all pure Nashville. The Monument studios played home to the cream of the Tennessee capital's sidemen: among the players rounded up for the Mitchum sessions was Charlie McCoy, who was then between working on the Bob Dylan albums *Blonde on Blonde* and *John Wesley Harding*.

The album Mitchum recorded is the aural equivalent to a slowed-down, weather-beaten, but still kicking *Thunder Road*, that is, it's an artefact designed for and exploring a certain, strange kind of America. His choice of songs – many by the husband and wife song-writing team of Boudleaux and Felice Bryant, who provided the Everly Brothers with their most memorable hits – come from a hopeless backroads place full of country, out-of-the-way roadhouse jukeboxes, knotty black woods, homesick convicts, broken hearts, idle dreamers, murderers and boozy losers. *That Man* is a record full of miles and miles of road-going. As if to underline the point, and the personal nature of the undertaking, both *The Ballad of Thunder Road* – recast as a rattling acoustic thing – and the love song from that movie, *Whippoorwill* are present.

The first track, a coolly pissed-off version of John D Loudermilk's *You Deserve Each Other* is a laid-back, but disgusted brush-off song, spat out by a Mitchum as sick of a girl as the Mitchum of *Out of the Past* was of Jane Greer by the end of that movie. The next is an insane thing called *Walker's Woods* a weirdly sprightly song with a lyric that sounds as if it was conceived by a drunken William Faulkner trying out the pop market. Mitchum happily narrates from the point of view of a man lying dying in the middle of a Southern swamp, having been bitten by a cottonmouth. Just before the snake got him, he'd murdered the woman he's been having an affair with. They had fled from her husband into the lightless tangle of the swamp, but when she decided she wanted to go back home, Mitchum killed her and dumped her body in a quicksand pool. As he dies, he notices her headscarf still floating on the surface and laughs because he knows that the snake's poison will have killed him before her husband, who's been chasing them with a shotgun, has the chance to shoot him.

Elsewhere, on *That Man Right There* and *Little Ole Wine Drinker Me* come lazy, wistful laments from a downbeat, washed-up boozer hoping that the right girl might still come by and save him, or sailing into the bottle because the right girl has left him. There are tales of failed love and weird schemers on *Ricardo's Mountain*; weird spartan country-soul pop celebrations that sounds like a lament on Mitchum's mournful glide through *Sunny*; and broody, country-punk attitude on *In My Place*, a song from a man who doesn't care about the mess he's making of his life and is sneering at the very idea that his all busy friends think they have any advice worth offering.

The cover of the record is a great, merciless, *are-you-talking-to-me-pal?* portrait of a just-up Mitchum, in a wood somewhere, saddlebags under his eyes, hair all messed up and shot with grey, a little scar and the break in his nose clearly visible. It's a face that's been through all the hangovers in the world, for all the reasons there are in the world, and is just groggily beginning to look forward to building up the next one. In a way the picture is reminiscent of the awkward blank-eyed self-portrait Bob Dylan – working with Charlie McCoy again – painted for the cover of his own

supremely odd Nashville-recorded collection of standards and Americana, *Self Portrait*.

The songs Dylan stuck together on that record in 1970 were a half-serious, often parodic jigsaw clue as to where he came from, and *That Man* represents a similar undertaking on Mitchum's part. In places, it even sounds the same. Dylan includes a cover of the track Mitchum's record closes with, Paul Clayton's restless outsider tune *Gotta Travel On* – a song regularly picked up by against-the-grain artists from Buddy Holly and Jerry Lee Lewis through to The Clash, who incorporate the main refrain of Clayton's song in their apocalyptic reggae tune of 1980, *Armagideon Time*.

Mitchum's record leaves off with his own road-rolling, finger clicking version of this hobo anthem, dropping in hillbilly beat flourishes – 'dad' – an unpretentious song all about a restless hungry feeling, the road, the big country, not fitting into the town with the rest of them, chain-gang time, trouble with the law. It could have been written for him, and he wanders through it like it was:

Laid around and I've played around this old town too long

Summer's almost gone, winter's comin' on

Laid around and I've played around this old town too long

And I feel like I gotta travel on...

The song doesn't come to an end; it fades into the distance. It takes nothing with it, and all it leaves is dust.

Miles and miles
of road-going:
Nashville, 1967.

Walking the Via Dolorosa, I began to have a great respect for Jesus Christ, because I tell you, if I was packing that cross I'd have said, 'Fellas, do what you have to do, but I'm not packing this cross another foot.' Mitchum.[7]

Footnotes

Acknowledgements

1   Lee Marvin, quoted in David Shipman, Movie talk: *Who Said What About Whom in the Movies*, New York, St. Martin's Press, 1988

Introducing

1   Howard Hughes to Robert Mitchum, during a discussion as to whether or not, should the situation arise, the latter should sleep with Ava Gardner, during the filming of *My Forbidden Past*. Quoted in various, including Jane Ellen Wayne *Ava's Men* (London, Sphere Books Ltd, 1991)

2   *Holiday Affair* (1949), for all of a deathless second or two.

3   Robert Mitchum to Michael Parkinson. *Parkinson*, BBC television, broadcast 1972.

4   Mitchum to Roger Ebert in *Robert Mitchum: Against the Grain*. Reprinted in *Close-Ups: The Movie Star Book*. (New York, Simon and Schuster Inc, 1978).

5   Robert Mitchum. I Know What I'm Doing, *Movieland* magazine, 1948.

6   Ibid.

Chapter 1: ChronoMitchology

1   This chronology is in a large part based on material assembled by Jerry Roberts in his *Robert Mitchum: A Bio-Bibliography* (Westport CN, Greenwood Press, 1992), in part on stories told by John Mitchum in his *Them 'Ornery Mitchum Boys* (Pacifica CA, Creatures at Large Press, 1989) and in part on George Eells' *Robert Mitchum* (London, Robson Books Ltd, 1984).

2   Jack Black: *You Can't Win*. Published 1926. Reprinted, San Francisco, AK Press, 1999.

Chapter 2: About a Photograph

1   Mitchum to various, including Jerry Roberts in his *Robert Mitchum: A Bio-Bibliography*. Westport CN, Greenwood Press, 1992.

2   In the first volume of which Robert Mitchum, courtesy of his marijuana bust, would find a featured role.

3   In truth, the *Hopalong Cassidy* movie of 1943 that gave Mitchum his feature debut, *Hoppy Serves A Writ*, wasn't his actual screen debut. In 1942 he had appeared as a model in a short something called *The Magic of Make-Up*. Among the demonstrations, Model Mitchum has his chest hair shaved and then replaced with a chest hairpiece.

4   Earl Wilson: *The Show Business Nobody Knows*. Chicago and New York: Cowles Book Company Inc, 1971.

5   Mitchum to Grover Lewis, 'The Last Celluloid Desperado', *Rolling Stone*, March 1973.

6   Mitchum, quoted in David Downing: *Robert Mitchum*. London: WH Allen & Co, 1985.

7   Brando to Vivian Leigh; Alexander Walker: *Vivian: The Life of Vivian Leigh*. New York, Weidenfeld & Nicolson, 1987.

8   Mitchum to Los Angeles Times 1956. Quoted in George Eells: *Robert Mitchum*. London, Robson Books Ltd, 1984.

9   Mitchum, quoted in David Downing.

10 Brando to Louis Levitas, New York Post 1958.

11 Mitchum to Alan Ebert, *In the Know* December 1975.

12 Brando to Joe Hyams, *Los Angeles Times* circa 1958.

13 Mitchum to Aline Mosby, *Los Angeles Daily News* 1952.

14 Nicolas Cage would later don as a mark of personal freedom the snakeskin jacket in David Lynch's *Wild at Heart* (1990).

15 Excepting, that is, the backstage musical *Follow the Band* (1943) and the limp war musical *Doughboys in Ireland* (1943). In both of these films, Mitchum played a minor supporting role and sang in neither of them.

16 Sinatra quoted in Mike Tomkies: The *Robert Mitchum Story*. Chicago, Henry Regnery Company, 1972.

Chapter 3: About a Drugs Bust

1   'Man With the Immoral Face' Bobby-soxed Mitchum Droolettes outside a screening of *GI Joe*, quoted by Eleanor Harris, *Photoplay*, December 1945.

2   Michael Starks: *Cocaine Fiends and Reefer Madness*, East Brunswick, New Jersey, Cornwall Books, 1982.

3   Ibid.

4   Publicity ad for MGM's *The Lady in the Lake* (1947).

5   The director Delmar Daves came closer than Montgomery had to making it work in his own subjective-camera movie, *Dark Passage* (1947), starring that other Marlowe, Humphrey Bogart. For the first third of that movie, only Bogart's Bugs Bunny voice stars, as we see the world through his eyes, before he gets the plastic surgery that finally makes him look like Humphrey Bogart; when Lauren Bacall speaks to him, she speaks to us, looking into the camera. At one point, she ties him to her bed.

Chapter 4: Mitchum in Pictures

1   Interviewed by Tony Crawley, *Ritz* Newspaper, London, 1989.

2   Sterling Hayden: *Wanderer*. New York, Alfred A Knopf, 1963.

3   Interviewed by James W Seymour, *People Weekly*, 1983.

4   Martin Scorsese, writing in *Roberto Rossellini: Magician of the Real*. Eds David Forgacs, Sarah Lutton and Geoffrey Nowell-Smith. London, BFI Publishing, 2000.

5   Robert Warshow: The Gangster as Tragic Hero. *Partisan Review*, 1947.

Chapter 5: *When Strangers Marry*

1   Lewton is best remembered for *Cat People* (1942), on which he worked with the director Jacques Tourneur, who would later direct Mitchum in *Out of the Past* (1947). His unorthodox and highly lyrical horror cycle also includes *I Walked with a Zombie* (1943), *The Leopard Man* (1943), *The Ghost Ship* (1943), *The Curse of the Cat People* (1944), *Isle of the Dead* (1945), *The Body Snatcher* (1945) and *Bedlam* (1946). In these succinct (rarely more than 75 minutes long) poverty row B-poems, Lewton established himself as a producer—*auteur* with an fascination for the dim and unknown areas of life, and one filled with a deep and melancholy sympathy for his strange and fated characters. Earlier in his career, he had written pornographic novels.

Chapter 5: *The Big Steal*

1   Don Siegel to Peter Bogdanovich: *Who the Devil Made It*. New York, Ballantine Books, 1997.

Chapter 5: *His Kind of Woman*

1   Robert Mitchum to various, including Michael Parkinson, *Parkinson*, BBC television, broadcast 1972.

2   Richard Fleischer: *Just Tell Me When to Cry: A Memoir*. New York, Carroll & Graff, 1993.

3   Albert Camus: *The Myth of Sisyphus*, translation, London, Hamish Hamilton, 1955.

Chapter 5: *Macao*

1   Mitchum talking to Derek Malcolm, Guardian Film Lecture, 1984. Reprinted in *Talking Films*. Ed Andrew Britton. London, Fourth Estate, 1991.

2   Grahame partially re-shot certain scenes under the direction of Robert Stevenson and Mel Ferrer.

3   Guardian Film Lecture

Chapter 5: *Angel Face*

1   Otto Preminger, interviewed by Peter Bogdanovich in Bogdanovich's *Who the Devil Made It?* New York, Ballantine Publishing Group, 1998.

2   Stewart Granger: *Sparks Fly Upward*. New York, GP Putnam's Sons, 1981.

3   Preminger's film wouldn't be the last pairing of Mitchum and Simmons either; eight years later they teamed up with his favourite leading lady, Deborah Kerr, and Cary Grant for Stanley Donen's starchy, stagy romantic drawing room comedy, *The Grass is Greener* — considering the mutual mischievousness and empathy of Simmons and Mitchum, it's a pity they were never given a better comedy script. In 1985, Mitchum and Simmons were also among the cameo faces blowing through the epic Civil War miniseries *North and South*, along with Gene Kelly, Johnny Cash and Elizabeth Taylor.

Chapter 5: *Cape Fear*

1   In the *Cape Fear* remake, the threatened daughter of the family is played by Juliette Lewis, who worked with Mitchum regularly, if briefly, in one of the most bizarre segments of his career, when he was called on in 1990 to helm a Saturday night TV sitcom, *A Family for Joe*, in which he played a misfit crusty vagrant, adopted as cuddly grandfather by a middle-class family of children about to be split up by the courts after the death of their parents. Lewis played one of the kids. It lasted nine episodes.

2   Polly Bergen interviewed in *Hollywood Legends: Robert Mitchum*. BBC TV, 1999.

Chapter 5: *The Friends of Eddie Coyle*

1   Manny Farber: *Negative Space: Manny Farber on the Movies*. New York, Da Capo Press, 1998.

2   Jordan's offbeat, watchful acting complemented Mitchum well; they teamed up again for *The Yakuza*, then reunited in 1987 when Mitchum was asked to step in for an ailing Edward Woodward as guest lead on two episodes of Woodward's espionage show *The Equalizer*.

Chapter 5: Farewell, My Lovely

1   *The Raymond Chandler Papers: Selected Letters and Non-fiction 1909 - 1959*, Ed Tom Hiney and Frank McShane, London, Hamish Hamilton Ltd., 2000.

Chapter 6: *War Movies*

1   Mitchum quoted in *Robert Mitchum*, George Eells.

Chapter 6: *The Story of GI Joe*

1   James Agee: *Agee on Film*. New York, Modern Library, 2000.

2   Sam Fuller quoted in Clyde Jevons: *A Pictorial History of War Films*. Secaucus, NJ, Citadel Press, 1974.

3   William Wellman: *A Short Time For Insanity*. New York, Hawthorn Books, 1974.

Chapter 6: *Heaven Knows, Mr Allison*

1   Production secretary Jilda Smith, interviewed by John Grobel: *The Hustons*. London, Bloomsbury Publishing Ltd, 1990.

2   John Huston: *An Open Book*. London, Columbus Books, 1988.

Chapter 7: *The Night of the Hunter*

1   Charles Laughton, quoted in Simon Callow: *Charles Laughton: A Difficult Actor*. London, Vintage, 1995.

2   Davis Grubb: *The Night of the Hunter*. London, Prion Books, 1999.

3   Francois Truffaut: *The Films in My Life*. London, Penguin Books, 1982.

4   Charles Laughton interviewed in *Esquire* magazine, 1964.

Chapter 7: *Ryan's Daughter*

1   Robert Mitchum to various, including Michael Parkinson, *Parkinson*, BBC TV, broadcast 1972.

2   David Lean interviewed in *Rolling Stone*, 1973.

3   Sarah Miles: *Serves Me Right*. London, Macmillan, 1994.

Chapter 8: *Westerns*

1   Mitchum to various, including Geoff Brown in *The Times*, 1984.

Chapter 8: *Rachel and the Stranger*

1   Sections of Norman Foster's My Friend Bonito can be seen in the 1993 documentary *It's All True: Based on an Unfinished Film by Orson Welles* (Paramount Pictures).

Chapter 8: *Track of the Cat*

1   The film was actually filmed on Mount Rainier in Washington.

2   In 1972, Rettig was busted for growing marijuana.

3   Switzer had turned up in the background of the Mitchum universe 11 years earlier in *The Human Comedy*.

Chapter 8: *El Dorado*

1   Howard Hawks to Joseph McBride: *Hawks on Hawks*. London, University of California Press Ltd, 1982.

2   As told by Mitchum to various, including Peter Bogdanovich: *Who the Devil Made It*. New York, Ballantine Books, 1997.

3   *Hawks on Hawks*.

Chapter 9: *That Man Sings*

1   Of the 10 cuts on Wayne's album, nine were by John Mitchum.

2   *The Scorn Papers*, printed in *Psychotic Reactions and Carburettor Dung*, Ed Lester Bangs and Greil Marcus. New York, Vintage Books, 1988.

3   Sinatra's magazine article is quoted in Linda Martin and Kerry Seagrave: *Anti-Rock: The Opposition to Rock 'n' Roll*. Hamden, CN, Shoe String Press, Archon Books, 1988.

4   Jack Lemmon quoted in George Eells: *Robert Mitchum*. London, Robson Books Ltd, 1984.

5   Bass player, Irving Manning, in Robert Hilbert: *Pee Wee Russell: The Life of a Jazzman*. New York, Oxford University Press, 1993.

6   Mitchum's stop–start jazz rehearsal, along with the tracks he cut for *Rachel and the Stranger* and the title song of *Young Billy Young* are collected on the CD *Tall Dark Stranger*, issued by Bear Family Records (BCD 16 223 AJ) 1997.

7   Mitchum talking to Derek Malcolm, Guardian Film Lecture, 1984, reprinted in *Talking Films*. Ed Andrew Britton. London, Fourth Estate, 1991.

Index